REAL-TIME SYSTEMS

Edited by **Kuodi Jian**

Real-time Systems
http://dx.doi.org/10.5772/61695
Edited by Kuodi Jian

Contributors

Daniel Bernardon, Ana Mello, Luciano Pfitscher, Martijn Van Den Heuvel, Reinder Jaap Bril, Johan Lukkien, Moris Behnam, Thomas Nolte, Ming Fan, Vinicius Jacques Garcia, Iochane Guimarães, Júlio Fonini, Lim Chot Hun, Lim Tien Sze, Koo Voon Chet, Lee Yeng Ong, Truong Quang Dinh, Jong Il Yoon, Cheolkeun Ha, James Marco, Alessandro Carbonari, Massimo Vaccarini, Mikko Valta, Maddalena Nurchis, Kuodi Jian

Published by InTech

Janeza Trdine 9, 51000 Rijeka, Croatia

Publishing Process Manager Andrea Koric
Technical Editor InTech DTP team
Cover InTech Design team

First published June, 2016
Printed in Croatia

Additional hard copies can be obtained from orders@intechopen.com

Real-time Systems, Edited by Kuodi Jian
p. cm.
Print ISBN 978-953-51-2398-9
Online ISBN 978-953-51-2397-2

For EU product safety concerns:
IN TECH d.o.o., Prolaz Marije Krucifikse Kozulić 3, 51000 Rijeka, Croatia,
info@intechopen.com or visit our website at intechopen.com.

Meet the editor

Dr. Kuodi Jian holds B.S. degree in Computer Science from the University of Mary Hardin-Baylor, and the M.S. degree in Computer Science and the Ph. D. degrees in Computer Science and Operations Research from the North Dakota State University. He worked as a Computer System Architect at the Banner Health System, Fargo, North Dakota. He is the Associate Professor (ICS Graduate Director) in Metropolitan State University since 2003. His research interests are in the areas of algorithms, programming languages, real-time operating systems, operations research, database systems, web service–oriented architecture (SOA), artificial intelligence, computer hardware, and computer simulation.

Contents

Preface

The history of humanity is the history of progress and improvement. From the use of primitive tools such as stone axes to bronze utensils, from observing individual phenomenon to the understanding of systems, human history is littered with social progress and technological improvement. The focal point shift from individual events to systems represents a quantum leap in understanding. The subject of this book "real-time systems" is a branch of the study about systems and their behaviors. A lot of times, the cumulative behaviors of a system are not a simple addition of individual parts. For example, the collective behavior of a neural network exhibits intelligence while its individual node does not. Thus, the study of systems (all kinds of systems such as bio-systems, ecosystems, social systems, computer systems, and the weather system to name just a few) is much more complex and interesting than the study of individual object and its behaviors.

Real-time systems (discussed in this book) are special kind of systems that have some unique characteristics:

• These systems are subject to real-time constraints. The time constraints are represented as deadlines. In this context, systems interact with environments by acquiring data from the environment (through sensors, cameras, etc.), processing (interpreting) the data, and affecting (taking actions based on the processed data) the environment before the deadlines. Of course, in real situations, deadlines can be further categorized as hard deadlines or soft deadlines.

• The parts in these systems are connected and can communicate either synchronously or asynchronously.

• Flexible architectures that can be applied to different domains and be adapted to changing environments.

• Systems that are able to display cognitive behaviors (intelligence) by self-learning and self-organizing.

It's exciting to know that the content presented in this book is the work of practitioners, researchers, scientists, and scholars from many countries, like Brazil, Finland, Italy, Korea, Malaysia, Spain, Sweden, the United Kingdom, and the United States. This book will be useful to a wide range of audiences: university students/professors, engineers, and businessmen who are interested in real-time systems and future innovations.

Dr. Kuodi Jian
Metropolitan State University, Computer Science Faculty,
Department of Information and Computer Sciences,
Minnesota, The United States of America

Chapter 1

Introductory Chapter: Real-Time Systems

Kuodi Jian

Additional information is available at the end of the chapter

http://dx.doi.org/10.5772/63443

1. Introduction

In nature, we encounter a lot of things: some are single objects (such as rocks, water, and air) while others are systems (such as weather systems, cooling systems in cars, and electric power systems). In general, systems consist of many objects. Thus, systems are more complex than single objects. To understand how things work, we need to study not only the characteristics of single objects but also the collective behaviors of systems. This book focuses on the study of systems and their characteristics. Specifically, we discuss a subset of systems called "real-time systems" that meet certain time constraints.

The dividing line of single objects and systems also depends on the viewpoint. For example, when looking at a car as a single object (from a car user's points of view), we only see its functionalities as a vehicle (its driving wheel to control direction, its brake pedal to control stop, etc.); on the other hand, when looking at a car's break system (from a car mechanic's point of view), we see the mechanical details of the brake system such as hydraulic ducts, boosters, and brake pads. Figure 1 shows the different points of views.

Figure 1(a) shows an object viewpoint; Figure 1(b) shows the car's brake from a system point of view. Understanding these different views is very important in dealing with the complexity. In fact, these viewpoint shiftings mimic the human brain strategy (the strategy that is also adopted by software engineering and design) in dealing with complex tasks.

The strategy is to abstract away the details when they are not needed, and to microscope the details when they are needed. For example, to use a car, we do not need to know how the combustion engine works, neither do we need to know how the brake system works (all we need to know is that pressing the gas pedal to accelerate the car and pressing the brake pedal to stop the car). As a car user, we simplify the car by abstracting away the details of mechanical details. Here the mechanical details are irrelevant to operate a car. On the other hand, to repair a car, we have to know different systems in a car. As a mechanic, the knowledge of how each system works is vital to perform his job. At system level, we have to go extra mile to understand different parts and the interaction among these parts (as mentioned before, systems consist of parts). This viewpoint shifting is necessary for a mechanic. By microscoping into the details, a mechanic is able to isolate and fix a problem occurred in a car system.

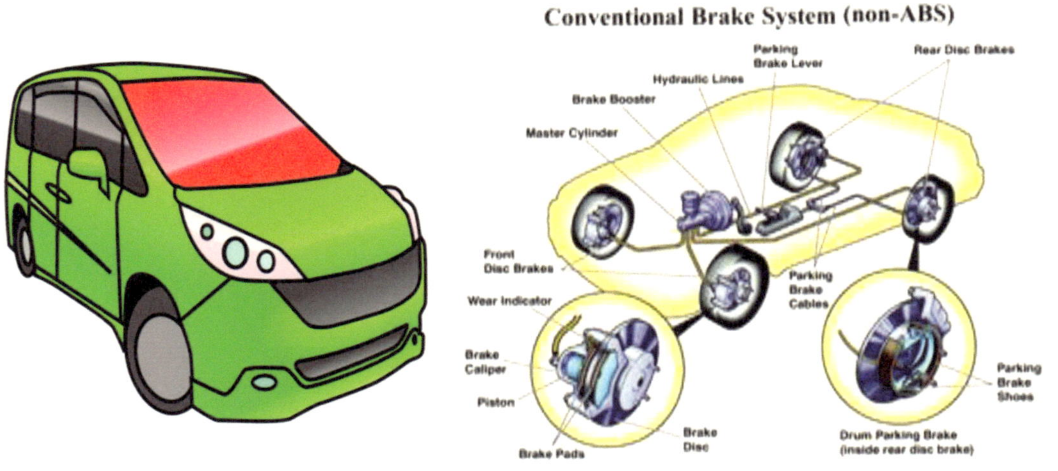

a) Object view b) System view of break

Figure 1. Object view and system view of a car. (a) Object view, (b) system view of brake.

2. Systems are more than simple addition of parts

Often, we assume that systems are made of parts and collective behavior of a system is the addition of its parts. This assumption stems from our intuition and experiences. For example, if one chopstick can sustain 1 lb, then a bundle of ten can sustain 10 lbs.

But that assumption does not tell the whole story. We claim that **a system is more than the addition of its parts**. In other words, the whole is greater than the sum of its parts. "The whole is more than the sum of its parts. It is more correct to say that the whole is something else than the sum of its parts, because summing up is a meaningless procedure, whereas the whole-part relationship is meaningful" [1].

The importance of studying systems instead of individual parts is the implication of our claim: the **synergy**. Let us take an example to illustrate how this is the case. Human body can be viewed differently. If our focus is on the parts, we will see organs such as heart, liver, kidney, and head; if our focus is on the whole (holistic/system view) body, we actually see a complex organism that is made of many systems (digestive system, cardiovascular system, nerve system, etc.). Figure 2 shows the structure parts of a human body.

http://dx.doi.org/10.5772/63443

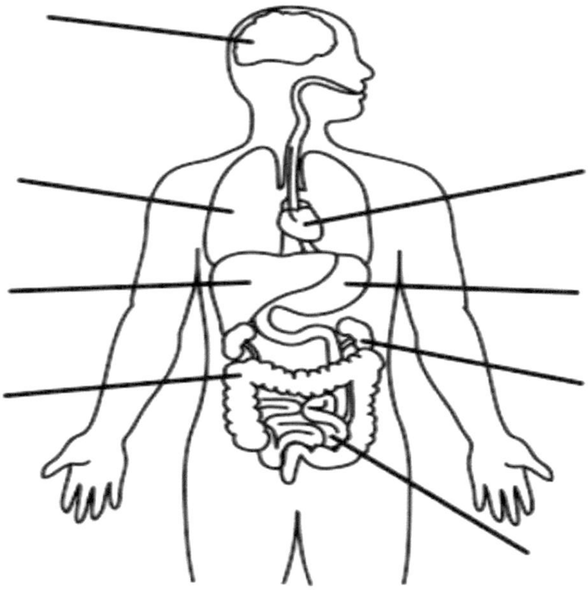

Figure 2. The structure parts of a human body.

One of the most amazing synergistic effects of a human body is the soul (or abstract thinking). Human soul is the thing that is above and beyond any body parts. In fact, it belongs to a different domain (body parts belong to a concrete physical domain, while soul belongs to a cognitive/spiritual domain). I want to point out that only from a holistic/system point of view, we are able to see the effect of synergy (the spiritual side of our body).

Another example of our claim is the neural networks. When focusing on an individual neural node, we see only simple behavior of conducting information from point A to point B; but when focusing on the whole system, we are able to see the synergy of intelligence.

Synergy gives us the reason to study systems.

3. Real-time systems

In this book, we focus on the discussion of a subset of systems: real-time systems. Real-time systems are those systems that have certain requirements on the timing. In this type of systems, responses to environment's stimuli must be done before certain deadlines. The characteristics of real-time systems are:

- The usefulness of a system is judged not only by the correctness of the system behaviors but also by the time these behaviors are initiated.
- Different parts of a system will communicate and the communication among the parts also satisfies certain time requirements. The typical communication timing requirements are:

1. Synchronous--- the communication must be done at the real-time (no delay or the delay can be ignored in a practical sense). This is the most stringent time requirement. One of the examples is the video conferencing (in this situation, real-time data must be delivered without delay).

2. Isochronous--- real-time data must be delivered in a fixed period of time. This is a quasi real-time requirement. Isochronous is the requirement that is not as rigid as synchronous but not as lenient as asynchronous (kind of in the middle). This mode of communication meets the need of those applications that a steady data stream is more important than completeness and accuracy. One of the examples is the digitized voice communication (in this case, dropping of packets is acceptable).

3. Asynchronous--- the communication can be done later. This is the most flexible time requirement. One of the examples is the email (no guarantee how fast the message will be delivered to the recipient).

- Failure to take a required action is as bad as the wrong action. For instance, the consequence of a delayed car brake action may cause an accident (in this case, it is almost as bad as the wrong action).

To make the concept of real-time system more concrete, let us look at some examples of real-time systems:

3.1. Air traffic control system

Air traffic control system contains multiple function units. The main objective is to regulate the airplane traffic so that the operation is safe and efficient. To achieve that, multiple functional units (parts) of the system must communicate and cooperate among themselves. For

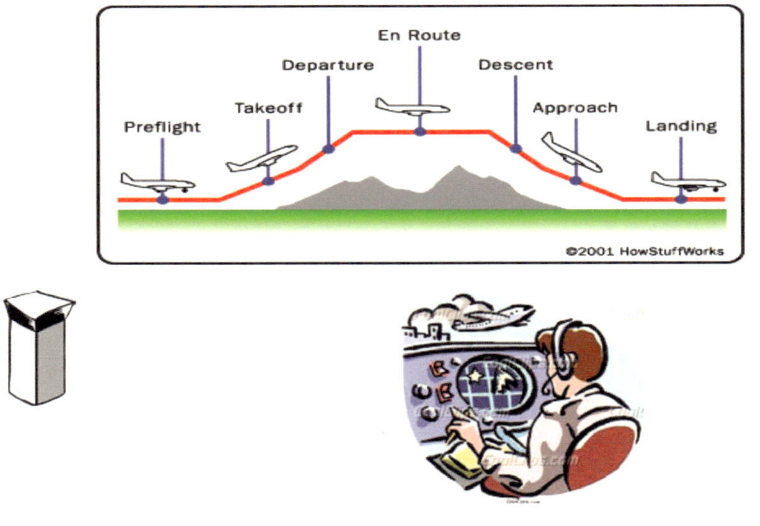

Figure 3. An air traffic control system.

example, the radar tower will send information of airplane positions to the air traffic controllers and the air controller will tell airplanes to maintain certain speed, altitude, and direction. Figure 3 shows the parts involved in this system.

As shown in Figure 3, the air controller needs to monitor and control airplanes (such as knowing the stages of takeoff, departure, en route, approaching, and landing). Since the speed of a typical commercial airplane is in the range of 600–700 miles per hour, the system works in strict time constraint. Thus, it is a real-time system.

3.2. Energy demand management system

Another example of real-time system is the electric distributing and energy demand management system also known as demand side management (DSM) [2]. Figure 4 shows the parts involved in this system.

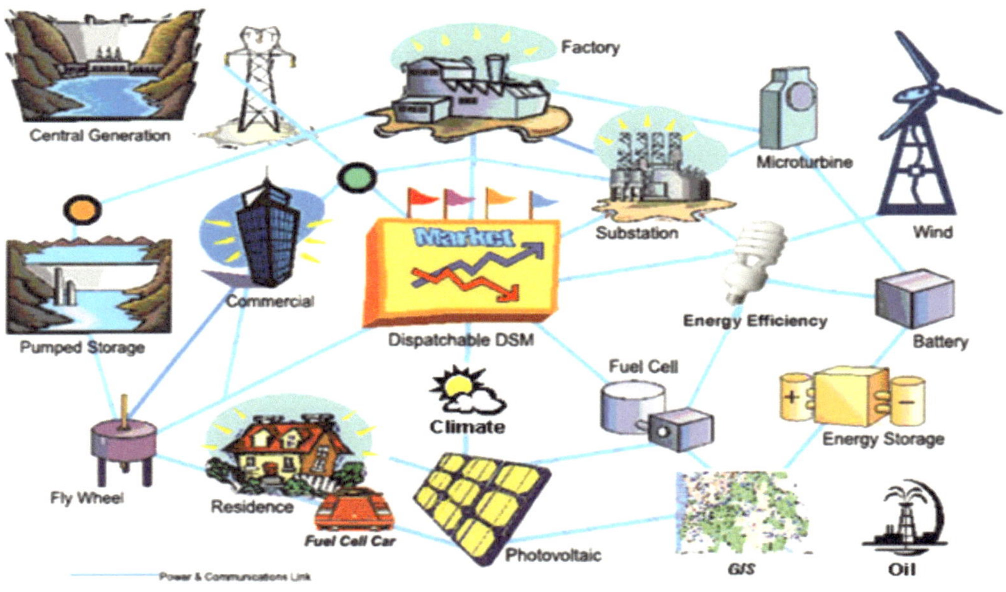

Figure 4. An electric distributing and energy demand management system.

As shown in Figure 4, the electric power distributing system has many parts and is a complex system. To optimize the power efficiency, modern power systems use both fossil energy and reusable energy such as hydraulic power, photovoltaic energy, and wind energy. The main functionality of the system is to regulate the power source by using energy storage and by switching on and off power generators. Since we are not able to store large portion of electricity, the system must monitor the supply and demand data in real-time. Sometimes, the configuration of the power grid needs to be changed to accommodate the power demand surge (all these need to be done with a time limit).

4. Overview of the chapters

In this book, we carefully selected a set of manual scripts that are written by authors with different backgrounds. The selected articles have a broad spectrum of topics ranging from theory to application. At the mean time, all the topics are centered on the main theme of real-time systems. In this way, readers get the benefit of wide exposure to the issues and information related to the subject. In the following, I give you a brief introduction to each of the remaining chapters.

Chapter 2 "**Real-Time Reconfiguration of Distribution Network with Distributed Generation**" wrote by Daniel Bernardon, Ana Paula Carboni de Mello, and Luciano Pfitscher. The main contribution of the chapter is the presentation of "a new methodology to perform the real-time reconfiguration of distribution networks incorporating distributed generation in normal operation". The research method used belongs to empirical and scientific (according to [3], research methods can be put into a set of predefined categories).

Chapter 3 "**Uniform Interfaces for Resource-Sharing Components in Hierarchically Scheduled Real-Time Systems"** wrote by Martijn M. H. P. Van Den Heuvel, Reinder J. Bril, Johan J. Lukkien, Moris Behnam, and Thomas Nolte. The main contribution of the chapter is the proposing of "uniform interfaces to integrate resource-sharing components into Hierarchical Scheduling Frameworks (HSFs) on a uni-processor platform". The contribution is significant to the field of real-time operating systems. The research method used belongs to experimental research [I].

Chapter 4 "**Thermal and Energy Analysis for Periodic Scheduling on Multi-Core Real-Time Systems"** wrote by Ming Fan. The main contribution of the chapter is the analysis of the thermal behavior on multi-core real-time systems and the energy consumption for a given speed scheduling on multi-core systems.

Chapter 5 "**Multi-objective Real-time Dispatching Problem in Electric Utilities: an Application to Emergency Service Routing"** wrote by Vinicius Jacques Garcia, Daniel Bernardon, Iochane Guimaraes, and Julilo Fonini. The main contribution of the chapter is the presentation of a novel application of real-time dispatching problem to electric utilities when multi-objectives are involved. It presents a heuristic approach to solve the emergency dispatching and routing problem.

Chapter 6 "**Kalman Filtering and Its Real-Time Applications"** wrote by Lim Chot Hun, Ong Lee Yeng, Lim Tien Sze, and Koo Voon Chet. The main contribution of the chapter is the demonstration of different use of Kalman filtering. The authors outlined and explained the fundamental Kalman filtering model in real-time discrete form, and devised two real-time applications that implemented Kalman filtering.

Chapter 7 "**A Real-Time Bilateral Teleoperation Control System over Imperfect Network"** wrote by Truong Quang Dinh, Yong II Yoon, Cheolkeun Ha, and James Marco. The main contribution of the chapter is the introduction of an advanced bilateral teleoperation networked control system; the introduction of an approach to develop a force-sensorless feedback

http://dx.doi.org/10.5772/63443

control (FSFC) that is able to simplify the sensor requirement in designing the Bilateral Teleoperation Networked Control System (BTNCS).

Chapter 8 "**Wireless Real Time Monitoring System for the Implementation of Intelligent Control in Subways**" wrote by Alessandro Carbonari, Massimo Vaccarini, Mikko Valta, and Maddalena Nurchis. The main contribution of the chapter is the presentation of the technical features of state-of-the-art Wireless Sensors Networks (WSN) for environmental monitoring. Specifically, this article presents the application of WSN to the Passeig de Gracia (PdG) subway station in Barcelona using a Model-based Predictive Control system (MPC).

The above-mentioned chapters cover a wide range of topics that are centered on the theme of real-time systems [4, 5]. We wish you enjoy reading rest of the book.

Author details

Kuodi Jian

Address all correspondence to: Kuodi.jian@metrostate.edu

Metropolitan State University, Saint Paul, MN, USA

References

[1] Koffka, K. (1935). *Principles of Gestalt Psychology*. New York: Harcourt, Brace, & World.

[2] Internet source: Wikipedia, Energy Demand Management. Retrieved on April 22, 2016.

[3] Pattten, M. 2014. *Understanding Research Methods Ninth Edition*. Glendale, CA, Pyrczak Publishing.

[4] Mello, AP, Sperandio, M, Bernardon, DP, Pfitscher, LL, Canha, LN, Ramos, M, Porto, D, Pressi, R. (2015). Intelligent system for automatic reconfiguration of distribution network with distributed generation. *2015 IEEE 5th International Conference on Power Engineering, Energy and Electrical Drives (POWERENG)*, pp.383–388, 11–13.

[5] Bernardon, DP, Mello, APC, Pfitscher, LL, Canha, LN, Abaide, AR, Ferreira, AAB. (2014). Real-time reconfiguration of distribution network with distributed generation. *Electric Power Systems Research*, 107, pp.59–67.

Chapter 2

Real-Time Reconfiguration of Distribution Network with Distributed Generation

Daniel Bernardon, Ana Paula Carboni de Mello and
Luciano Pfitscher

Additional information is available at the end of the chapter

http://dx.doi.org/10.5772/62632

Abstract

This chapter shows a methodology to accomplish the real-time reconfiguration of distribution networks considering distributed generation in normal operating conditions. The availability of the wind power generation, solar photovoltaic power generation, and hydroelectric power generation is considered in the reconfiguration procedure. The real-time reconfiguration methodology is based on the branch-exchange technique and assumes that only remote-controlled switches are considered in the analysis. The multicriteria analysis, analytic hierarchy process (AHP) method, is used to determine the best switching sequence. The developed algorithms are integrated into a supervisory system, which allows real-time communication with the network equipment. The methodology is verified in a real network of a power utility in Brazil with different typical daily demand curves and distributed generation scenarios.

Keywords: distributed generation, distribution network, real-time reconfiguration, remote-controlled switches, smart grid

1. Introduction

The electric power system, especially the distribution system, is undergoing major changes in its current structure. This new concept of smarter grids, known as smart grids, is incorporating automation technologies and communication in real time to the grid, with more intelligent devices, distributed generators' connection and instant forward actions to electrical problems. These changes in the distribution system enable greater diversity in services related to energy, such as demand management, the use of distributed generation from renewable sources, connection of electric vehicles, and voltage maintenance after self-healing, among others.

In this sense, this chapter presents a new methodology and a software tool for real-time reconfiguration of distribution network considering distributed generation units the renewable sources. The work of [1, 2] indicates that this system has a good performance, applying smart grids concepts, from the information and functionality of remote-controlled equipment installed in the distribution test systems.

This chapter is divided into five sections. The second section presents the main concepts that guide the smart grids. Following is shown the distributed generation technologies to the application exposed in this work. The fourth section presents the reconfiguration methodology developed in real time. Then, the results and discussions are exposed considering a large real distribution system. Finally, the main conclusions are presented in the last section.

2. Smart grids concepts

The smart grids represent a new paradigm in the way power systems are designed and operated. They are characterized by the integration of well-established technologies and concepts that together seek to respond to the increased demand and requirements regarding quality and sustainability in the energy sector [3]. The resources available from technological advances in telecommunication and automation have brought benefits to the grid, especially: fast processing and information exchange between network devices, allowing real-time monitoring and control; cost and time reduction with maintenance teams; the possibility of creating more robust and reliable systems and less susceptible to human limitations; and the integration of network structures, such as distributed generation, stability control, and demand control.

However, the benefits of the technology are often economically viable only if the automated system is part of a larger whole, provided with a degree of intelligence. This applies, for example, for the automatic network restoration, in which the automatic operation of remotely controlled switches must be integrated with the detection and isolation of the fault systems, ensuring the restoration of the largest possible number of consumers. In this case, the system's intelligence can be represented by the response of computer programs that employ optimization techniques and support decision-making.

A general illustration of some features and elements of the smart grids is highlighted in **Figure 1**. From the bottom to the top, the figure shows the main interfaces between the power utility services and equipment, and the consumer and/or micro generator. The middle layer of the figure gives some examples of structures that can be related either to power utilities or to consumers. A brief discussion on the main concepts shown in the **Figure 1** is presented in this section.

http://dx.doi.org/10.5772/62632

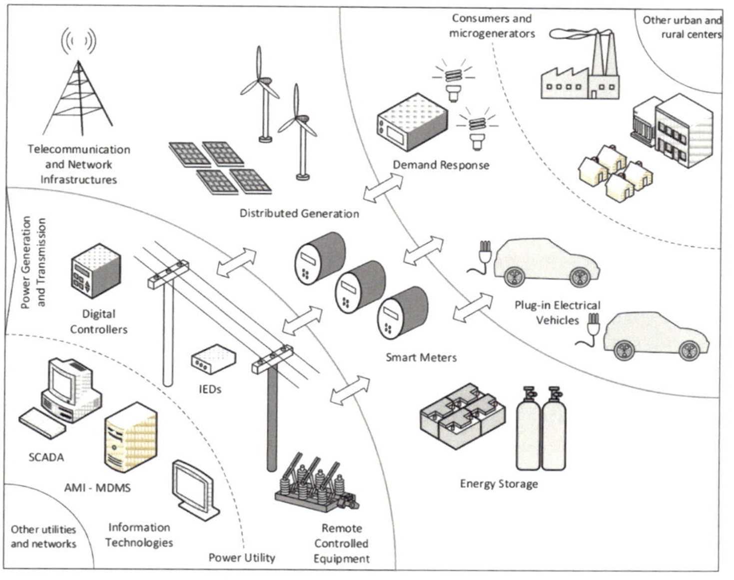

Figure 1. A general view of a smart grid.

2.1. Response demand

The demand response refers to the ability of management and control of power system loads. The primary goal of DR was to reduce peak consumption by turning off loads in higher power consumption schedules. Alternatively, consumption can be shifted to off-peak periods or even can be increased at certain periods, to maintain the stability of generation or to make the most of the available resources, such as energy from distributed generation [4].

The implementation of DR is done through electronic devices that communicate with the power utility and receive commands to turn off the loads connected to them, according to the request of the utility or to the energy rate variation. Previously, a priority study of the loads must be done to avoid interruptions that may harm important services to the consumer.

The demand response is one of the challenges of the energy market facing the smart grids. It can promote greater pressure to reduce prices and increase concern about the use of energy by consumers. From the utility's viewpoint, it may result in a change in load curves and reduction of the peak consumption, which implies lower need for investment in energy reserves. On the other hand, the biggest challenges are the consumers' behavior change, the need for compatible technology—such as advanced metering structures—and the efficiency of government agencies in regulating and supervising the process.

2.2. Advanced metering infrastructures (AMIs)

Advanced metering infrastructure comprises all the elements needed for the measurement and communication between consumers and suppliers. The communication in this case is bidirectional and allows, for example, that a power utility sends to the consumer the real-time energy pricing. Integration with demand response devices allows load management according to the change in the price or according to the need of the power utility.

The advanced metering infrastructure consists of electronic meters, communication networks, and a data management system (MDMS, meter data management system), which is responsible for storing and managing the large amount of data from the power meters and establish interface between the data collected and other features of the network, such as the billing system and maintenance teams, for example.

The advantages of AMIs include the possibility of monitoring the energy billing in real time by the consumer, fast detection of measurement failures and non-technical losses, and the creation of consumer profiles for demand response programs and fast response to energy restoration systems. AMIs also allow the creation of more accurate consumer databases for profiles and demand estimation studies and provide real-time measurements that help in decision-making regarding the system operation. The technological challenges of AMIs include the need for standardization of communication and interfaces between devices, and security issues to ensure that only authorized devices could access the network information [5].

2.3. Smart meters

The smart meter may be considered as an evolution of the automatic electronic power meter. The main feature of smart meters is the two-way communication, which makes it possible to receive real-time power utility commands.

The standard of communication varies depending on the smart meter application project. In some countries, for example, power meters communicate through wire with a data concentrator and the data concentrator communicates with a central by a wireless network. Many smart meters, however, have wireless communication capability directly to the operation center.

Communication can be considered the biggest challenge of deploying smart meters. A wide variety of protocols and possible ways of communication is used, and there is no universal standardization of power meters. Possible arrangements of networks include the use of cellular networks, satellite communications, radio frequency, Wi-Fi, power line communication, directly to a central or a data concentrator, or in cascade mode communicating through a mesh network. The main protocols used are defined by ANSI C12.18 standard in the United States, and IEC 61107/62056 in Europe. Regardless of the type of communication, the discussion about the project to be adopted involves cost, safety, and health.

Some common features in smart meters include possibility of remote connection and shutdown of the energy point, grid failure warning, fraud warning, real-time monitoring of energy bill, and demand control. In some projects, smart meters also have the ability to communicate with user internal devices. For example, in a residence, the smart meter can receive or send information to and from appliances, air-conditioning units. This concept is based on the home area network and enables the timely management of user loads.

http://dx.doi.org/10.5772/62632

2.4. Plug-in electric vehicles

The smart grids led to concerns about changes in consumer load profiles, and the prospect of increased plug-in hybrid electric vehicles (PHEV) connected to the power system is one of the most discussed points [6]. Electric vehicles are characterized by substituting fully or partially (in case of hybrid vehicles) the traditional internal combustion motor by electric motors for vehicle propulsion. Electric motors are typically powered by batteries; and if the batteries are recharged through the electric distribution network, the vehicles are called plug-in.

The impact of PHEVs in power systems is significant, and several studies highlight the need for planning of battery recharges, to avoid concentration of PHEVs overloading the system, and solutions based on the use of the vehicle to inject energy into the network during peak periods (vehicle-to-grid).

The smart grids shall be prepared to absorb this new type of demand. Some aggravating quality factors in power systems can be cited: power imbalances (in case of single-phase chargers), harmonics, and increased voltage drops and losses, particularly in feeders with large extensions. Furthermore, the capacity of distributions transformers may be easily extrapolated if a large amount of PHEVs is loaded simultaneously.

2.5. Small-scale distributed generation

Distributed generation (DG) normally employs renewable energy sources, mainly wind and photovoltaic, due to difficulties of building small conventional power plants, such as hydro and thermal coal, close to consumption centers.

In residences, photovoltaic energy has the advantages of cost and modularity to install in roofs —in the power range up to 10 kW. **Figure 2** shows a typical arrangement of a photovoltaic microgeneration connected to the grid, which includes a set of batteries for energy storage, power electronics circuits (charge control and inverters), and a bidirectional power meter.

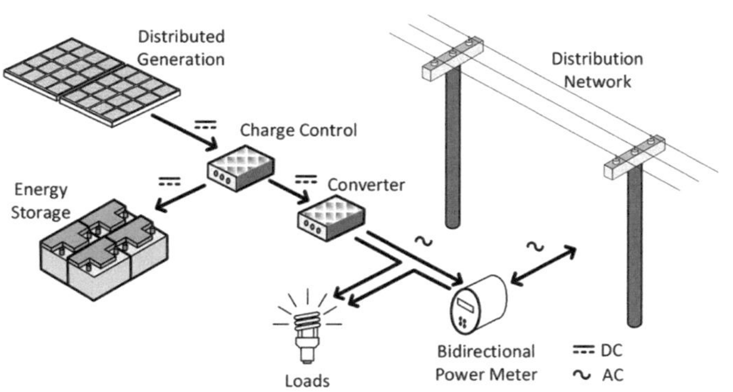

Figure 2. Small-scale generation connected to the grid.

To take advantage of DG, smart grids have to include advanced mechanisms of generation estimation, short- and long-term ability to quickly regulate power and energy storage, and management of distributed resources in conjunction with the demand response [7]. The main technical issues involved are related to power quality, stability, and protection, due to the intermittent characteristic of the primary sources.

2.6. Automation and information technology

A high level of automation and information technology (IT) is expected in a smart grid. The network infrastructure must support data management of electronic meters (MDMS), monitoring and control of network status (overload, reactive power control, etc.), load and distributed generation management, charging of PHEVs, among other features. Information systems should communicate with each other at different levels of implementation, such as power regulation strategies, billing, maintenance management, consumer and network databases, geographic information systems (GIS), among others. Interoperability between standards and communication protocols plays a critical role in the advancement of smart grids. An important reference guide is published by the National Institute of Standards and Technology (NIST) [8].

At the operation center, the supervisory systems (SCADA) perform the interface between the technical team (operator, planner, supervisor, etc.) and the network devices. At the distribution network, some automation features may include automatic adjustment of protection devices, automatic regulation of voltage levels, control of capacitor banks and transformers' taps, control of distributed generation, self-reconfiguration, in addition to the automatic management of loads and consumption measurements. Furthermore, the automation requires the employment of remote-controlled equipment (switches, reclosers, circuit breakers, etc.), and digital controllers and intelligent electronic devices (IEDs).

With the advancement of the smart grids, the profile of the load curves of distribution feeders will be subject to a different dynamic behavior. Some features, such as increased use of distributed generation, demand response, and charging of electric vehicles, will require a fast network response for new generation and load scenarios. The automatic reconfiguration in real time will help to improve the network performance and to promote more efficient use of the smart grids resources.

3. Distributed generation technologies

The concept of distributed generation refers to the use of small generators directly connected to the distribution network or the local network of consumers. Among the current generation sources stand out wind power, photovoltaic, hydroelectric, and diesel. Thermal power plants and biomass have also been employed in DG, but on a smaller scale.

3.1. Wind power

The wind power harnessing is obtained from the kinetic energy conversion of the air masses through translational movement in rotational kinetic energy, using a wind turbine or wind generator for electricity generation. **Figure 3** illustrates the typical components of a wind turbine: rotor, nacelle, generator, sensors, among others.

The rotor is responsible for transforming the kinetic energy of wind in mechanical energy of rotation. The turbine blades are fixed in the rotor, which in turn is connected to a hub interconnected to the generator through a gearbox. The mechanisms to allow operation of the generator are located in the nacelle, for example, the turning control, the brake system, the wind sensors, among others.

3.1.1. Determination of wind power

Only part of the extracted wind power can be used to generate electricity. The amount of energy that can be converted into electricity is obtained by the power coefficient of the wind turbine C_p, which is the ratio between the possible power to be extracted from the wind and the total amount of power contained therein [9, 10]. Equation (1) defines the effective output power of a wind turbine (kg m/s) (where 1 kg m/s is 9.81 W):

$$P_t = \frac{1}{2} \cdot C_p \cdot \rho \cdot A \cdot v^3 \tag{1}$$

where ρ is the specific air density (kg/m³), A is the cross-sectional area (m²) swept by the propeller blades or the turbine blades, e v is the wind speed (m/s).

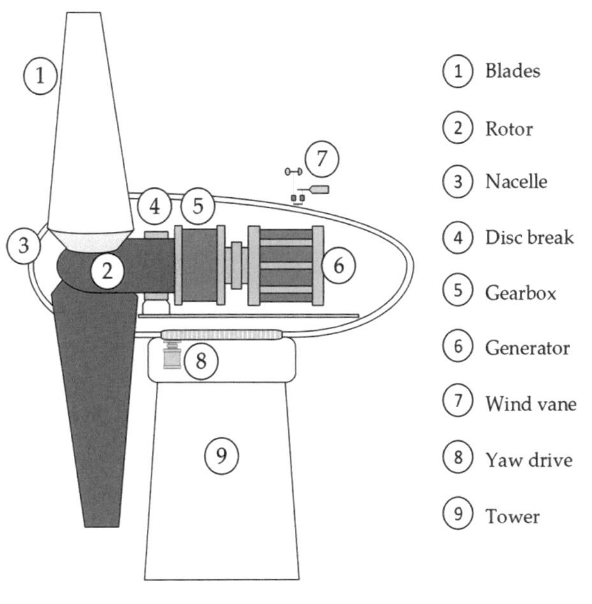

Figure 3. Schematic of a wind turbine generating power.

3.2. Photovoltaic power

Photovoltaic generation uses semiconductor elements capable to generate electricity from the direct conversion of solar energy in electrical energy through solar cells (photovoltaic). Although it can be straightforward, this conversion process depends on the characteristics of each semiconductor and quality of the materials employed in manufacturing technology.

One of the key aspects for the photovoltaic systems implementation is the knowledge of local solar radiation characteristics. These data may be obtained through the meteorological data base information. Solar radiation and temperature are the major variables that affect the generated power of the photovoltaic cells. To illustrate these effects, characteristic curves were obtained with the PV module parameters (245 W KD245GH) of the Kyocera manufacturer [11]. **Figure 4a** shows the *I–V* curves as a function of solar radiation. As can be seen, the solar radiation modifies the available power by changing the output current of a photovoltaic module. Besides to the solar radiation, the operating temperature of the cells also influences the amount of generated power, since the output voltage of the photovoltaic cell is changed depending on the ambient temperature. **Figure 4b** shows the *I–V* characteristic curve considering the temperature variation.

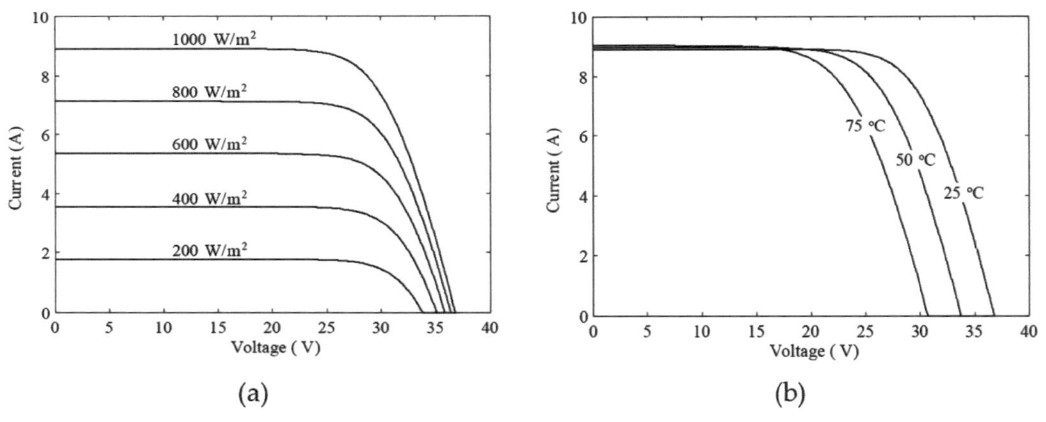

Figure 4. (a) Current and (b) voltage characteristics for the KD245GH module.

3.2.1. Determination of the solar photovoltaic power

The photovoltaic systems' behavior is usually characterized by measuring the voltage and current curves (*I–V* curves) of the PV modules from standard test conditions (STC). These conditions establish the reference values for the radiation (*L*) 1000 W/m^2, temperature (*T*) 25°C, and air mass (*AM*) 1.5.

However, STC conditions rarely occur in real operating conditions. Consequently, the estimation of the PV modules behavior requires extrapolation from the standpoint of real operating conditions.

http://dx.doi.org/10.5772/62632

Currently, there is no standard methodology for assessing the electricity production of PV modules. There are typically two methods of assessing the amount of maximum power that modules produce numerical methods and algebraic methods [12, 13]. The numerical procedures are used to calculate the instantaneous power peak of the curve *I–V* in specific conditions, such as STC. Since the algebraic procedures use data regression analysis using historical data and can be used for any operating condition, they are more suitable for real data applications.

The method of Osterwald is one of the algebraic methods most commonly used because of the simplicity. It allows calculating the output power of a photovoltaic system for any amount of irradiation and cell temperature. Equation (2) shows the method of Osterwald [14]:

$$P_{Máx} = P_{STC} \cdot \frac{G_i}{G_{STC}} \cdot \left[1 - \gamma \cdot (T_i - T_{STC})\right] \tag{2}$$

where P_{STC} is the maximum power generated by the module (Watts), usually being the rated power of the manufacturer datasheet. G_{STC} is the overall radiation to the condition of the STC; G_i and T_i is the overall radiation; and air temperature condition T_{STC} is measured and the temperature for STC condition. Knowing that the STC conditions are given in restricted conditions, it is necessary to apply a power factor correction for temperature, which is represented by γ and corresponds to the value of the interval -0.005 to -0.003°C^{-1}.

3.3. Hydroelectric generation

The energy generation through the hydraulic potential for exploitation in a river can be characterized in different ways: When there is a concentrated unevenness in a waterfall, featuring a natural advantage, through a barrage with small unevenness, or through diversion of river from its natural course. The water is conducted through canals, tunnels, or penstocks and transformed into kinetic energy by spinning of turbine blades; this motion produces electrical power from the drive shaft of a generator.

Small hydro power (SHP) currently accounts for a fast and efficient way to promote the expansion of supply of electricity. This type of project enables better compliance with the consumers' requirement of small urban centers and rural areas, complementing the power supply performed by the conventional system.

Regarding operating philosophies, SHPs have great flexibility, having two main forms of reservoirs regularization: the river or storage, with daily regulation reservoir, and the dispatched power depends on the physical characteristics and techniques and also the central philosophy of the undertaking that holds.

3.3.1. Power extracted from a hydraulic turbine

The estimated output power for a hydraulic turbine can be obtained in relation to the height of the available downfall and of the flow of the hydraulic turbine, considered constant. Generally, the turbines models of Pelton, Francis, Kaplan, and Bulb are used for small hydro projects. The choice considering one or other model is defined according to the height of fall characteristics, water flow, and rotation of the turbine generator set.

In general terms, the power of a turbine can be expressed as the sum of the three forms of energy of Bernoulli's theorem [9], as represented in Eq. (3).

$$\frac{v^2}{2g}+\frac{p}{\rho g}+h=\frac{P}{\rho g Q} \tag{3}$$

where v is the flow velocity (m/s), g represents the gravitational constant (m/s), p is the water pressure (N/m^2) at a height h of water (m) with ρ density (kg/m^3) and a water flow Q (m^3/s).

The output power of the turbine shaft in a hydroelectric system can be obtained through **Eq. (4)** [15].

$$P_e=\rho\cdot g\cdot Q\cdot H_{liq}\cdot\eta_T \tag{4}$$

where ρ represents the specific mass of water (1000 kg/m^3), g is the gravity acceleration (9.81 m/s^2), Q is the flow rate (m^3/s) of the turbine at a drop height H_{liq} (m) with an efficiency of η_T, which depend on the chosen hydraulic turbine model.

4. Automatic reconfiguration of distribution network in real time

4.1. Problem formulation

The reconfiguration of the distribution network is considered an optimization problem in that search, among the various solutions (topologies) possible, the solution that leads to better performance, considering the ultimate goal of reconfiguration and observing the network constraints. One factor that increases the complexity of the problem is the high number of switching devices in a real network, which results in a lot of different possible configurations to be analyzed.

In general, it may be impractical to test all possible combinations and perform, for each of the calculations needed—such as power flow and reliability indicators—in order to identify the setting that results in the best performance. To solve the problem, optimization methods that reduce the search space of the optimal solution are used.

Another problem is that the optimal solution found meets a given situation of power generation and consumption, which typically varies over a period. The load variation during the day, for example, can modify the parameters for which the topology is optimized, resulting in a new optimum configuration. At this point, the solution for the reconfiguration of the network must come from at least two premises:

http://dx.doi.org/10.5772/62632

a. The network must be flexible to allow the reconfiguration, whenever observed the need; and

b. It is necessary to establish a cost–benefit relationship to determine the necessity and the effectiveness of the reconfiguration;

The diagram in **Figure 5** shows the architecture employed in this work to meet these premises. The SCADA program is the main interface between the real-time reconfiguration program developed and the equipment in distribution network.

The first premise is to facilitate the implementation of the reconfiguration, so there is an effective gain with the network topology change. The use of remote-controlled equipment such as switches and reclosers is a solution that meets this premise on two aspects: The reconfiguration can be automated without the need to displacement teams to operate the equipment, and immediate, or can be performed at the time wherein determining its need.

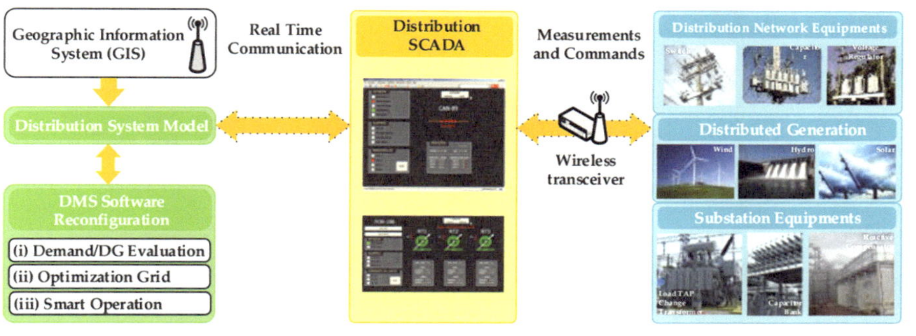

Figure 5. Architecture of the developed system.

The second premise aims to limit the wear of the switching equipment. One solution is to establish relevant levels change in the network (e.g., demand) and parameters utilized as the aim of reconfiguration (e.g., energy losses), and conditioning reset only to cases in which the alteration levels exceed the reference values.

4.1.1. Demand rate evaluation and profile of distributed generation

In order to obtain a good discretization of the demand curve and generation curve to avoid frequent reconfigurations in the network, it is employed a set of six demand rates. The rates are constructed from the average of historical data (typical daily demand curve). The representative demand for one entire period is the maximum value observed in it and the case of generation curve it is used the average output power.

Figure 6 exemplifies the discretization of typical curves; **Figure 6a** shows the demand curves of an industrial feeder; and **Figure 6b** shows a wind turbine generation curve.

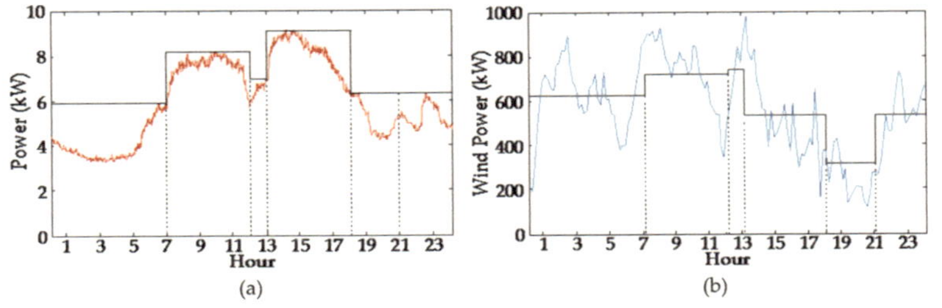

Figure 6. Discretization of typical curves of (a) an industrial feeder, (b) a wind turbine.

4.1.2. Objective functions and constraints

The first stage of the optimization process is to define the objective function (FO) and constraints of the problem. The OF includes the minimization of network indicators:

i. Expected loss of energy in the primary network (*ELosses*);

ii. Expected index of interruption frequency in the system (*ESAIFI*); and

iii. Expected value of energy not supplied (*EENS*).

These three indicators can identify each of the alternatives, and reconfiguration is shown in **Eq. (5)**.

$$OF = \min \left(ELosses_i^* .w_1 + ESAIFI_i^* .w_2 + EENS_i^* .w_3 \right) \tag{5}$$

Subject to:

$$\begin{aligned} |I_i| &\leq I_{i\max} \\ V_{j\min} \leq V_j &\leq V_{j\max} \\ P_{\min} \leq P_{DG_n} &\leq P_{\max} \end{aligned} \tag{6}$$

where i corresponds to the period of analysis: 1...6; $w_1...w_3$ are weights of the criteria in multicriteria method; I_i is current equipment or driver; V_j is operating voltage in permanent state; P_{DGn} is active and reactive power limits provided by the distributed generator, the minimum power equations P_{min}, and maximum power P_{max} presented in Section 3, depend on the DG technology considered.

4.1.3. Optimization technique for selecting configurations

Several optimization methods are proposed to solve the reconfiguration problem of distribution networks. The search techniques can be classified into different categories: heuristics, meta-heuristics, expert systems, and mathematical programming [16]. Following is detailed

http://dx.doi.org/10.5772/62632

one of heuristic search techniques, and considerations are then presented to illustrate a reconfiguration of application example using this technique in a real network model. The heuristic search technique, also known as branch exchange, is based on a local search, where the algorithm looks for a new solution from neighboring configurations in each iteration.

In power systems, the method is premised on the radial configuration of the network. This method consists in carrying out successive changes in network configuration (e.g., opening a switch and closing another), so that each search tree node represents a possible solution of the problem. If the objective function indicators decrease, there is a new solution, and the algorithm continues the search process until no further improvement occurs. The technique can best be understood in two stages:

i. Step A: Analysis of interconnections between feeders in situations where there are not distributed generators connected to the distribution network [17] and

ii. Step B: Analysis of interconnections in situations where there are distributed generators connected to the distribution network [1, 2].

Figure 7 illustrates the flow chart includes the Stage A and Stage B of heuristic search technique for reconfiguration of distribution networks.

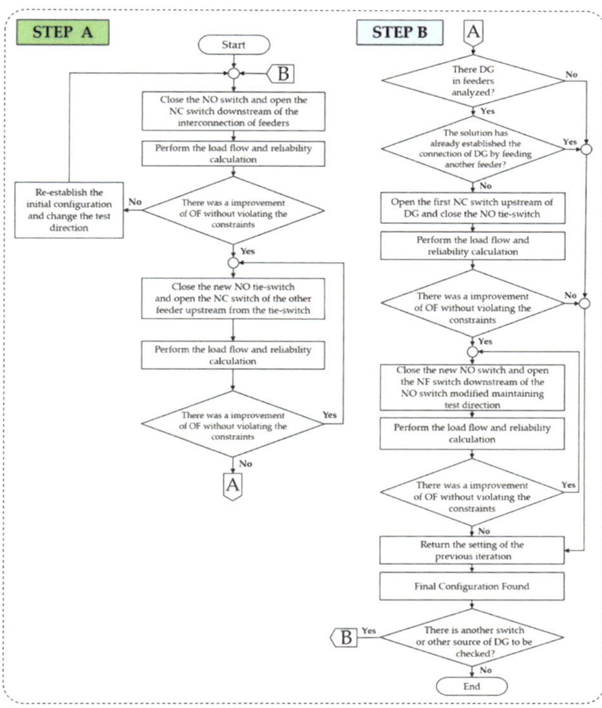

Figure 7. Flowchart from step A and step B of heuristic search technique for reconfiguration of distribution networks.

4.1.4. Decision-making method of multicriteria

The reconfiguration of the distribution network can involve optimization criteria that result in conflicting solutions. For example, considering the minimization of losses and increased reliability, a network topology can represent the optimal solution that meets the first criterion is, however, not represent the optimum solution to the second criterion.

A usual method of multicriteria analysis-based decision-making is the analytic hierarchy process (AHP) proposed by Saaty [18]. In AHP, the degree of preference of one over another objective is quantified through a table of the method suggested by the author, and the relationship between alternatives is represented by a matrix. A detailed description of AHP calculation methodology used in this work is presented in [17], which obtained as results for the indicators of the OF: w_1 (*ELosses*) = 0.64; w_2 (*ESAIFI*) = 0.26 and w_3 (*EENS*) = 0.10.

5. Experimental analysis

The proposed methodology was verified through several tests on the concession area of a power utility of Brazil. The real distribution network model presented in **Figure 8** is used as a case study, and this network has the following:

- Two substations with voltage 69/13.8 kV;
- Five feeders: FD-101; FD-102; and FD 103 connected from the Substation A; and FD-104 and FD-105 connected from the Substation B;
- 15 tie-switches remote-controlled (TS) in normally open state, named and numbered as TS-1 to TS-15;
- 143 remote-controlled switches (S) in normally closed state[1];
- Solar photovoltaic plant of 500 kW, located between the S11 and S12 switches;
- Wind power plant of 1600 kW, located between the TS-10 and S39 switches;
- Hydroelectric power plant (SHP) of 1000 kW, located between the TS-15 and S61 switches.

The original configuration of this system is shown in **Figure 8**, where it is important to highlight the interconnection switches and the distributed generation plants.

5.1. System evaluation

The analysis is done considering the expected maximum values of demand feeders and the average availability of active power generation by source of DG during the period corresponding to each of the six levels, as shown in **Figure 9**. For the developed methodology exemplification, only the results of level 5 are detailed (18h00–20h59).

[1] The manual switches which are not part of the tests are omitted in the representation of the network.

http://dx.doi.org/10.5772/62632

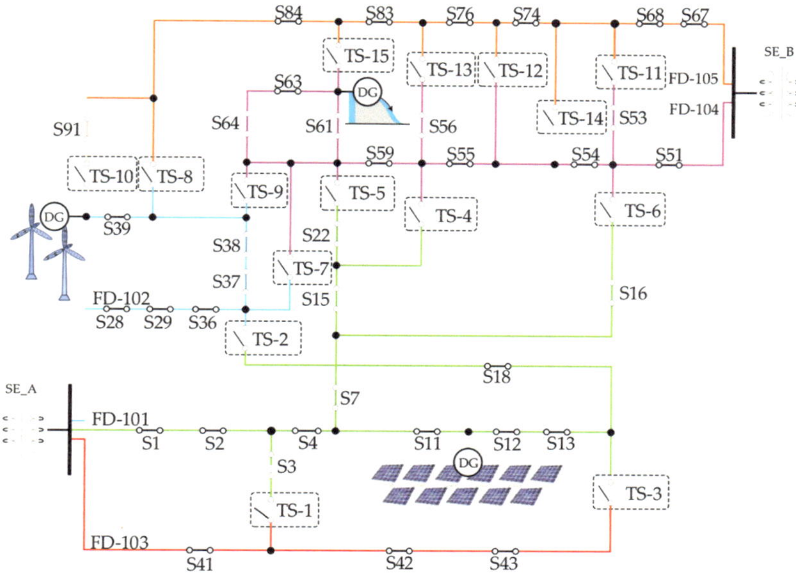

Figure 8. Network distribution with DG.

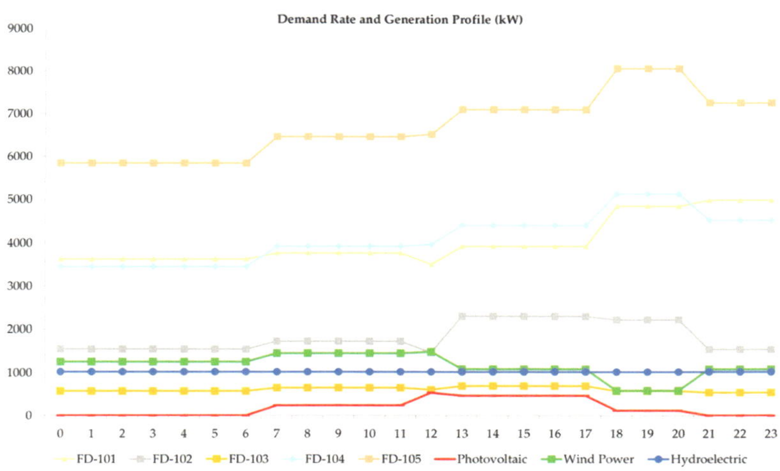

Figure 9. Demand evaluation and generation.

5.2. System optimization

The reconfiguration algorithm is applied considering the individual analysis of each switch interconnection shown in **Figure 8**. The individual analysis of the tie-switches leads to the results shown in **Figure 10**. Only the cases where the objective functions analyzed presented positive evolution are shown.

The results of objective function in **Eq. (5)** are sorted from lowest to highest value to give the best switching sequence. These results of the objective function represent the individual changes made in the network and its effects, as can be seen in **Figure 10a** for energy losses, **Figure 10b** for ESAIFI and **Figure 10c** for EENS.

These sorted results represent one switching sequence that should be performed by reapplying the branch exchange according to the defined order. The best configuration achieved with one tie-switch is preserved as the initial configuration to the following tie-switch to be tested. The final result of the network optimization to the analyzed rate demand is shown in **Figure 11**.

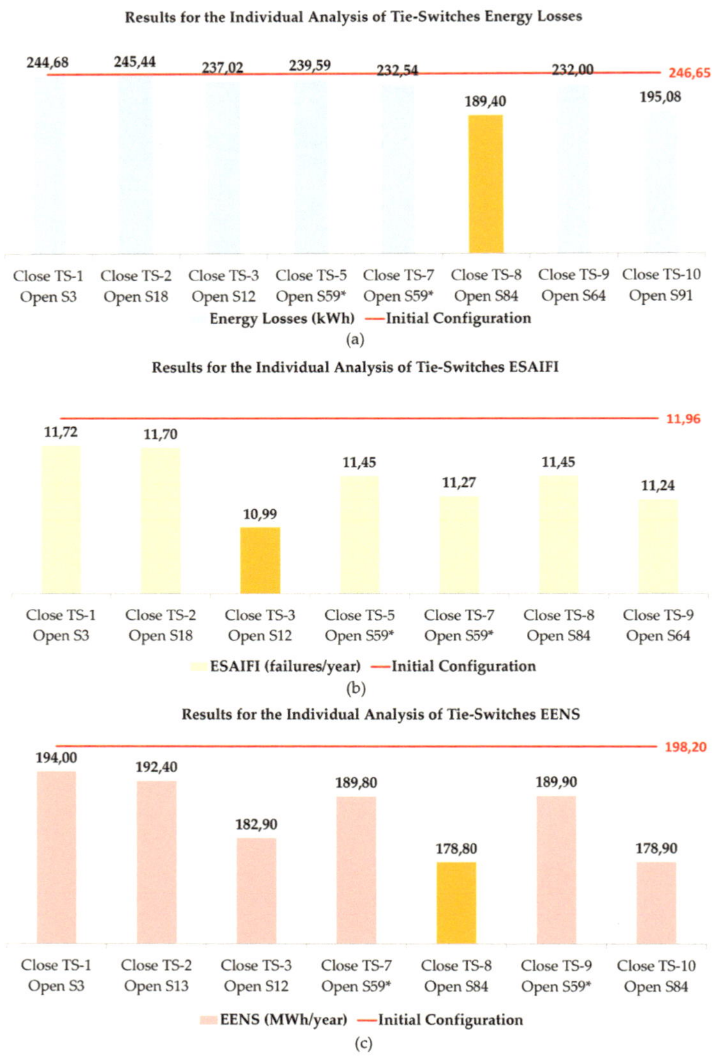

Figure 10. Results for the individual analysis of tie-switches. (a) Energy losses. (b) ESAIFI. (c) EENS.

http://dx.doi.org/10.5772/62632

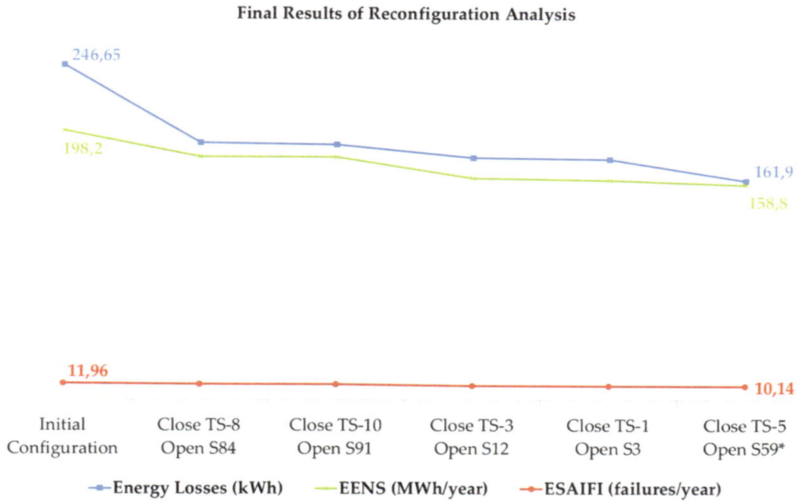

Figure 11. Final results of reconfiguration analysis.

The final result of the optimization of the network to the rate demand analyzed is shown in **Figure 12** which shows the loads distribution between the analyzed feeders; **Figure 12a** shows the original configuration; and **Figure 12b** shows the network configuration after changes. All procedures of the main software were successfully performed to give the best network topology that improves the FO indicators.

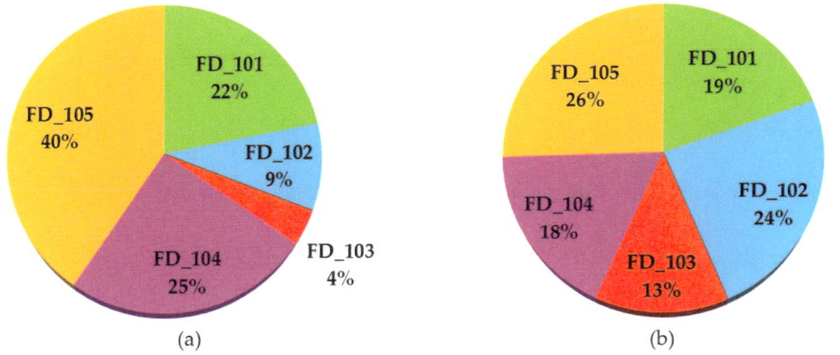

Figure 12. Load distribution between the distribution network feeders: (a) original configuration and (b) after changes reconfiguration.

6. Conclusion

In this chapter, a novel methodology for real-time reconfiguration of power distribution networks considering distributed generation units was presented. The main advantages of the proposed system are automatic change of the network topology based on load rate analysis, modelling, and DG profile from distinct generation sources; multicriteria decision-making is given by the AHP method to choose the switching sequence and, finally, the computational analysis, the supervisory control, and the data acquisition of remote-controlled switches are integrated to perform the real-time reconfiguration. The switching is performed automatically, in the sequence determined by the software. Additionally, case studies are performed with real data from a power utility in Brazil, with the use of different operational scenarios that guarantee a real evaluation of the developed software performance. The results included in this chapter shown the feasibility of the proposed methodology, which assure the use of this system to other real networks with DG.

Acknowledgements

The authors would like to thank the technical and financial support of AES Sul Distribuidora Gaúcha de Energia SA by project "Solução Inovadora para Gerenciamento Ativo de Sistemas de Distribuição" (P&D/ANEEL), Conselho Nacional de Desenvolvimento Científico e Tecnológico (CNPq), Fundação de Amparo à Pesquisa do Estado do Rio Grande do Sul (FAPERGS) and Coordenação de Aperfeiçoamento de Pessoal de Nível Superior (CAPES).

Author details

Daniel Bernardon[1*], Ana Paula Carboni de Mello[1,2] and Luciano Pfitscher[3]

*Address all correspondence to: dpbernardon@ufsm.br

1 Federal University of Santa Maria, Santa Maria, Rio Grande do Sul, Brazil

2 Federal University of Pampa, Alegrete, Rio Grande do Sul, Brazil

3 Federal University of Santa Catarina, Florianópolis, Rio Grande do Sul, Brazil

References

[1] Mello, A.P., Sperandio, M., Bernardon, D.P., Pfitscher, L.L., Canha, L.N., Ramos, M., Porto, D., Pressi, R. "Intelligent system for automatic reconfiguration of distribution network with distributed generation." In: IEEE 5th International Conference on Power Engineering, Energy and Electrical Drives (POWERENG), Riga, Latvia. 11–13 May 2015, pp. 383–388.

[2] Bernardon, D.P., Mello, A.P.C., Pfitscher, L.L. Canha, L.N. Abaide, A.R. Ferreira, A.A.B. Real-time reconfiguration of distribution network with distributed generation. Electric Power Systems Research. 2014;107:59–67.

[3] Brown, R.E. Impact of smart grid on distribution system design. In: Power and Energy Society General Meeting—IEEE Conversion and Delivery of Electrical Energy in the 21st Century, 2008. Pittsburg: IEEE; 2008, pp. 1–4.

[4] Rahimi, F., Ipakchi, A. Demand response as a market resource under the smart grid paradigm. IEEE Transacions on Smart Grid. 2010;1(1):82–88.

[5] Bouhafs, F., Mackay, M., Merabti, M. Links to the future: communication requirements and challenges in the smart grid. IEEE Power & Energy Magazine. 2012;10(1):27–28.

[6] Boulanger, A.G., et al. Vehicle electrification: status and issues. Proceedings of the IEEE. 2011;99(6):116–1138.

[7] Atzeni, I., et al. Demand-side management via distributed energy generation and storage optimization. IEEE Transactions on Smart Grid. 2013;4(2):866–875.

[8] National Institute of Standards and Technology. NIST Framework and Roadmap for Smart Grid Interoperability Standards, Release 2.0. NIST Special Publication 1108R2, 2012.

[9] Farret, F.A., Simões, M.G. Integration of Alternative Sources of Energy. Hoboken, NJ: John Wiley & Sons, Inc., 2006.

[10] Masters, G.M. Renewable and Efficient Electric Power Systems. Hoboken, NJ: John Wiley & Sons, Inc., 2004.

[11] Kyocera Solar. High Efficiency Multi-Crystalline Photovoltaic Module (MODEL KD245GH). Available from: http: //www.kyocerasolar.com.br/pdf/KD245GH-4FB.pdf. [Access: 2015-01-13].

[12] Fuentes, M., et al. Application and validation of algebraic methods to predict the behaviour of crystalline silicon PV modules in Mediterranean climates. Solar Energy. 2007;81(11):1396–1408.

[13] Kroposki, B., et al. A comparison of photovoltaic module performance evaluation methodologies for energy ratings. In: Photovoltaic Energy Conversion 1994, Conference Record of the Twenty Fourth, vol. 1. Waikoloa, HI: IEEE; 1994, pp. 858–862.

[14] Osterwald, C.R. Translation of device performance measurements to reference conditions. Solar Cells. 1986;80401:269–279.

[15] Paish, O. Small hydro power: technology and current status. Renewable and Sustainable Energy Reviews. 2002;6(6):537–556.

[16] Nagata, T., Sasaki, H. An Efficient Algorithm for Distribution Network Restoration. In: IEEE Power Engineering Society Summer Meeting 2001, vol. 1. Vancouver, BC; 2001, pp. 54–59.

[17] Pfitscher, L.L., Bernardon, D.P., Canha, L., Montagner, V., Garcia, V., Abaide, A. "Intelligent system for automatic reconfiguration of distribution network in real time." Electric Power Systems Research. 2013;97:84–92.

[18] Saaty, T.L. The Analytic Hierarchy Process: Planning, Priority Setting, Resource Allocation, New York: McGraw-Hill, 1980.

Chapter 3

Uniform Interfaces for Resource-Sharing Components in Hierarchically Scheduled Real-Time Systems

Martijn M. H. P. van den Heuvel, Reinder J. Bril,
Johan J. Lukkien, Moris Behnam and Thomas Nolte

Additional information is available at the end of the chapter

http://dx.doi.org/10.5772/62691

Abstract

In literature, several hierarchical scheduling frameworks (HSFs) have been proposed for enabling resource sharing between components on a uni-processor system. Each HSF comes with its own set of composition rules which take into account a specific synchronization protocol for arbitrating access to resources. However, the inventors of these synchronization protocols have also chosen to describe these composition rules with the help of protocol-specific component interfaces. This creates unnecessary framework dependencies on components.

In this chapter, we review existing interfaces and propose uniform interfaces to integrate resource-sharing components into HSFs. For the purpose of computing uniform interfaces, we introduce a local (component-level) timing analysis for components which is independent (or agnostic) of the global synchronization protocol being used for arbitrating access to shared resources. An individual component can therefore be analyzed as if all resources are entirely dedicated to it. Given its interface, the component can then be used with an arbitrary global synchronization protocol. This increases the reusability of a component's timing interface, because the interface can still be fed to protocol-specific composition rules when components are integrated.

Keywords: hierarchical scheduling frameworks, resource sharing, component composition, real-time interfaces, synchronization protocol

1. Introduction

Hierarchical scheduling frameworks (HSFs) have been developed to enable composition and reusability of real-time components in complex systems, for example, as described by Holenderski et al. [1] for the automotive domain. During the development of such systems, component models have become important in order to separate and structure the development of system parts over engineering teams (or third parties). The increasing system complexity therefore demands a decoupling of (*i*) development and analysis of individual components and (*ii*) integration of components on a shared platform. This decoupling requires component interfaces covering both functional aspects as well as non-functional aspects, such as timing. An HSF supports system composition from a timing perspective because it isolates components by allocating a *processor budget* to each component. A component that is validated to meet its timing constraints when executed in isolation will continue meeting its timing constraints after integration (or admission) on a shared uni-processor platform. The HSF is therefore a promising solution for industrial standards, e.g., the AUTomotive Open System ARchitecture (AUTOSAR), which more and more specify that an underlying operating system should prevent timing faults in any component to propagate to other components on the same processor.

Independent analysis of components and their integration in HSFs is enabled through a set of composition rules (e.g., as proposed by Shin and Lee [2]). By splitting the timing analysis in complementary parts, one could establish global (system level) timing properties by composing independently specified and analyzed local (component level) timing properties. Local timing properties are analyzed by assuming a worst-case supply of processor resources to a component. The way of modeling the provisioning of the processor budget to a component is defined by a resource-supply model, e.g., the periodic resource model by Shin and Lee [2] or the bounded-delay model by Feng and Mok [3]. These models make it possible to combine the timing constraints of the tasks within a component (typically deadlines) and abstract from the way tasks are locally scheduled. A component can therefore be represented by a single real-time constraint, called *a real-time interface*. Components can be composed into an HSF by combining a set of real-time interfaces, which will treat each component as a single task by itself. This enables reuse of components.

The global scheduling environment (a parent component) can provide more resources to its (child) components than just processor resources. For example, components may use operating system services, memory mapped devices, and shared communication devices requiring mutually exclusive access. An HSF with support for resource sharing makes it possible to share serially accessible resources (from now on referred to as resources) between arbitrary tasks, which are located in arbitrary components, in a mutually exclusive manner. A resource that is only shared by tasks within a single component is a *local shared resource*. Their local scheduling impact can be easily abstracted by real-time interfaces. A resource that is used in more than one component is a *globally shared resource*.

Any access to a resource (local or global) is assumed to be arbitrated by a synchronization protocol. In practical situations, a component developer is typically unconcerned about the sharing scope of resources. A component may access resources for which just local usage or global usage is determined only upon integration of components into the HSF. Fortunately, the syntax of the primitives for accessing local and global resources can be the same, even though the synchronization protocols are different (e.g., as implemented by van den Heuvel,

http://dx.doi.org/10.5772/62691

et al. [4]). The actual binding of function calls to scope-dependent synchronization primitives, that arbitrate either global or local resource access, can be done at compile time or when the component is loaded. Dynamic binding of primitives makes it possible to decouple the specification of global resources in the interface from their use in the implementation. This flexible decoupling of the sharing scope of resources in the application's programming interface is called *opacity* by Martinez et al. [5] and it abstracts whether or not a resource is globally shared in the system.

This chapter presents an extension of this notion of opacity to component analysis and the corresponding derivation of a real-time interface of a component. Opacity requires that the implementation of a component, as well as the way in which interface parameters are derived (the local analysis), are unaware of the global synchronization protocol. In this way, components cannot make use of any knowledge about the constraints and modifications to a component imposed by the global synchronization protocol. By definition of opacity, all computed interface parameters of a component are made independent of a global synchronization protocol.

Based on this observation, we present the following contributions:

- We present a uniform representation of component interfaces and a corresponding opaque analysis to derive these interfaces.
- We survey the existing analyses for components that are assumed to run in HSFs with a particular synchronization protocol. We characterize the opacity compliance of their analyses.

2. Related work

In hierarchically scheduled systems, a group of recurring tasks, forming a component, is mapped on a reservation; reservations were originally introduced by Mercer et al. [6] and Rajkumar et al. [7]. We first review existing works on hierarchical scheduling of independent components. Secondly, we lift the assumption on the independence of components, so that tasks may share resources with other tasks, either within the same component or located in other components. This means that resource sharing expands across reservations which calls for specialized synchronization protocols for arbitrating access to resources. Finally, we discuss the extension of real-time interface representations for components requiring access to shared resources through a synchronization protocol.

2.1. Timing interfaces of independent real-time components

The increasing complexity of real-time systems led to a growing attention for component-based systems. Deng and Liu [8] therefore proposed a two-level HSF for open systems, where components may be independently developed and validated. The corresponding timing analysis of the HSF has been presented by Kuo and Li [9] for fixed-priority preemptive scheduling (FPPS) and by Lipari and Baruah [10] for earliest-deadline-first (EDF) global schedulers.

Later, the research community identified the challenges of separating the timing analysis of the HSF by means of real-time interfaces for components. A real-time interface separates the component's internals (i.e., its tasks and scheduling policy) from its global resource allocation strategy. Wandeler and Thiele [11] calculate demand and service curves for components using real-time calculus. Shin and Lee [2] proposed the periodic resource model to specify periodic processor allocations to components. The explicit-deadline periodic (EDP) resource model by Easwaran et al. [12] extends the periodic resource model of Shin and Lee [2] by distinguishing the relative deadline for the allocation time of budgets explicitly. The bounded-delay model by Feng and Mok [3] describes linear service curves with a bounded initial service delay.

Many works presented approximated [e.g., 13–15] and exact [e.g., 2,12,14] budget allocations for the bounded-delay and periodic resource models under preemptive scheduling policies. Both Lipari and Bini [14] and Shin and Lee [16] have presented methods to convert the bounded-delay model into a periodic resource model. In our chapter, we extend these models in order to support task synchronization.

2.2. Task synchronization in hierarchically scheduled systems

In literature, several alternatives are presented to accommodate resource sharing between tasks in reservation-based systems. de Niz et al. [17] support this in their fixed-priority preemptively scheduled (FPPS) Linux/RK resource kernel based on the immediate priority ceiling protocol (IPCP) by Sha et al. [18]. Steinberg et al. [19] implemented a capacity-reserve donation protocol to solve the problem of priority inversion for tasks scheduled in a fixed-priority reservation-based system. A similar approach is described by Lipari et al. [20] for EDF-based systems and termed bandwidth inheritance (BWI).

BWI regulates resource access between tasks that each have their dedicated budget. It works similar to the priority-inheritance protocol (PIP) by Sha et al. [18], and when a task blocks on a resource, it donates its remaining budget to the task that causes the blocking. BWI does not require a priori knowledge of tasks, i.e., no ceilings need to be precalculated. BWI-like protocols are therefore not very suitable for arbitrating hard real-time tasks in HSFs, because the worst-case interference of all tasks in other components that access global resources needs to be added to a component's budget at integration time in order to guarantee its internal tasks' schedulability also in case budget needs to be donated. This leads to pessimistic budget allocations for hard real-time components. To accommodate resource sharing in HSFs, three synchronization protocols have therefore been proposed based on the stack resource policy (SRP) from Baker [21], i.e., HSRP by Davis and Burns [22], SIRAP by Behnam et al. [23], and BROE by Bertogna et al. [24].

2.3. Timing interfaces for resource-sharing components

Global resource sharing in HSFs is often based on the SRP by Baker [21] in order to compute blocking delays in the schedule; these computations follow a similar approach as the SRP, which is then re-used at the various scheduling levels in the HSF. In addition, resource sharing requires scheduling mechanisms which have an impact on the local scheduling of a component. If a task that accesses a globally shared resource is suspended during its execution due to the exhaustion of its (processor) budget, excessive blocking periods can occur which may hamper the correct timeliness of other components (see Ghazalie and Baker [25]). To prevent such budget depletion during global resource access (see **Figure 1**), four synchronization protocols have been proposed. These are based on two general mechanisms to prevent budget depletion during the execution of a task's critical section:

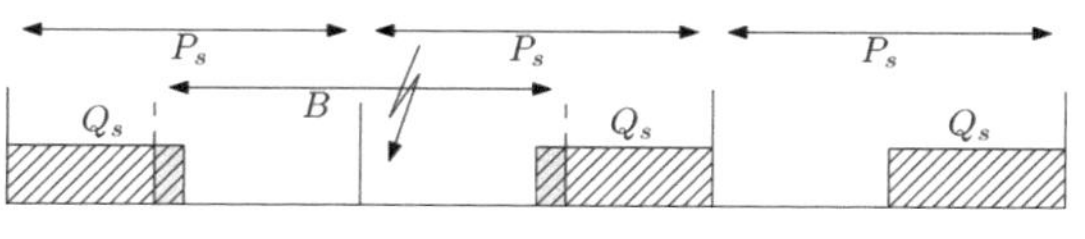

Figure 1. When the budget Q_s (allocated every period P_s) of a task depletes while a task executes on a global resource, tasks in other components may experience excessive blocking durations, B.

1. *self-blocking:* wait with accessing a resource when the remaining budget is insufficient to complete a resource access entirely. Self-blocking comes in two flavors: (*i*) the subsystem integration and resource allocation policy (SIRAP) by Behnam et al. [23] and (*ii*) the bounded-delay resource open environment (BROE) by Bertogna et al. [24]. With SIRAP, a self-blocked task essentially spin locks, i.e., it idles the component's budget away, while the task is waiting for its budget to replenish. Instead, BROE delays the remaining processor's resource supply to a component if there is insufficient budget to complete the entire critical section and if the budget supplied so far is running ahead with respect to the guaranteed processor utilization.

   The idea of self-blocking has also been considered in different contexts, e.g., see [26] for supporting soft real-time tasks and see Holman and Anderson [27] for a zone-based protocol in a pfair scheduling environment. SIRAP by Behnam et al. [23] and BROE by Bertogna et al. [24] use self-blocking for hard real-time tasks in HSFs on a single processor and their associated analysis supports composition. Behnam et al. [28] have significantly improved the original SIRAP analysis by Behnam et al. [23] for arbitrating multiple shared resources; similarly, Biondi et al. [29] have improved the analysis of BROE for arbitrating multiple shared resources. However, these improvements also complicate the analysis and they make the timing analysis more protocol specific.

2. *overrun:* execute over the budget boundary until the resource is released—called the hierarchical stack resource policy (HSRP) by Davis and Burns [22]. HSRP has two flavors: overrun with payback (OWP) and overrun without payback (ONP). The term *without payback* means that the additional amount of budget consumed during an overrun does not have to be returned in the next budget period.

   The overrun mechanism (with payback) was first introduced by Ghazalie and Baker [25] in the context of aperiodic servers. This mechanism was later re-used in HSRP in the context of two-level HSFs by Davis and Burns [22] and complemented with a variant *without* payback. Although the analysis presented by Davis and Burns [22] does not integrate in HSFs due to the lacking support for independent analysis of components, this limitation is lifted by Behnam et al. [30].

Although these four resource-arbitration protocols prevent budget depletion during a task's resource access, in order to do so, processor resources may need to be delivered differently. This, on its turn, may add constraints to the supply of processor resources in order to preserve local deadline constraints of tasks. Protocol developers deal with these constraints in different ways and sometimes these are already taken into account in the local analysis of a component (e.g., see [28–30]). This may therefore result in protocol-specific interfaces of components.

We present a uniform way to model the local constraints on the component's processor supply imposed by resource sharing by extending the periodically constrained model of Feng and Mok [3], as presented for independent components by Shin and Lee [16]. It is therefore important to know which resources a task will access in order to support independent analysis of each of the resource-sharing components. Our local analysis then yields the same timing interface, regardless of the protocol being used for global resource synchronization. During the integration of components, we take those interfaces and we analyze the impact of synchronization penalties with the help of protocol-specific composition rules.

3. Real-time scheduling model

A system contains a single processor and a set $\mathcal{R}$ of M resources $R_1, \ldots, R_M$. The processor and (some of) these resources need to be shared by N components, $C_1, \ldots, C_N$, and each component executes its work through a set of (concurrent) tasks (as depicted in **Figure 2**).

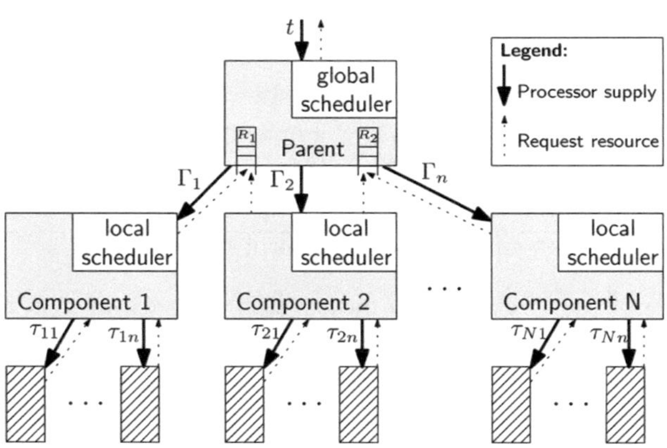

Figure 2. Overview of our system model. A parent component implements a global scheduler to allocate a share of the processor and a share of other resources, e.g., R_1 and R_2, to each of its child components, $C_1 \ldots C_N$. Each child component, C_s, contains a set of tasks, $\tau_{s1} \ldots \tau_{sn}$, and a local scheduler. Tasks, located in arbitrary components, may share resources. Tasks receive their share of the resources as specified by their component interface, Γ_s.

3.1. Component and task model

Each component C_s contains a set T_s of n_s sporadic, deadline-constrained tasks $\tau_{s1}, \ldots, \tau_{sn_s}$. A sporadic task generates an infinite sequence of jobs which are activated at least T_{si} time units separated from each other. Each sporadic job may arrive at an arbitrary moment in time, i.e., it may delay its arrival for an arbitrarily long period. A sporadic task can be seen as a sporadically periodic task which exhibits its worst-case processor demand when subsequent jobs arrive separated minimally in time, i.e., similar to a periodic task under arbitrary phasing (see Liu and Layland [31]).

We extend the timing characteristics of a sporadic task, as introduced by Mok [32], with a parameter to capture its resource requirements. The timing characteristics of a task $\tau_{si} \in \mathsf{T}_s$ are therefore specified by means of a quadruple $(T_{si}, E_{si}, D_{si}, \mathcal{H}_{si})$, where $T_{si} \in \mathrm{IR}^+$ denotes its minimum inter-arrival time, $E_{si} \in \mathrm{IR}^+$ its worst-case execution time (WCET), $D_{si} \in \mathrm{IR}^+$ its (relative) deadline (where $0 < E_{si} \leq D_{si} \leq T_{si}$), and $\mathcal{H}_{si}$ denotes the set of its WCETs of critical sections. The WCET of task τ_{si} within a critical section accessing global resource R_ℓ is denoted $h_{si\ell}$ (i.e., a value contained in $\mathcal{H}_{si}$), where $h_{si\ell} \in \mathbb{R}^+ \cup \{0\}$, $E_{si} \geq h_{si\ell}$. For tasks, we also adopt the basic assumptions by Liu and Layland [31], i.e., jobs do not suspend themselves, a job of a task does not start before its previous job is completed, and the overhead of context switching and task scheduling is ignored. For notational convenience, tasks (and components) are given in deadline-monotonic order, i.e., τ_{s1} has the smallest deadline and τ_{sn_s} has the largest deadline. A task set is said to be schedulable if all jobs of the tasks are able to complete their WCET of E_{si} time units within D_{si} time units from their arrival. The tasks of this component have to meet their deadlines with a particular budget on the processor and each resource being used. These budgets specify the periodically guaranteed fraction of the resource that the tasks may use. The timing interface of a component C_s specifies this budget, i.e., the interface is denoted by a triple $\Gamma_s = (P_s, Q_s, \mathsf{X}_s)$, where $P_s \in \mathrm{IR}^+$ denotes the component's period, $Q_s \in \mathrm{IR}^+$ denotes its budget on the processor, and X_s denotes the set of resource holding times to global resources (which may be seen as budgets on resources). The maximum value in X_s is denoted by X_s and, just like any budget, the resource holding time must fit in the components budget: $0 \leq X_s \leq P_s$. The period P_s therefore serves as an implicit deadline of the component.

The set $\mathcal{R}_s$ denotes the subset of global resources accessed by component C_s, so that $h_{si\ell} > 0 \Leftrightarrow R_\ell \in \mathcal{R}_s$ and the cardinality of $\mathcal{R}_s$ is denoted by m_s (just like the cardinality of X_s). The maximum time that a component C_s executes on the processor while accessing resource $R_\ell \in \mathcal{R}_s$ is called the resource holding time which is denoted by $X_{s\ell}$, where $X_{s\ell} \in \mathrm{IR}^+ \cup \{0\}$ and $X_{s\ell} > 0 \Leftrightarrow R_\ell \in \mathcal{R}_s$. The relation between the WCET of a critical section ($h_{si\ell}$) and the resource holding times ($X_{s\ell}$) of a component is further explained in Section 4.1.

3.2. Scheduling model

A unique system-level (global) scheduler selects which component, and when a component, is executed on the shared processor. The component-level (local) scheduler decides which of the tasks of the executing component is allocated the processor. The global scheduler and each of the local schedulers of individual components may apply different scheduling policies. As scheduling policies, we consider EDF, an optimal dynamic uniprocessor scheduling algorithm, and the deadline-monotonic (DM) algorithm, an optimal priority assignment for FPPS of deadline-constrained tasks. The SRP by Baker [21] is used to arbitrate access to shared resources between components at the global level; similarly, the SRP is used at the local level to arbitrate access to shared resources between tasks locally.

3.3. Synchronization protocol

This chapter focuses on arbitrating *global* shared resources using the SRP. To be able to use the SRP for synchronizing global resources, its associated ceiling terms need to be extended.

3.3.1. Preemption levels

With the SRP, each task τ_{si} is assigned a static preemption level equal to $\pi_{si} = 1/D_{si}$. Similarly, we assign a component a preemption level equal to $\Pi_s = 1/P_s$, where period P_s serves as a relative deadline. If components (or tasks) have the same calculated preemption level, then the smallest index determines the highest preemption level.

3.3.2. Resource ceilings

With every global resource R_ℓ two types of resource ceilings are associated; a *global* resource ceiling RC_ℓ for global scheduling and a *local* resource ceiling $rc_{s\ell}$ for local scheduling. These ceilings are statically calculated values, which are defined as the highest preemption level of any component or task that shares the resource. According to the SRP, these ceilings are defined as:

$$RC_\ell = \max(\Pi_N, \max\{\Pi_s \mid R_\ell \in \mathcal{R}_s\}), \tag{1}$$

$$rc_{s\ell} = \max(\pi_{sn_s}, \max\{\pi_{si} \mid h_{si\ell} > 0\}). \tag{2}$$

We use the outermost max in (1) and (2) to define RC_ℓ and $rc_{s\ell}$ in those situations where no component or task uses R_ℓ. The values of the local and global ceilings as defined in (1) and (2) by definition guarantee mutual exclusive access to their corresponding resource R_ℓ by the sharing tasks and components and, therefore, the values of these ceilings cannot be further decreased. In some situations—as further investigated by Shin et al. [33] and van den Heuvel et al. [34]—it might be desirable to limit preemptions more than is strictly required for mutual exclusive resource access, which can be established by increasing the value of the local resource ceilings in (2) artificially. On the contrary, increasing the global ceiling, i.e., the value of RC_ℓ in (1), never returns schedulability improvements.

http://dx.doi.org/10.5772/62691

3.3.3. System and component ceilings

The system ceiling and the component ceiling are dynamic parameters that change during execution. The system ceiling is equal to the highest global resource ceiling of a currently locked resource in the system. Similarly, the component ceiling is equal to the highest local resource ceiling of a currently locked resource within a component. Under the SRP, a task can only preempt the currently executing task if its preemption level is higher than its component ceiling. A similar condition for preemption holds for components.

4. Opaque schedulability analysis of a component

After developing a component and before publishing it to a framework integrator, a component is packaged as a re-usable entity. This includes deriving a timing interface to abstract from deadline constraints of tasks. Such an abstraction requires an explicit choice for a resource-supply model, capturing the processor supply to a component. Moreover, a component specifies what it needs in terms of resources and exposes those resources that may be shared globally in its interface. Whether or not a global resource is actually used by other components is unknown within the context of a component.

There are several ways to account for local scheduling penalties due to global resource sharing. One might assume that each resource must be globally shared and, subsequently, account for the worst-case overhead inside the local analysis. Alternatively, we opt for the assumption that all resources are just locally shared during the local analysis and we compensate for global sharing between components at integration time. These assumptions are often made tacitly.

The latter alternative presents the same view as during component development, i.e., a component has the entire platform at its disposal and all resources. Whenever a synchronization protocol for global resources is used that is compliant with a synchronization protocol for local resources, the local analysis of a component can be based on local properties only. We call such a local analysis *opaque* because it separates local and global resource arbitration.

Definition 1*An opaque analysis provides a sufficient local schedulability condition for an individual component. It treats all resources accessed by the component as local, so that, even under global sharing, properties of the global synchronization protocol do not influence the computed interface parameters.*

The key consequence of an opaque local analysis is the absence of assumptions on the global synchronization protocol. Section 4.1 shows how resource holding times, $X_{s\ell} \in \mathsf{X}_s$, can be computed without making assumptions on the global synchronization protocol. Next, we accomplish the same for budget parameter Q_s in the interface of the component. This means that the values of the resource holding times should be absent in the equations that validate the local tasks' schedulability. **Table 1** gives an overview of local analyses found in literature by indicating their opacity. This section proceeds with an opaque analysis which ultimately results in a uniform representation of component interfaces, $\Gamma(P_s, Q_s, X_s)$.

Analysis of resource-sharing strategies	Authors	Opacity	Impact on local analysis
BROE	Bertogna et al. [24]	Yes	–
Enhanced BROE	Biondi et al. [29]	No	Proc.-supply model uses RHTs
HSRP—overrun without payback (ONP)	Davis and Burns [22]	No	Not compositional
HSRP—overrun without payback (ONP)	Behnam et al. [30]	Yes	–
Enhanced overrun	Behnam et al. [30]	No	Proc.-supply model uses RHTs
Improved overrun without payback	Behnam et al. [35]	No	Proc.-supply model uses RHTs
HSRP—overrun with payback (OWP)	Davis and Burns [22]	No	Not compositional
HSRP—overrun with payback (OWP)	Behnam et al. [30]	No	Proc.-supply model uses RHTs
SIRAP	Behnam et al. [23,28]	No	Proc.-supply model uses RHTs

Table 1. Overview of the synchronization protocol's support for integrating resource-sharing components into the HSF with opaque analysis.

4.1. Computing resource holding times

The resource holding times were introduced by Bertogna et al. [36] in order to represent the cumulative processor time consumed by the tasks within the same component C_s that can preempt a task τ_i while it is holding a resource R_ℓ. The way of computing resource holding times of tasks therefore depends on the local scheduling policy, because the scheduling policy determines possible preemptions. Besides the scheduling policy, preemptions may be limited by a resource ceiling, i.e., the value of the local resource ceiling $rc_{s\ell}$ also influences the *resource holding times* (see **Figure 3**). In an HSF, the resource holding time represents the longest critical-section length as experienced by blocked tasks in other components.

In literature, various system assumptions in the description of a particular global synchronization protocol have shown to affect the way of computing resource holding times [e.g., see 23, 24, 30]. However, all these methods can be simplified and unified (independent of the local scheduling policy and the global synchronization protocol) by assuming that the component's period P_s is smaller than the tasks' periods.

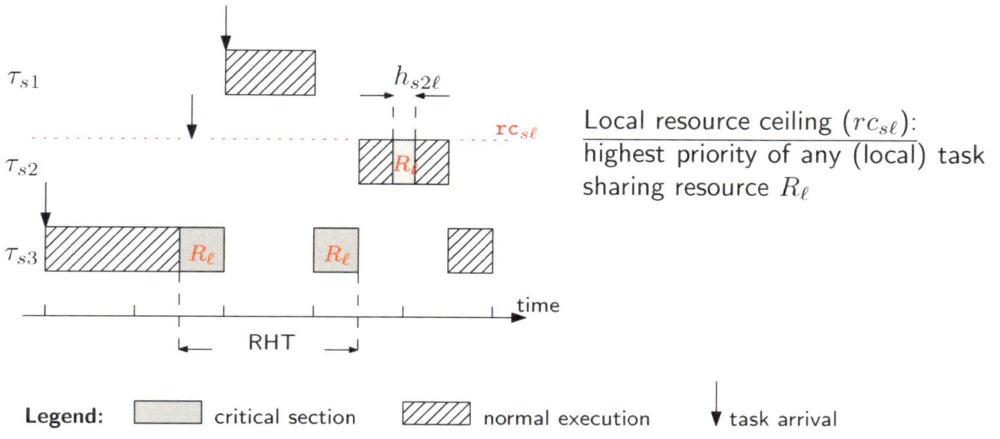

Figure 3. The resource holding time (RHT) represents the cumulatively consumed processor time by any task of a component while one task holds a resource. In order to guarantee mutual-exclusive access to resource R_ℓ, the associated resource ceiling ($rc_{s\ell}$) is at least equal to the highest preemption level of any (local) task sharing resource R_ℓ. One may consider to further limit preemptions during critical sections by increasing the resource ceiling. On the one hand, this may lead to longer blocking delays to tasks with a higher preemption level (in this case: τ_{s1}). On the other hand, this decreases the tasks' RHTs (in this case: τ_{s2} or τ_{s3}).

The main observation leading to this simplification is that an access to a global resource must be followed by a release of the resource in the same component period, for example, established by the self-blocking mechanisms or the overrun mechanisms considered in real-time literature. If a resource must be accessed and released in the same component period which is smaller than the task periods, then we can limit the number of preemptions within a critical section and this, on its turn, will lead to a smaller resource holding time. The resource holding time of a task τ_i accessing a resource R_ℓ is captured by a value $X_{si\ell}$, which represents the amount of processor time supplied to component C_s from the access until the release of task τ_{si} to resource R_ℓ. We now present a lemma that captures the possible preemptions of task τ_i, regardless of other system assumptions.

Lemma 1 (Taken from van den Heuvel et al. [34]). *Given $P_s < T_s^{\min}$ and $T_s^{\min} = \min\{T_{si} \mid 1 \le i \le n_s\}$, all tasks τ_{sj} that are allowed to preempt a critical section accessing a global shared resource R_ℓ, i.e., $\pi_{sj} > rc_{s\ell}$, can preempt at most once during an access to resource R_ℓ when using any global SRP-compliant protocol, independent if the local scheduler is EDF or FPPS.*

Lemma 1 makes it possible to compute the *resource holding time*, $X_{si\ell}$ of task τ_{si} to resource R_ℓ as follows:

$$X_{si\ell} = h_{si\ell} + \sum_{\pi_{sj} > rc_{s\ell}} E_{sj}, \tag{3}$$

and the maximum resource holding time within a component C_s is computed as

$$X_{s\ell} = \max\{X_{si\ell} \mid 1 \le i \le n_s\}. \tag{4}$$

The computed values of $X_{s\ell}$ are included in the set X_s which is part of the component's interface, Γ_s. We recall that opacity requires that the way of computing the interface parameters Q_s and X_s of a component is independent of the global synchronization protocol; Lemma 1 establishes this requirement for the set of resource holding times, X_s, of a component.

4.2. Computing a processor budget

The traditional schedulability analysis of tasks fills in task characteristics in a demand-bound function or a request bound function and compares the tasks' requirements with the supplied processor resources. The same schedulability analysis holds for tasks executing within a component, although the processor supply is modeled in a more complicated way.

The *processor supply* refers to the amount of processor resources that a component C_s can provide to its tasks in order to satisfy deadline constraints. The linear lower bound of the processor resources supplied to a component with a periodically assigned processor (specified by an interface $\Gamma_s = (P_s, Q_s, \mathrm{X}_s)$) is given by [2]:

$$\mathtt{lsbf}_{\Gamma_s}(t) = \frac{Q_s}{P_s}\left(t - 2\left(P_s - Q_s\right)\right). \tag{5}$$

The longest interval a component may receive no processor supply on a periodic resource $\Gamma_s = (P_s, Q_s, \mathrm{X}_s)$ is named the *blackout duration*, i.e.,

$$BD_s = \max\left\{t \mid \mathtt{lsbf}_{\Gamma_s}(t) = 0\right\} = 2(P_s - Q_s). \tag{6}$$

The $\mathtt{lsbf}_{\Gamma_s}(t)$ in (5) is not only a linear approximation of the supplied processor resources in an interval of length t, it also models a bounded-delay resource supply as defined by [3] with a continuous, fractional provisioning of $\frac{Q_s}{P_s}$ of the shared processor (also referred to as the virtual processor speed) and a longest initial service delay of BD_s time units.

4.2.1. Testing interfaces with earliest-deadline-first scheduling of tasks

Assume we are given a component C_s and its tasks have to execute on a periodic budget Q_s every period P_s. If this processor budget is allocated to the tasks according to an EDF scheduling policy, then the following sufficient schedulability condition holds (as described by Shin and Lee [16]):

http://dx.doi.org/10.5772/62691

$$\forall t : t \in S_s : dbf_s(t) \leq lsbf_{\Gamma_s}(t), \tag{7}$$

where $\texttt{dbf}_s(t)$ denotes the cumulative processor demand of all tasks of component C_s for a time interval of length t and the set S_s denotes a non-empty finite set of time-interval lengths (see Baruah [37]), i.e.,

$$\mathsf{S}_s \stackrel{\text{def}}{=} \left\{ t = b \cdot T_{si} + D_{si} \mid 1 \leq i \leq n_s; b \in \mathrm{N}^+; t \in \left(0, \mathrm{lcm}\left\{T_{s1}, \ldots, T_{sn_s}\right\}\right]\right\}. \tag{8}$$

The $\texttt{dbf}_s(t)$ is fully compliant to the schedulability analysis for task sets on a dedicated unit-speed processor, i.e.,

$$\texttt{dbf}_s(t) = b_s(t) + \sum_{1 \leq i \leq n_s} \left\lfloor \frac{t - D_{si} + T_{si}}{T_{si}} \right\rfloor E_{si}. \tag{9}$$

The blocking term, $b_s(t)$, is defined according to the SRP, as described by Baruah [37]:

$$b_s(t) = \max\{h_{sj\ell} \mid \exists k : h_{sk\ell} > 0 \wedge D_{sk} \leq t < D_{sj}\}. \tag{10}$$

The algorithmic complexity of verifying the scheduling condition in (7) is pseudo-polynomial in the number of tasks.

4.2.2. *Testing interfaces with fixed-priority preemptive scheduling of tasks*

Assume we are given a component C_s and its tasks have to execute on a periodic budget Q_s every period P_s. If this processor budget is allocated to the tasks according to a FPPS policy, then the following sufficient schedulability condition holds (as described by Shin and Lee [16]):

$$\forall 1 \leq i \leq n_s : \exists t \in \mathsf{S}_{si} : \texttt{rbf}_s(t,i) \leq \texttt{lsbf}_{\Gamma_s}(t), \tag{11}$$

where $\texttt{rbf}_s(t, i)$ denotes the worst-case cumulative processor request of τ_{si} for a time interval of length t and the set S_{si} denotes a non-empty finite set of time-interval lengths (see Lehoczky et al. [38]), i.e.,

$$\mathsf{S}_{si} \stackrel{\text{def}}{=} \left\{ t = b \cdot T_{sa} \mid a < i; b \in \mathbf{N}^+; t \in (0, D_{si}] \right\} \cup \{D_{si}\}. \tag{12}$$

The $\texttt{rbf}_s(t, i)$ is fully compliant to the schedulability analysis for task sets on a dedicated unit-speed processor, i.e.,

$$\texttt{rbf}_s(t,i) = b_{si} + \sum_{1 \le j \le i} \left\lceil \frac{t}{T_{sj}} \right\rceil E_{sj}. \tag{13}$$

The blocking term, b_{si}, is defined according to the SRP, as described by Baker [21]:

$$b_{si} = \max\{h_{sj\ell} \mid \pi_{sj} < \pi_{si} \le rc_{s\ell}\}. \tag{14}$$

The algorithmic complexity of verifying the scheduling condition in (11) is pseudo-polynomial in the number of tasks.

4.2.3. *Deriving the processor budget from the scheduling test*

Computing a processor budget for a component C_s involves a function that takes a fixed period P_s, a task set and a local scheduling policy as input and returns the smallest component budget Q_s. The function should satisfy, dependent on the local scheduling policy, the condition in (7) or (11).

One may approximate the size of the smallest required processor budget by means of a binary search in the range $Q_s \in (0, P_s)$. As amongst others suggested by Shin and Lee [2], the smallest value of budget Q_s can be found by means of taking an intersection between the left-hand sides and the right-hand sides of the inequalities. This intersection concerns solving a simple quadratic equation (e.g., see Lipari and Bini [14]).

5. Integration of components and global schedulability

In this section, we present the composition rules of components in HSFs in the presence of global shared resources. A global integration test implements the admission control for components based on the resource requirements specified in their interfaces. The global analysis explicitly takes into account the corresponding penalties for global resource sharing which depend on the synchronization protocol applied at the top-level scheduler. These penalties include (*i*) blocking between components and (*ii*) protocol-specific penalties (in our case, either BROE, ONP, OWP, or SIRAP). Dependent on the chosen global synchronization protocol, the latter influences the processor requests by a component or it influences the processor supplies to a component. To analyze these scheduling penalties appropriately, it is reasonable to assume that during component-integration in the HSF, the synchronization protocol of the HSF is known.

http://dx.doi.org/10.5772/62691

Looking at resource sharing between components, the effectively used processor bandwidth of a component therefore depends on two parts (see Section 3.1): the processor budget (denoted by Q_s in interface Γ_s) and the set of budgets on global resources (which are the resource holding times denoted by X_s in interface Γ_s). The budget Q_s should be sufficient to meet the deadline constraints of the tasks and no other constraints should influence the size of Q_s (e.g., constraints related to global synchronization should be avoided). The resource holding times define the amount of execution time that a component receives for an accessing a global resource. In other words, if component C_s is granted access to resource R_ℓ, it receives $X_{s\ell}$ time units of execution time on resource R_ℓ prior to the implicit deadline P_s. The global synchronization protocol defines how this is established and the run-time rules of the protocol may or may not lead to an overlap of the processor allocation times to a component as contained in Q_s and X_s. In the remainder of this section, we show the integration of components for two scheduling policies (EDF and FPPS) applied to the allocated bandwidth of the components.

5.1. Earliest-deadline-first scheduling of components

In the processor supply model, we assumed that the component's period also serves as a deadline for the provisioning of its processor budget. The following utilization-based schedulability condition, as defined by Baruah [37], can therefore be applied to the top-level EDF-scheduler:

$$\forall w : 1 \le w \le N : \frac{B(P_w)}{P_w} + \sum_{1 \le s \le w} \frac{Q_s + O_s(P_s)}{P_s} \le 1. \tag{15}$$

The blocking term, $B(t)$, presents the resource holding time of a potentially interfering, resource-sharing component with a deadline beyond the considered component, C_w; it is defined by Baruah [37]:

$$B(t) = \max\{X_{u\ell} \mid \exists s : R_\ell \in \mathrm{R}_u \cap \mathrm{R}_s \wedge P_s \le t < P_u\}. \tag{16}$$

The term $O_s(t)$ defines the additional amount of budget that a component C_s requires under a certain global synchronization protocol in order to prevent excessive blocking durations for other components in the system.

With ONP, a component can request for an additional amount of X_s time units of processor time each period P_s. Similarly, with SIRAP, a task of a component may idle away at most X_s time units of processor time each period P_s. Hence, the synchronization penalties of both SIRAP and ONP can be modeled by allocating X_s time units of processor time in addition to the regular processor budget Q_s in each period P_s, so that the term $O_s(t)$ is defined by Behnam et al. [30] for ONP and van den Heuvel et al. [39] for SIRAP:

$$O_s(t) = \left\lfloor \frac{t}{P_s} \right\rfloor X_s. \tag{17}$$

With OWP, a component can only request an additional amount of X_s time units of processor time once. Hence, the term $O_s(t)$ is defined by [30]:

$$O_s(t) = \begin{cases} X_s & \text{if } t \geq P_s \\ 0 & \text{otherwise.} \end{cases} \tag{18}$$

For both SIRAP and BROE, it is required that $X_s \leq Q_s$ in order to be able to complete an entire critical section within a single budget of size Q_s. For SIRAP, we establish this condition by allocating $Q_s + X_s$ time units of processor budget every period P_s. For BROE, however, we increase Q_s with $O_s(t)$ time units if it is too small to fit X_s time units contiguously, where $O_s(t)$ is defined as follows:

$$O_s(t) = \left\lfloor \frac{t}{P_s} \right\rfloor \max\left(0, X_s - Q_s\right). \tag{19}$$

5.2. Fixed-priority preemptive scheduling of components

For global FPPS of components—by definition disallowing BROE—the following sufficient scheduling condition can be applied (as defined by Lehoczky et al. [38]):

$$\forall 1 \leq s \leq N : \exists t \in (0, P_s] : B_s + \sum_{1 \leq r \leq s} \left(O_r(t) + \left\lceil \frac{t}{P_r} \right\rceil Q_r \right) \leq t. \tag{20}$$

The blocking term, B_s, is defined by the resource holding time of a lower-priority, resource-sharing component (in line with Baker [21]):

$$B_s = \max\{X_{u\ell} \mid \Pi_u < \Pi_s \leq RC_\ell\} \tag{21}$$

and the term $O_r(t)$ defines the additional amount of budget that a component C_s requires under a certain global synchronization protocol in order to prevent excessive blocking durations for other components in the system.

Similar to EDF, under global FPPS the term $O_r(t)$ is defined by Behnam et al. [30] for ONP and by van den Heuvel et al. [39] for SIRAP:

http://dx.doi.org/10.5772/62691

$$O_r(t) = \left\lceil \frac{t}{P_r} \right\rceil X_r. \tag{22}$$

Also under FPPS, a component arbitrated by OWP can only request an additional amount of X_s time units of processor time once. Hence, the term $O_r(t)$ becomes time independent and it is defined by [30]:

$$O_r(t) = X_r. \tag{23}$$

Just like with tasks, a finite set of time-interval lengths t can be tested in order to determine the schedulability of a set of components, i.e., the set can be specified as in (12) using component period P_s as the deadline for the execution of budget (WCET) Q_s. The algorithmic complexity of verifying the scheduling condition in (20) is then pseudo-polynomial in the number of components.

6. On the importance of opacity and its properties

Traditional protocols such as the PCP by Sha et al. [18] and the SRP by Baker [21] can be used for *local* resource sharing in HSFs, as observed by Almeida and Peidreiras [13]. With an opaque local analysis, we can re-use the same local analysis of components in the presence of global shared resources. The local analysis for HSFs with the ONP protocol, as presented by [30], already satisfied the notion of opacity because it uses a simple overrun upon integration and nothing else locally. In the previous sections, we also unified the local analysis of HSFs with other resource-sharing protocols (OWP, SIRAP, and BROE). This means that the interface of a component is independent of the resource-arbitration protocol. In this section, we briefly review non-opaque analysis and we highlight some important properties of opacity.

6.1. Monotonicity of the analysis

In Sections 4 and 5, we have summarized the compositional timing analysis of an HSF: the global analysis verifies the admission of a set of components into the HSF and the local analysis verifies the deadline constraints of tasks of each component in isolation on a periodically allocated budget, Q_s. The local scheduling conditions in (7) and (13) determine the smallest size of Q_s. For analyzing these conditions, we observe that increasing a local resource ceiling $rc_{s\ell}$ cannot lead to less blocking of local tasks (term $b_s(t)$ or b_{si}) and, thus, it cannot lead to a smaller budget Q_s. As a result, we have the following property.

Property 1*In an analysis satisfying* (7) *for EDF or* (13) *for FPPS, the total requested resources of a component reflected in the allocated budget* Q_s *is monotonically non-decreasing with an increase of a local resource ceilings* $rc_{s\ell}$, $\forall R_\ell \in \mathcal{R}_s$.

Although not mentioned explicitly, this property is tacitly assumed in some analysis (e.g., by Shin et al. [33], Behnam et al. [40] and Behnam et al. [30]) and our analysis supports it as well. It holds for all global synchronization protocols except for some non-opaque analysis (see **Table 1**).

6.1.1. SIRAP and its opacity

The analysis as traditionally presented for SIRAP is non-opaque. However, SIRAP is an important and widely used protocol, so we side-step this problem by applying the same local and global analysis of ONP also to SIRAP, i.e., inserting X_s units of idle time every period P_s. The intuition behind this idea is that SIRAP never idles away more processor time in one component period P_s than ONP requires for overrun (see van den Heuvel et al. [39] for the details). This adjusted analysis of SIRAP satisfies Property 1.

6.1.2. How Property 1 could be violated

Since global resources may need to be shared with tasks in other components, the ideas underlying most of the non-opaque analyses (like the non-opaque ones in **Table 1**) is to use the resource holding times of local tasks to tighten the analysis of wasted resources. Often this means that the tasks of a component are penalized by changes in the processor supply due to arbitrated accesses to global resources. The properties of a synchronization protocol are then reflected on the computed value of budget Q_s of a component. For example, this could work based on the following observations:

- With OWP, see Behnam et al. [30], the resource holding time can be used to account for the processor time that is being exchanged between two consecutive component periods due to overruns and paybacks.
- With ONP, see Behnam et al. [35], the resource holding times can be used to tighten the delivery of budget Q_s in component period P_s, because an overrun must fit in each component period as well.
- With SIRAP, see Behnam et al. [23], the resource holding times can be used to determine the amount of resources that can be idled away by the tasks in each component period.
- With BROE, see Biondi et al. [29], the resource holding times can be used to bound an additional delay due to resource sharing experienced by tasks compared to the regular delay of their resource supply (BD_s).

Intuitively, resource sharing comes with penalties to the tasks involved. However, sometimes the local tasks may also benefit from resource sharing, i.e., the tasks may require less processor resources. Section 6.1.3 presents an example of such a scenario using a non-opaque analysis of ONP. This clearly shows that a non-opaque analysis may violate our monotonicity property (Property 1).

6.1.3. Motivating example

We now demonstrate the effect of using properties of the global synchronization protocol for optimizing the parameters of the component's interface in the local analysis. We consider a simple non-opaque analysis for ONP. Behnam et al. [35] improved ONP by observing that the normal budget Q_s of a component C_s has to be served at least before $P_s - X_s$ instead of the regular relative deadline P_s (as we assumed for our analysis). The reason is that an overrun of at most length X_s must also fit in each period P_s after budget Q_s has been depleted. This means that the blackout duration of the processor supply becomes shorter, so that tasks have to wait shorter until they get selected for execution by the local scheduler. Behnam et al. [35] model their idea with the help of the explicit deadline periodic resource model by Easwaran et al. [12]. The explicit deadline $P_s - X_s$ improves the required budget of the tasks in a non-opaque way because it uses resource holding times to tighten the deadline.

Example 1*Consider a component $C_1$with a period $P_1 = 10$ and a single task $\tau_{11} = (27, 5, 27, \{0.5\})$ which specifies an access to a global resource R_ℓ for a duration of $h_{11\ell} = X_{11\ell} = X_1 = 0.5$ time units. We use ONP for arbitrating access to global resources.*

According to the improved ONP analysis of Behnam et al. [35] *where the resource holding time of* 0.5 *time units is exploited to tighten the deadline for budget Q_1, it is sufficient to allocate $Q_1 = 2.5$ time units every period of 10 time units. This budget allocation can be captured by interface $\Gamma_1 = (P_1, Q_1, \mathsf{X}_1) = (10, 2.5, \{0.5\})$ with explicit deadline $P_1 - X_1$. This interface is derived based on the assumption that an additional amount of 0.5 time units may need to be supplied within one component period to complete resource access by means of a budget overrun.*

If resource $R_\ell$turns out to be local to component C_1, i.e., component $C_1$is independent of other components in the system, then budget overruns are unnecessary for accessing resource R_ℓ. An independent component C_1would have required a periodic budget of$Q_1 = \frac{8}{3}$time units every period of 10 time units. We recall, however, the 2.5 time units must be supplied within 9.5 time units from the budget's release, leading to a density of processor allocations of$\frac{2.5}{9.5}$. This density is higher than the one without resource sharing, i.e.,$\frac{8/3}{10} < \frac{2.5}{9.5}$.

Once the HSF is composed, one may admit a component into the system requiring$\frac{8}{3}$time units every 10 time units while one may need to reject a component requiring 2.5 time units before relative deadline 9.5 every 10 time units. This depends on the resources requirements of other components in the HSF. Hence, a non-opaque analysis may give the illusion of resource efficiency by artificially creating resource dependencies.

By making assumptions in the local analysis on how ONP changes the processor supply to a component, a manufacturer may give an untruthful impression on the efficiency of the component. Such impressions cannot be given through an opaque analysis due to its monotonicity property. For some protocol-specific local analysis, monotonicity of the local analysis is hard to prove or disprove. Nevertheless, the above example clearly shows the importance of monotonicity for multi-vendor environments, for example, obtained through an opaque local analysis.

6.2. Detecting and accounting for shared resources

An additional problem with a non-opaque analysis (e.g., see the analyses in **Table 1**) is that it impacts the budget of a component with synchronization penalties, no matter whether or not an accessed resource is shared with other components. As a result, the synchronization penalties are incorporated in the component's timing interface and they cannot be taken out any longer. Hence, it disallows us to account for the synchronization penalties corresponding to the resources that really need to be shared between components as detected at integration time.

Since a component is unaware of other components, it is also unknown which resources actually need to be shared. Instead of directly deriving the interface of a component, one may therefore perform an intermediate step. One may specify partial interfaces for components for each of the resources the component requires. Upon integration of components, these partial interfaces can then be combined into a true interface by selecting just the interfaces corresponding to the resources that are globally shared with other components.

This procedure works intuitively with an opaque analysis and works as follows. Given a component C_s, we assume that P_s is given by the system designer and is fixed during the whole process of merging partial interfaces into a single interface. A partial interface $\Gamma_{s\ell}$ considers one global resource R_ℓ in isolation, i.e., R_ℓ can be globally shared or it can be local to the component.

Definition 2 (Partial interface candidate)(*Taken from van den Heuvel et al.* [34]) *A partial interface candidate* $\Gamma_{s\ell} = (P_s, Q_{s\ell}, \{X_{s\ell}\})$ *of component* C_s *accessing resource* R_ℓ *is a valid interface* Γ_s *for component* C_s*—i.e., an interface that satisfies the local scheduling condition in (7) for EDF or (11) for FPPS—under the assumption that only resource* R_ℓ *may be globally shared with other components.*

A partial interface $\Gamma_{s\ell}$ is a valid interface for the restrictive case that resource R_ℓ is the only resource being exposed globally. It specifies the budget and the resource holding time to resource R_ℓ of the component, but other resources accessed by the same component are excluded from the interface. The remaining problem is to derive one interface for the case a component accesses more than one globally shared resource. Lemma 2 shows how to merge partial interfaces into a single interface.

Lemma 2 (Taken from van den Heuvel et al. [34]). *Assume a component* C_s *accesses* m_s *resources. Let a selection of partial interfaces of component* C_s *be a series of* $\Gamma_{s\ell} = (P_s, Q_{s\ell}, \{X_{s\ell}\})$*, i.e., one partial interface* $\Gamma_{s\ell}$ *is selected for each resource* R_ℓ*. The local tasks' deadlines of component* C_s *are met by interface* $\Gamma_s = (P_s, Q_s, \{X_{s\ell} \mid R_\ell \in \mathcal{R}_s\})$*, where* $Q_s = \max\{Q_{s\ell} \mid R_\ell \in \mathcal{R}_s\}$.

The intuition behind this lemma is as follows. By virtue of the SRP [21], a task τ_{si} can be blocked by just one (outermost) critical section of task τ_{sj} with a lower preemption level (where $\pi_{si} \geq \pi_{sj}$) before τ_{si} can start its execution. Hence, it is sufficient to add the largest difference in budget to the value of $Q_{s\ell}$ in order to accommodate for one local blocking occurrence.

Lemma 2 presents an important result for open environments in which components may be loaded or removed from the platform after deployment. It enables us to incrementally analyze the resource dependencies of the components in the HSF. Prior to the integration of components, it is still unclear which of the global resources need to be shared with other components and which resources can be treated as local. Upon integration of components, the sets $\mathcal{R}_s$ of accessed resources by component C_s with the resources that truly need to be shared globally are known. We can then make an appropriate selection of partial interfaces and combine them into a single interface for each component. **Figure 4** illustrates this procedure as defined by Lemma 2. The result is that we account for the synchronization penalties of just the globally shared resources. If components enter or leave the HSF, one may use the partial interfaces to detect the updated resource dependencies between the components in the HSF.

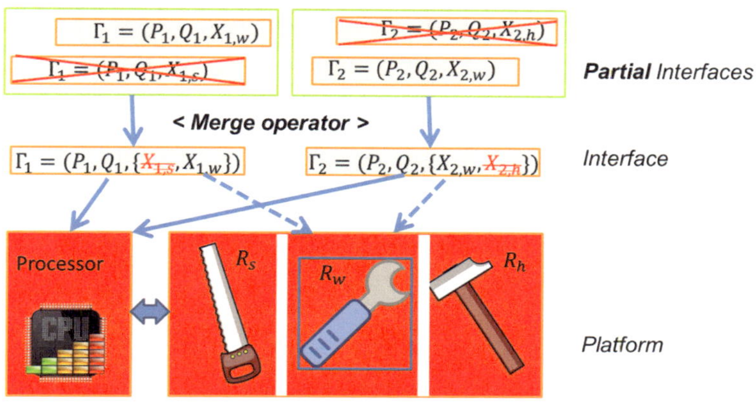

Figure 4. Partial interfaces define the resource requirements of a component on each accessed resource separately. They can be combined into a single interface which captures all resource requirements of a component. The resources that do not need to be shared between components can be ignored (in this example, R_s and R_h can be ignored), so that resource arbitration and the corresponding penalties can be avoided for those resources.

7. Conclusion

This chapter introduced the notion of uniform interfaces for resource-sharing components that need to be integrated on a uni-processor platform. The interface of a component abstracts from global resource sharing until component integration. The local timing analysis of a component that returns such an interface is called *opaque*. Sufficient conditions for opacity are

- component periods are smaller than the local tasks' periods, so that resource holding times of a component are defined independently of the global synchronization protocol;
- resource holding times must disappear from the local schedulability test, so that the budget parameter of a component can be solely computed with the purpose of meeting deadline constraints of tasks (and independently of the global synchronization protocol).

As a result of both conditions, when the SRP arbitrates access to shared resources between periodic components, the necessary condition of opacity is satisfied: all interface parameters of a component are computed independently of a global synchronization protocol. Moreover, component dependencies on shared resources and the corresponding synchronization penalties can be optimized at component integration.

We applied opacity to four existing global synchronization protocols: SIRAP, ONP, OWP, and BROE. For some systems that deploy such a protocol, a non-opaque analysis has shown to significantly improve schedulability (e.g., as demonstrated by Behnam et al. [28], Biondi et al. [29]). However, this requires that components are delivered to system integrators with an interface that includes worst-case synchronization penalties, which in practice may never occur. We therefore believe that the simplicity of opaque analysis and its opportunities to analyze systems incrementally may be beneficial for complex systems in which component development, test, analysis, and integration is spread over different research and development teams.

8. Glossary

This section gives an overview of the abbreviations and the symbols being used throughout this chapter.

Abbreviation	Description
AUTOSAR	AUTomotive Open System Architecture
BROE	Bounded-delay resource open environment
BD	Blackout duration
BWI	Bandwidth inheritance
DM	Deadline monotonic
EDF	Earliest-deadline-first
EDP	Explicit-deadline periodic
FPPS	Fixed-priority preemptive scheduling
HSFs	Hierarchical scheduling frameworks
HSRP	Hierarchical SRP
IPCP	Immediate PCP
LCM	Least common multiple
ONP	Overrun and no payback
OWP	Overrun with payback
PCP	Priority ceiling protocol
RHT	Resource holding time
LSBF	Linear supply-bound function
SIRAP	Subsystem integration and resource allocation policy

http://dx.doi.org/10.5772/62691

Abbreviation	Description
SRP	Stack resource policy
WCET	Worst-case execution time

Symbol	Description
N	Number of components in the system
M	Number of global resources
$\mathcal{R}$	Set of global resources
R_ℓ	ℓ-th global resource
RC_ℓ	Global resource ceiling of R_ℓ
C_s	s-th component
Π_s	Preemption level of C_s
P_s	Period of the resource allocations to component C_s
D_s	Relative deadline for the resource allocations to component C_s
Q_s	Periodically allocated processor time for C_s
$\mathcal{R}_s$	Set of global resources accessed by C_s
X_s	Set of holding times to global resources accessed by C_s
$X_{s\ell}$	the resource holding time of C_s for R_ℓ
X_s	Maximum of the resource holding times of C_s
O_s	Processor time for C_s merely dedicated to prevent excessive blocking
Γ_s	Interface of C_s defining periodic resource demands of C_s
$\Gamma_{s\ell}$	Partial interface defining C_s' demands for a given resource R_ℓ
BD_s	Longest duration for C_s without any processor supply
$\mathtt{dbf}_s(t)$	Demand-bound function of the tasks of C_s in an interval t
$\mathtt{rbf}_s(t, i)$	Request-bound function of task τ_{si} and its higher priorities in an interval t
$\mathtt{lsbf}(t)$	Linear lower bound of the processor supply in any sliding window of length t
T_s	Task set of a component
n_s	Number of tasks composing component C_s
τ_{si}	i-th task of component C_s
T_{si}	Minimal inter-arrival time of task τ_{si}
E_{si}	WCET of τ_{si}
D_{si}	(Relative) deadline of τ_{si}
S_{si}	Set of time instances that to determine schedulability of a task τ_{si}
$\mathcal{H}_{si}$	Set of WCETs of task τ_{si} on resources

Symbol	Description
$rc_{s\ell}$	Local resource ceiling of resource R_ℓ
π_{si}	Preemption level of task τ_{si}
$h_{si\ell}$	WCET of τ_{si}'s largest critical section to R_ℓ
$X_{si\ell}$	Largest resource holding time of τ_{si} to R_ℓ

Author details

Martijn M. H. P. van den Heuvel[1], Reinder J. Bril[1*], Johan J. Lukkien[1], Moris Behnam [2] and Thomas Nolte[2]

*Address all correspondence to: r.j.bril@tue.nl

1 Eindhoven University of Technology, Eindhoven, Netherlands

2 The Netherlands Mälardalen University, Västerås, Sweden

References

[1] HolenderskiM., BrilR. J., and LukkienJ. J.. An efficient hierarchical scheduling framework for the automotive domain. In Morteza BabamirSeyed, editor, *Real-Time Systems, Architecture, Scheduling, and Application*, pages 67–94. InTech, 2012.

[2] ShinI. and LeeI.. Compositional real-time scheduling framework with periodic model. *ACM Trans. on Embedded Computing Systems (TECS)*, 70 (3):0 1–39, April 2008.

[3] FengX.A. and MokA.K.. A model of hierarchical real-time virtual resources. In *Real-Time Systems Symposium (RTSS)*, pages 26–35, December 2002.

[4] van den HeuvelM. M. H. P., BrilR. J., and LukkienJ. J.. Transparent synchronization protocols for compositional real-time systems. *IEEE Transactions on Industrial Informatics (TII)*, 80 (2):0 322–336, May 2012.

[5] López MartinezP., BarrosL., and DrakeJ.. Scheduling configuration of real-time component-based applications. In *Reliable Software Technology—Ada-Europe*, volume 6106 of *Lecture Notes in Computer Science (LNCS)*, pages 181–195. Springer, 2010.

[6] MercerC.W., SavageS., and TokudaH.. Processor capability reserves: operating system support for multimedia applications. In *International Conf. on Multimedia Computing and Systems (ICMCS)*, pages 90–99, May 1994.

[7] RajkumarR., JuvvaK., MolanoA., and OikawaS.. Resource kernels: a resource-centric approach to real-time and multimedia systems. In *SPIE/ACM Conference on Multimedia Computing and Networking (CMCN)*, pages 150–164, January 1998.

[8] DengZ. and LiuJ.W.-S.. Scheduling real-time applications in open environment. In *Real-Time Systems Symposium (RTSS)*, pages 308–319, December 1997.

[9] KuoT.-W. and LiC.-H.. A fixed-priority-driven open environment for real-time applications. In *Real-Time Systems Symposium (RTSS)*, pages 256–267, December 1999.

[10] LipariG. and BaruahS.K.. Efficient scheduling of real-time multi-task applications in dynamic systems. In *Real-Time Technology and Applications Symposium (RTAS)*, pages 166–175, May 2000.

[11] WandelerE. and ThieleL.. Real-time interfaces for interface-based design of real-time systems with fixed priority scheduling. In *Conference on Embedded Software (EMSOFT)*, pages 80–89, September 2005.

[12] EaswaranA., AnandM., and LeeI.. Compositional analysis framework using EDP resource models. In *Real-Time Systems Symposium (RTSS)*, pages 129–138, December 2007.

[13] AlmeidaL. and PeidreirasP.. Scheduling with temporal partitions: response-time analysis and server design. In *Conference on Embedded Software (EMSOFT)*, pages 95–103, September 2004.

[14] LipariG. and BiniE.. A methodology for designing hierarchical scheduling systems. *Journal of Embedded Computing (JEC)*, 10(2):257–269, April 2005.

[15] FisherN. and DewanF.. A bandwidth allocation scheme for compositional real-time systems with periodic resources. *Real-Time Systems*, 480(3):223–263, 2012.

[16] ShinI. and LeeI.. Compositional real-time scheduling framework. In *Real-Time Systems Symposium (RTSS)*, pages 57–67, December 2004.

[17] de NizD., AbeniL., SaewongS., and RajkumarR.. Resource sharing in reservation-based systems. In *Real-Time Systems Symposium (RTSS)*, pages 171–180, December 2001.

[18] ShaL., RajkumarR., and J.P. Lehoczky. Priority inheritance protocols: an approach to real-time synchronisation. *IEEE Transactions on Computers (TC)*, 390(9):1175–1185, September 1990.

[19] SteinbergU., WolterJ., and HärtigH.. Fast component interaction for real-time systems. In *Euromicro Conference on Real-Time Systems (ECRTS)*, pages 89–97, July 2005.

[20] LipariG., LamastraG., and AbeniL.. Task synchronization in reservation-based real-time systems. *IEEE Transactions on Computers (TC)*, 530(12):1591–1601, December 2004.

[21] BakerT.P.. Stack-based scheduling of realtime processes. *Real-Time Systems*, 30(1):67–99, March 1991.

[22] DavisR.I. and BurnsA.. Resource sharing in hierarchical fixed priority pre-emptive systems. In *Real-Time Systems Symposium (RTSS)*, pages 257–267, December 2006.

[23] BehnamM., ShinI., NolteT., and NolinM.. SIRAP: a synchronization protocol for hierarchical resource sharing in real-time open systems. In *Conference on Embedded Software (EMSOFT)*, pages 279–288, October 2007.

[24] BertognaM., FisherN., and BaruahS.. Resource-sharing servers for open environments. *IEEE Transactions on Industrial Informatics (TII)*, 50(3):202–219, August 2009.

[25] GhazalieT. M. and BakerT. P.. Aperiodic servers in a deadline scheduling environment. *Real-time Systems*, 90(1):31–67, July 1995.

[26] CaccamoM. and ShaL.. Aperiodic servers with resource constraints. In *Real-Time Systems Symposium (RTSS)*, pages 161–170, December 2001.

[27] HolmanP. and AndersonJ.H.. Locking in pfair-scheduled multiprocessor systems. In *Real-Time Systems Symposium (RTSS)*, pages 149–158, December 2002.

[28] BehnamM., NolteT., and BrilR. J.. Bounding the number of self-blocking occurrences of SIRAP. In *Real-Time Systems Symposium (RTSS)*, pages 61–72, December 2010 a .

[29] BiondiA., MelaniA., BertognaM., and ButtazzoG.. Optimal design for reservation servers under shared resources. In *Euromicro Conf. on Real-Time Systems (ECRTS)*, pages 153–164, July 2014.

[30] BehnamM., NolteT., SjodinM., and ShinI.. Overrun methods and resource holding times for hierarchical scheduling of semi-independent real-time systems. *IEEE Transactions on Industrial Informatics (TII)*, 60 (1):93–104, February 2010 b.

[31] LiuC.L. and LaylandJ.W.. Scheduling algorithms for multiprogramming in a real-time environment. *Journal of the ACM*, 200(1):46–61, January 1973.

[32] MokA.K.-L.. *Fundamental design problems of distributed systems for the hard-real-time environment*. Phd thesis, Massachusetts Institute of Technology, May 1983. http://www.lcs.mit.edu/publications/pubs/pdf/MIT-LCS-TR-297.pdf.

[33] ShinI., BehnamM., NolteT., and NolinM.. Synthesis of optimal interfaces for hierarchical scheduling with resources. In *Real-Time Systems Symposium (RTSS)*, pages 209–220, December 2008.

[34] M. M. H. P. van den Heuvel, BehnamM., BrilR. J., LukkienJ. J., and NolteT.. Optimal and fast composition of resource-sharing components in hierarchical real-time systems. In *IEEE Int. Conference on Embedded and Real-Time Computing Systems and Applications (RTCSA)*, pages 1–12, Aug. 2014.

[35] BehnamM., NolteT., and BrilR. J.. Tighter schedulability analysis of synchronization protocols based on overrun without payback for hierarchical scheduling frameworks. In *International Conference on Engineering of Complex Computer Systems (ICECCS)*, pages 35–44, April 2011.

http://dx.doi.org/10.5772/62691

[36] BertognaM., FisherN., and BaruahS.. Static-priority scheduling and resource hold times. In *Parallel and Distributed Processing Symposium (IPDPS)*, March 2007.

[37] BaruahS. K.. Resource sharing in EDF-scheduled systems: a closer look. In *Real-Time Systems Symposium (RTSS)*, pages 379–387, December 2006.

[38] LehoczkyJ. P., ShaL., and DingY.. The rate monotonic scheduling algorithm: exact characterization and average case behavior. In *Real-Time Systems Symposium (RTSS)*, pages 166–171, December 1989.

[39] M. M. H. P. van den Heuvel, BehnamM., BrilR. J., LukkienJ. J., and NolteT.. Opaque analysis for resource sharing in compositional real-time systems. In *4th Workshop on Compositional Theory and Technology for Real-Time Embedded Systems (CRTS)*, pages 3–10, Nov. 2011.

[40] BehnamM., NolteT., and FisherN.. On optimal real-time subsystem-interface generation in the presence of shared resources. In *Conference on Emerging Technologies and Factory Automation (ETFA)*, September 2010 c.

Chapter 4

Real-Time Systems

Ming Fan

Additional information is available at the end of the chapter

http://dx.doi.org/10.5772/63278

Abstract

Since 2004, most of chip vendors have begun to shift their major focus from single-core to multi-core architecture (W. Wolf. Signal Processing Magazine, IEEE, 26(6):50–54, 2009). One major reason of this shift is that it reaches a physical limit by scaling transistor size and increasing the clock frequency to improve the computing performance on a single-core architecture (Agarwal et al. Proceedings of the 27th International Symposium on, pages 248–259, June 2000), that is, the overall chip cannot be reached within a single clock cycle. Multi-core architecture, however, brings innovative and promising opportunities to further improve the computing performance. By providing multiple processing cores on a single chip, multi-core systems can dramatically increase the computing performance and mitigate the power and thermal issues with the same performance achievement as single-core systems. As multi-core architecture has been more and more dominant in the industrial market, there is an urgent demand for effective and efficient techniques for the design of multi-core systems.

In this chapter, we first analyze the thermal behavior on multi-core real-time systems by taking the heat transfer among different cores into consideration. Then we analyze the energy consumption for a given speed scheduling on multi-core systems.

Keywords: Real-Time, Multi-Core, Thermal, Power, Energy, Periodic Scheduling

1. Introduction

Today, multi-core architecture has been widely supported by most of major chip vendors, including Intel, AMD, IBM, Nvidia, ARM, Sum microsystems, Qualcomm, Broadcom, and so on. Some of the chip manufacturers have already launched 16-core chips into the market, that is, AMD OpteronTM 6300 Series [1]. It is not surprising that in the coming future, hundreds or even thousands of cores will be integrated into a single chip [22]. When moving toward multi-core architecture, it comes with new and critical challenges in design of multi-core systems, particularly multi-core real-time systems.

As architecture becomes more and more complicated, besides the timing constraint, many other design constraints are taken into consideration in real-time system design and development. Traditional approaches focus exclusively on timing constraints [3,4,6,7]. Today, many other design constraints (e.g. power/energy, thermal, and reliability) also need to be considered seriously in real-time system design [8,9,11,12,14].

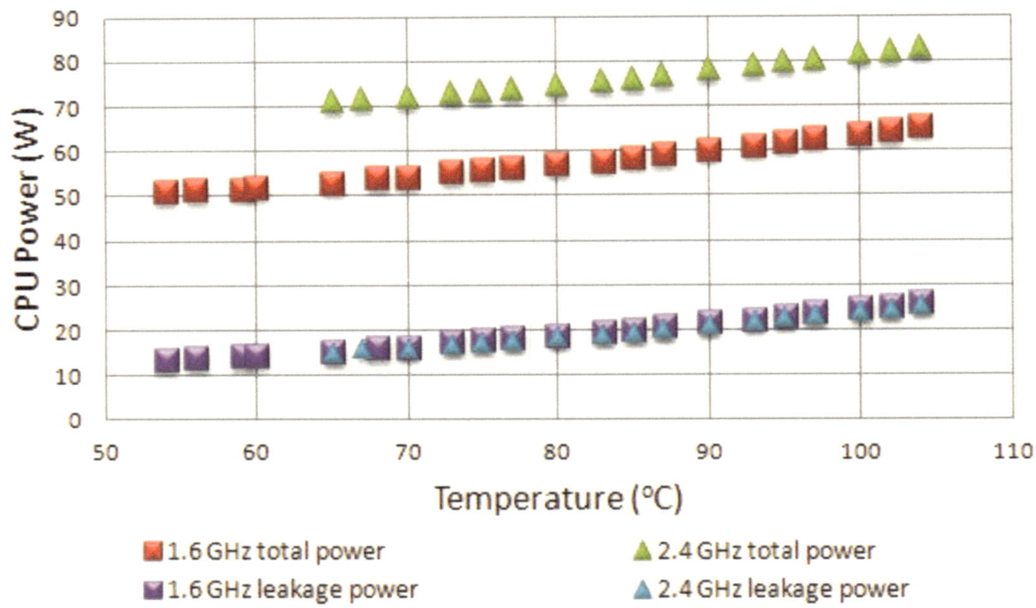

Figure 1. Power vs. Temperature [9]: Intel Core i5-2500K (32 nm Sandy Bridge), voltage 1.26 V, frequency at 1.6 GHz and 2.4 GHz, respectively.

1.1. Power/energy analysis in multi-core real-time systems

Catalyzed by continuous transistor scaling, hundreds of billions of transistors have been integrated on a single chip [13]. One of the immediate consequence caused by the tremendous increase of transistor density is the soaring power consumption [5], which further results in severe challenges in energy and temperature[11,17]. Today, power has become a critical and challenging design objective in front of system designers.

1.2. Thermal analysis in multi-core real-time systems

The continuously increased power consumption has resulted in a soaring chip temperature. Moreover, as design paradigm shifts to deep submicron domain, high chip temperature leads to a substantial increase in leakage power consumption [13], which in turn further deteriorates the power situation due to the interdependency between temperature and leakage power. For instance, with Intel core i5-2500K (32 nm Sandy Bridge), the leakage power roughly grows up to 2× from 55°C (13 W) to 105°C (26 W), see **Figure 1**. Furthermore, the soaring chip temperature adversely impacts the performance, reliability, and packaging/cooling costs [17]. As a result, power and thermal issues have become critical and significant for advanced multi-core system design. In next section, we introduce some necessary backgrounds of multi-core scheduling with power and thermal awareness, respectively.

The aggressive semiconductor technology scaling has pushed the chip power density doubled every two to three years [16,20], which immediately results in an exponential increasing in heat density. High temperature can degrade the performance of systems in various ways. Therefore, there is a great need of advanced techniques for thermal/temperature aware design of multi-core systems.

2. Preliminary

2.1. Multi-core platform and task model

The multi-core platform consists of M processing cores, $M \geq 2$, denoted as **P**, $\mathbf{P} = \{P_1,P_2,\ldots,P_M\}$. Each core P_i has N running modes, each of which is characterized by a 2-tuple set (v_k, f_k), where v_k represents the supply voltage and f_k represents the frequency under mode k, $1 \leq k \leq N$.

Let S represent a static and periodic speed schedule, which indicates how to vary the supply voltage and working frequency for each core at different time instants. A speed schedule S is constituted by several state intervals, which is described as below:

Definition 1 [25]: Given a speed schedule S for a multi-core system, an interval $[t_{q-1}, t_q]$ is called a state interval if each core runs only at one mode during that interval.

Recall that speed schedule S is a periodic schedule, let L denote the length of one scheduling period. According to Definition 1, a speed schedule S essentially consists of a number of non-overlapped state intervals. Let Q represent the number of non-overlapped state intervals within one scheduling period of S, then we have that [25]

1. $\cup_{q=1}^{Q}[t_{q-1}, t_q]=[0, L]$

2. $[t_{q-1}, t_q]\cap[t_{p-1}, t_p]=\varnothing$, if $q \neq p$

For a single state interval $[t_{q-1}, t_q]$, let $\mathbf{K}_q$ represent the interval mode, $\mathbf{K}_q = \{k_1,k_2,\ldots,k_M\}$, where ki denotes the running mode of core P_i in interval $[t_{q-1}, t_q]$.

2.2. Power model

The overall power consumption (in Watt) of each core is composed of two parts: dynamic power P_{dyn} and leakage power P_{leak}. We assume that: (1) P_{dyn} is varied with respect of supply voltage but independent of temperature, (2) P_{leak} is sensitive to both temperature and supply voltage. Specifically, for the dynamic power, we know that it is proportional to the square of supply voltage and linearity of working frequency. We assume that the working frequency is linearly proportional to supply voltage, thus the power consumption of the i-th core (P_i) under running mode k_i can be formulated as below [18].

$$P_{dyn,i} = \gamma_{ki} * v_{ki}^3 \tag{1}$$

where γ_{ki} is a constant value determined by the platform and running mode, and v_{ki} is the supply voltage of core P_i determined by the running mode.

For leakage power, although there is a very complicated relationship between leakage power and temperature from circuit level perspective, Liu et al. [23] found that a linear approximation of the leakage temperature dependency is fairly accurate. Work [12] further formulated the leakage power of core P_i as below:

$$P_{leak,i} = (\alpha_{ki} + \beta_{ki} * T_i(t)) * v_{ki} \tag{2}$$

where α_{ki} and $\beta_{ki}$are constants depending on the core running mode, that is, mode *ki*.

Consequently, the total power consumption of core P_i at time t, denoted as $P_i(t)$, can be formulated as:

$$P_i(t) = (\alpha_{ki} + \beta_{ki} * T_i(t)) * v_{ki} + \gamma_{ki} * v_{ki}^3 \tag{3}$$

For convenience in our presentation, we rewrite the above formula by separating the elements into temperature independent/dependent parts such that

$$P_i(t) = \psi_i + \phi_i * T_i(t) \tag{4}$$

where$\psi_i = \alpha_{ki} * v_{ki} + \gamma_{ki} * v_{ki}^3$ and $\phi_i = \beta_{ki} * v_{ki}$.

$$\begin{bmatrix} P_1(t) \\ \vdots \\ P_M(t) \end{bmatrix} = \begin{bmatrix} \psi_1 \\ \vdots \\ \psi_M \end{bmatrix} + \begin{bmatrix} \phi_1 & \cdots & 0 \\ \vdots & \ddots & \vdots \\ 0 & \cdots & \phi_M \end{bmatrix} \begin{bmatrix} T_1(t) \\ \\ T_M(t) \end{bmatrix} \tag{5}$$

Or

$$\mathbf{P}(t) = \mathbf{\Psi} + \mathbf{\Phi}\mathbf{T}(\mathrm{t}) \tag{6}$$

http://dx.doi.org/10.5772/63278

Note that we use the bold text for a vector/matrix and the unbolded text for a value, for example, **T** represents a temperature vector while T represents a temperature value.

2.3. Thermal model

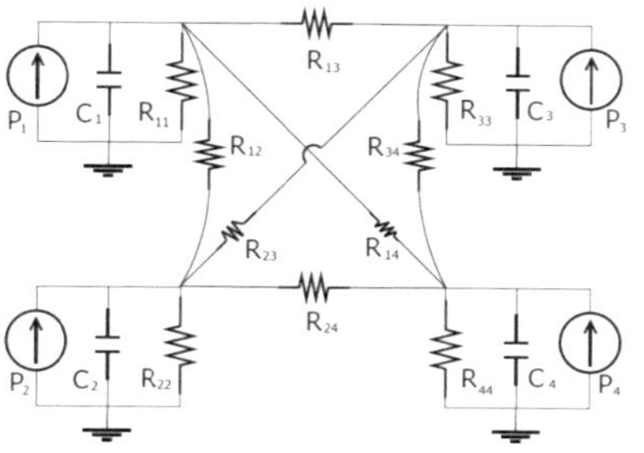

Figure 2. Illustration for thermal phenomena on multi-core system [26].

Figure 2 illustrates the thermal circuit model for a multi-core platform consisting of four processing cores. C_i represents the thermal capacitance (in Watt/°C) of core P_i, and R_{ij} represents the thermal resistance (in J/°C) between core P_i and P_j. Note that the thermal model adopted here is similar to the one used in related work [19,21]. Let T_{amb} represent the ambient temperature, then the thermal phenomena of core P_i in **Figure 2** can be formulated as

$$C_i \frac{dT_i(t)}{dt} + \frac{T_i(t) - T_{amb}}{R_{ii}} + \sum_{j \neq i} \frac{T_i(t) - T_j(t)}{R_{ij}} = P_i(t) \tag{7}$$

Let

$$\begin{cases} \delta i = \dfrac{T_{amb}}{R_{ii}} \\ g_{ij} = \begin{cases} \sum_{k=1}^{M} \dfrac{1}{R_{ik}}, \text{ if j=i} \\ \dfrac{-1}{R_{ij}}, \text{ otherwise} \end{cases} \end{cases} \tag{8}$$

Then the thermal model in equation (7) can be rewritten as

$$C_i \frac{dT_i(t)}{dt} + \sum_{j=1}^{M} g_{ij} T_j(t) = P_i(t) + \delta i \tag{9}$$

Accordingly, for the entire system, the thermal model can be represented as

$$\mathbf{C}\frac{d\mathbf{T}(t)}{dt} + \mathbf{g}\mathbf{T}(t) = \mathbf{P}(t) + \boldsymbol{\delta} \tag{10}$$

where **C** and **g** are MxM matrices

$$\mathbf{C} = \begin{bmatrix} C_1 & \cdots & 0 \\ \vdots & \ddots & \vdots \\ 0 & \cdots & C_M \end{bmatrix}, \mathbf{g} = \begin{bmatrix} g_{11} & \cdots & g_{1M} \\ \vdots & \ddots & \vdots \\ g_{M1} & \cdots & g_{MM} \end{bmatrix} \tag{11}$$

and $\boldsymbol{\delta}$ is an $Mx1$ vector

$$\boldsymbol{\delta} = \begin{bmatrix} \delta_1 \\ \vdots \\ \delta_M \end{bmatrix} \tag{12}$$

Note that **C, g,** and $\boldsymbol{\delta}$ are all constants that are determined by the multi-core platform only. Moreover, **C** is the thermal capacitance matrix with none zero values only on the diagonal, and **g** is a thermal conductance matrix. The thermal model adopted here is a generic model which takes the heat transfer among different cores into consideration. Thus, it can be directly applied on thermal analysis for both temperature transient state and temperature stable state.

3. Temperature analysis in multi-core real-time systems

There is an interactive effect between power and temperature, that is, high power leads to high temperature, which in turn further aggravates the power consumption. In order to calculate the energy consumption accurately and efficiently, it is necessary to develop an efficient solution to calculate the temperature first.

In this section, we first present a temperature formulation within thermal transient state for a constant speed schedule interval. Then we present an analytical solution to calculate the temperature within thermal steady state for a periodic speed schedule.

3.1. Temperature analysis in system thermal transient state

In this subsection, we will formulate the temperature variation [26] within one state interval $[t_{q-1}, t_q]$ in the system thermal transient state.

First, by applying power model given by equation (6) into thermal model given by equation (10), we can derive that

$$\mathbf{C}\frac{d\mathbf{T}(t)}{dt} + \mathbf{gT}(t) = \mathbf{\Psi} + \mathbf{\Phi T}(t) + \mathbf{\delta} \tag{13}$$

Then we simplify the above equation by letting $\mathbf{G}=\mathbf{g}-\mathbf{\Phi}$. Thus the above equation can be rewritten as

$$\mathbf{C}\frac{d\mathbf{T}(t)}{dt} + \mathbf{GT}(t) = \mathbf{\Psi} + \mathbf{\delta} \tag{14}$$

Since **C** represents the capacitance matrix, according to the circuit nature, we know that matrix **C** contains no zero values only on its diagonal. Thus, we can see matrix **C** is non-singular. Therefore, the inverse of **C**, that is, $\mathbf{C}^{-1}$ exists. Then we can further simplify equation (14) into below

$$\frac{d\mathbf{T}(t)}{dt} = \mathbf{AT}(t) + \mathbf{B} \tag{15}$$

where $\mathbf{A}=-\mathbf{C}^{-1}\mathbf{G}$ and $\mathbf{B}=\mathbf{C}^{-1}(\mathbf{\Psi}+\mathbf{\delta})$. The system thermal model formulated by equation (15) has a form of first order Ordinary Differential Equations (ODE). Particularly, if all coefficients are constant, then there exists a solution which can be formulated as

$$\mathbf{T}(t) = e^{t\mathbf{A}}\mathbf{T}_0 + \mathbf{A}^{-1}(e^{t\mathbf{A}} - \mathbf{I})\mathbf{B} \tag{16}$$

For a state interval $[t_{q-1},t_q]$, it is important to point out that all coefficients in the above are constant. Specifically, let K_q be the corresponding interval mode, and let $\mathbf{T}(t_{q-1})$ be the temperature at the starting point of that interval. Then according to equation (16), the ending temperature of that interval, that is, $\mathbf{T}(t_{q-1})$, can be directly formulated as

$$\mathbf{T}(t_q) = e^{\Delta t_q \mathbf{A}_{Kq}}\mathbf{T}(t_{q-1}) + \mathbf{A}_{Kq}^{-1}(e^{\Delta t_q \mathbf{A}_{Kq}} - \mathbf{I})\mathbf{B}_{Kq} \tag{17}$$

where $\Delta t_q = t_q - t_{q-1}$.

3.2. Temperature analysis in system thermal steady state

In this subsection, we will formulate the temperature variation [26] within one state interval $[t_{q-1}, t_q]$ in the system thermal steady state.

Consider a periodic speed schedule S, and let **T**(0) be the initial temperature at time instant 0. For an arbitrary state interval $[t_{q-1}, t_q]$ within speed schedule S, to obtain its steady-state temperature, one intuitive way is to trace the entire schedule S by consecutively calculating the temperature from the first scheduling period until system reaches its thermal steady state.

Although this approach works from theoretical point of view, when considering the practical computational time cost (which would be extremely expensive), it turns out that this intuitive approach would be inefficient or even impractical. Thus, it would be desirable and useful to develop an efficient solution to rapidly calculate steady-state temperatures for a periodic speed schedule.

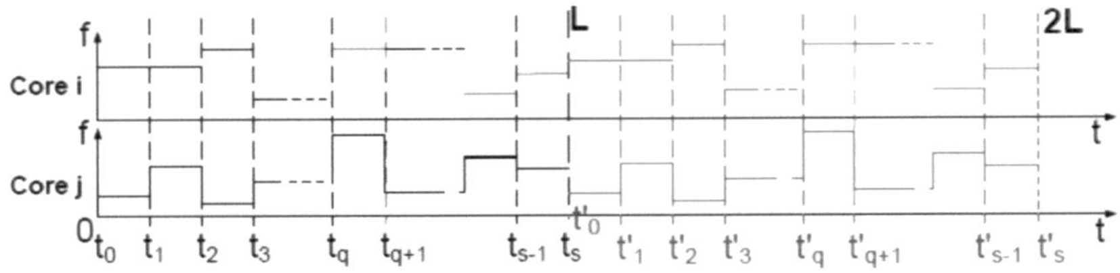

Figure 3. A speed schedule within two scheduling periods.

Let us first consider the temperature variation at the end of each scheduling period, that is, $t = n$L, where $n \geq 1$. Let the scheduling points of S(t) in the first period be $t_0, t_1, \ldots, t_s$, respectively. After repeating S(t), let the corresponding points in the second scheduling period be $t_0', t_1', \ldots, t_s'$, respectively (see **Figure 3**). Note that

$t_0 = 0$, $t_0' = t_s = L$, and $t_s' = 2L$. According to equation (17), at time t_1 and t_1', we have

$$\mathbf{T}(t_1) = e^{\Delta t_1 \mathbf{A}_{K1}} \mathbf{T}(t_0) + \mathbf{A}_{K1}^{-1} (e^{\Delta t_1 \mathbf{A}_{K1}} - \mathbf{I}) \mathbf{B}_{K1} \tag{18}$$

$$\mathbf{T}(t_1') = e^{\Delta t_1' \mathbf{A}_{K1}} \mathbf{T}(t_0') + \mathbf{A}_{K1}^{-1} (e^{\Delta t_1' \mathbf{A}_{K1}} - \mathbf{I}) \mathbf{B}_{K1} \tag{19}$$

Subtract equation (18) from (19) on both sides, and simplify the result by applying $\Delta t_1 = \Delta t_1'$, $t_0 = 0$ and $t_0' = L$, we get

$$\mathbf{T}(t_1') - \mathbf{T}(t_1) = e^{\Delta t_1 \mathbf{A}_{K1}} (\mathbf{T}(L) - \mathbf{T}(0)) \tag{20}$$

Follow the same trace of the above derivation, we have that

$$\begin{aligned} &\mathbf{T}(t_2') - \mathbf{T}(t_2) = e^{\Delta t_2 \mathbf{A}_{K2}} e^{\Delta t_1 \mathbf{A}_{K1}} (\mathbf{T}(L) - \mathbf{T}(0)) \\ &\cdots \\ &\mathbf{T}(t_s') - \mathbf{T}(t_s) = e^{\Delta t_s \mathbf{A}_{Ks}} \ldots e^{\Delta t_2 \mathbf{A}_{K2}} e^{\Delta t_1 \mathbf{A}_{K1}} (\mathbf{T}(L) - \mathbf{T}(0)) \end{aligned} \tag{21}$$

Since $t_s = L$, $t_s' = 2L$, and let $e^{\Delta t_s \mathbf{A}_{Ks}} \ldots e^{\Delta t_2 \mathbf{A}_{K2}} e^{\Delta t_1 \mathbf{A}_{K1}} = \mathbf{K}$, the last equation in (21) can be rewritten as

http://dx.doi.org/10.5772/63278

$$\mathbf{T}(2L) - \mathbf{T}(L) = \mathbf{K}(\mathbf{T}(L) - \mathbf{T}(0)) \tag{22}$$

In the same way, we can construct that

$$\mathbf{T}(xL) - \mathbf{T}((x-1)L) = \mathbf{K}^{x-1}(\mathbf{T}(L) - \mathbf{T}(0)) \tag{23}$$

where x = 1,2, …,n. Sum up the above n equations, we get

$$\mathbf{T}(nL) = \mathbf{T}(0) + \sum_{x=1}^{n} \mathbf{K}^{x-1}(\mathbf{T}(L) - \mathbf{T}(0)) \tag{24}$$

In the above, $\{\mathbf{K}^{x-1} | x = 1,2,\ldots,n\}$ forms a matrix geometric sequence. If $(\mathbf{I}-\mathbf{K})$ is invertible, then we have

$$\mathbf{T}(nL) = \mathbf{T}(0) + (\mathbf{I} - \mathbf{K})^{-1}(\mathbf{I} - \mathbf{K}^{n})(\mathbf{T}(L) - \mathbf{T}(0)) \tag{25}$$

Next, we consider the temperature variation for an arbitrary time instant when repeating a periodic speed schedule. Given a periodic speed schedule S(t), let t_q ($t_q \in [0,L]$) be an arbitrary time instant within schedule S(t). Moreover, let's repeat S(t) for n times, where $n \geq 1$. Let $\mathbf{T}(nL + t_q)$ denote the temperature of $\mathbf{T}(t_q)$ in the n-th scheduling period, by following the similar way of the above derivation, we can get that

$$\mathbf{T}(nL + t_q) = \mathbf{T}(t_q) + \mathbf{K}_q(\mathbf{I} - \mathbf{K})^{-1}(\mathbf{I} - \mathbf{K}^{n})(\mathbf{T}(L) - \mathbf{T}(0)) \tag{26}$$

where $\mathbf{K}_q = e^{\Delta t_q \mathbf{A}_{Kq}} \ldots e^{\Delta t_2 \mathbf{A}_{K2}} e^{\Delta t_1 \mathbf{A}_{K1}}$.

Until now, we have been able to formulate the temperature variation of an arbitrary time instant in the n-th scheduling period. Next, we will further formulate the temperature variation of an arbitrary time instant in the system steady state. Consider an arbitrary time instant, that is, t_q, $0 \leq t_q \leq L$, within the first scheduling period. The brief idea of calculating the steady-state temperature corresponding to t_q is to let n go to infinity in equation (27). We formally describe our method in Theorem 1.

Theorem 1 [25]: Given a periodic speed schedule S(t), let $\mathbf{T}(L)$ and $\mathbf{T}(t_q)$ be the temperatures at time instant L and t_q, $t_q \in [0,L]$, respectively. If for each eigenvalue λ_i of $\mathbf{K}$, we have $|\lambda_i| < 1$, then the steady-state temperature corresponding to t_q can be formulated as

$$\mathbf{T}_{ss}(t_q) = \mathbf{T}(t_q) + \mathbf{K}_q(\mathbf{I} - \mathbf{K})^{-1}(\mathbf{T}(L) - \mathbf{T}(0)) \tag{27}$$

Proof:

First, based on equation (26), by letting n→+∞, the steady-state temperature of the q-th scheduling point in S(t) can be represented as

$$\mathbf{T}_{ss}(t_q) = \mathbf{T}(t_q) + \mathbf{K}_q(\mathbf{I} - \mathbf{K})^{-1}(\mathbf{I} - \lim_{n\to\infty}\mathbf{K}^n)(\mathbf{T}(L) - \mathbf{T}(0)) \tag{28}$$

When n→+∞, the matrix sequence $\mathbf{K}^n$ converges if and only if $|\lambda_i| < 1$, for each eigenvalue λ_i of **K** [14]. Under this condition, we have $\lim_{n\to\infty}\mathbf{K}^n = 0$. Moreover, if $|\lambda_i| < 1$ holds, then (**I**-**K**) is invertible. Thus, the steady-state temperature of the q-th scheduling point in S(t) can be further formulated as

$$\mathbf{T}_{ss}(t_q) = \mathbf{T}(t_q) + \mathbf{K}_q(\mathbf{I} - \mathbf{K})^{-1}(\mathbf{T}(L) - \mathbf{T}(0)) \tag{29}$$

Note that as n→+∞, unless the temperature runs away and causes the system to break down, we know that the system could eventually achieve its thermal steady state. That means for each eigenvalue λi of **K**, the condition of $|\lambda i| < 1$ should always hold. Therefore, it is reasonable and practical to make such assumption shown in Theorem 1.

4. Energy analysis in multi-core real-time systems

Besides temperature, energy consumption is another important and challenging issue in the design of multi-core real-time systems. We have now been able to formulate the temperature variation in a multi-core system in the previous section. In this section, we will discuss how to formulate the energy consumption on multi-core systems with consideration of the inter-dependence between leakage power and temperature.

In the rest of this section, we first present an analytical solution to calculate energy consumption of an arbitrary state interval. Then we present a solution to calculate the total energy consumption of the entire speed schedule.

4.1. Energy analysis for one scheduling state interval

Consider a state interval, that is, $[t_{q-1}, t_q]$ with initial temperature of $\mathbf{T}(t_{q-1})$. The energy consumption of all cores within that interval can be simply formulated as

$$\mathbf{E}(t_{q-1}, t_q) = \int_{t_{q-1}}^{t_q} \mathbf{P}(t)dt \tag{30}$$

Based on our system power model, given by equation (6), we have

http://dx.doi.org/10.5772/63278

$$\mathbf{E}(t_{q-1}, t_q) = \Delta t_q \boldsymbol{\Psi} + \boldsymbol{\Phi}\int_{t_{q-1}}^{t_q} \mathbf{T}(t)dt \tag{31}$$

Theorem 2 given below is targeted to solve the above energy calculation problem.

Theorem 2 [25]: Given a state interval $[t_{q-1}, t_q]$, let $\mathbf{T}_{q-1}$ be the temperature at time t_{q-1}. Then the overall system energy consumption within interval $[t_{q-1}, t_q]$ can be formulated as

$$\mathbf{E}(t_{q-1}, t_q) = \Delta t_q \boldsymbol{\Psi} + \boldsymbol{\Phi}\mathbf{G}^{-1}\mathbf{H} \tag{32}$$

where $\Delta t_q = t_q - t_{q-1}$, and $\mathbf{H} = \Delta t_q(\boldsymbol{\Psi} + \boldsymbol{\delta}) - \mathbf{C}(\mathbf{T}(t_q) - \mathbf{T}(t_{q-1}))$.

Proof:

In equation (31), let $\mathbf{X} = \int_{t_{q-1}}^{t_q} \mathbf{T}(t)dt$, then the energy formula can be rewritten as

$$\mathbf{E}(t_{q-1}, t_q) = \Delta t_q \boldsymbol{\Psi} + \boldsymbol{\Phi}\mathbf{X} \tag{33}$$

On the other hand, according to the system thermal model given by equation (10), we have

$$\mathbf{C}\frac{d\mathbf{T}(t)}{dt} + \mathbf{G}\mathbf{T}(t) = \boldsymbol{\Psi} + \boldsymbol{\delta} \tag{34}$$

where $\mathbf{G} = \mathbf{g} - \boldsymbol{\Phi}$. By integrating on both sides of the above equation with respect to time t, where $t \in [t_{q-1}, t_q]$, we can get

$$\mathbf{C}(\mathbf{T}(t_q) - \mathbf{T}(t_{q-1})) + \mathbf{G}\int_{t_{q-1}}^{t_q} \mathbf{T}(t) = \Delta t_q(\boldsymbol{\Psi} + \boldsymbol{\delta}) \tag{35}$$

Note that $\mathbf{X} = \int_{t_{q-1}}^{t_q} \mathbf{T}(t)dt$; thus from the above, we can derive that

$$\mathbf{X} = \mathbf{G}^{-1}\mathbf{H} \tag{36}$$

where $\mathbf{H} = \Delta t_q(\boldsymbol{\Psi} + \boldsymbol{\delta}) - \mathbf{C}(\mathbf{T}(t_q) - \mathbf{T}(t_{q-1}))$

Applying equation (36) into (33), we can see that

$$\mathbf{E}(t_{q-1}, t_q) = \Delta t_q \boldsymbol{\Psi} + \boldsymbol{\Phi}\mathbf{G}^{-1}\mathbf{H} \tag{37}$$

From Theorem 2, we can see that for an arbitrary state interval $[t_{q-1}, t_q]$, once the beginning temperature $\mathbf{T}(t_{q-1})$ is known, the total energy consumption within $[t_{q-1}, t_q]$ can be easily and directly calculated.

Subsequently, given a periodic speed schedule S and an initial temperature $\mathbf{T}_0$, we are able to calculate the energy consumption within an arbitrary state interval in any scheduling period.

Corollary 1 [25]: Given a periodic speed schedule S(t) consisting of Q state intervals, let $\mathbf{T}_0$ be the initial temperature. Then the energy consumption within the q-th state interval in the n-th scheduling period, denoted as $\mathbf{E}(t_{q-1} + nL,\ t_q + nL)$, can be calculated as

$$\mathbf{E}(t_{q-1} + nL\ ,\ t_q + nL\ ) = \Delta t_q \mathbf{\Psi}_{Kq} + \mathbf{\Phi}_{Kq} \mathbf{G}_{Kq}^{-1} \mathbf{H}_{Kq} \tag{38}$$

where $\Delta t_q = t_q - t_{q-1}$, and $\mathbf{H}_{Kq} = \Delta t_q(\mathbf{\Psi}_{Kq} + \mathbf{\delta}) - \mathbf{C}(\mathbf{T}(t_q + nL\ ) - \mathbf{T}(t_{q-1} + nL\ ))$.

Corollary 1 can be easily derived from Theorem 2. With the help of Corollary 1, given any periodic speed schedule on a multi-core platform, when repeating that schedule, we can quickly calculate the energy consumption within any state interval.

Accordingly, given a periodic speed schedule, when analyzing the system thermal steady state, we can directly calculate the energy consumption of any state interval within the system steady state.

Corollary 2 [25]: Given a periodic speed schedule S(t) consisting of Q state intervals, let $\mathbf{T}_0$ be the initial temperature. Then the energy consumption within the q-th state interval in the system steady state, denoted as $\mathbf{E}_{ss}(t_{q-1}, t_q)$, can be calculated as

$$\mathbf{E}_{ss}(t_{q-1}, t_q) = \Delta t_q \mathbf{\Psi}_{Kq} + \mathbf{\Phi}_{Kq} \mathbf{G}_{Kq}^{-1} \mathbf{H}_{ss\ Kq} \tag{39}$$

where $\Delta t_q = t_q - t_{q-1}$, and $\mathbf{H}_{ssKq} = \Delta t_q(\mathbf{\Psi}_{Kq} + \mathbf{\delta}) - \mathbf{C}(\mathbf{T}_{ss}(t_q) - \mathbf{T}_{ss}(t_{q-1}))$.

Corollary 2 is directly derived from Corollary 1 by replacing the transient temperatures with steady-state temperatures.

Author details

Ming Fan*

Address all correspondence to: mf.mingfan@gmail.com

Broadcom Ltd, 3151 Zanker Road, San Jose, CA, United States of America

http://dx.doi.org/10.5772/63278

References

[1] AMD. Amd server processor series. pages http://www.amd.com/US/PRODUCTS/SERVER/PROCESSORS/6000–SERIES–PLATFORM/6300/Pages/6300–series–processors.aspx, 2013.

[2] J.H. Anderson, V. Bud, and U.C. Devi. An EDF-Based Scheduling Algorithm for Multiprocessor Soft Real-Time Systems. In Proceedings of Euromicro Conference on Real-Time Systems (ECRTS), July 2005.

[3] B. Andersson, S. Baruah, and J. Jonsson. Static-Priority Scheduling on Multiprocessors. In Proceedings of IEEE Real-Time Systems Symposium (RTSS), December 2001.

[4] M. Bao, A. Andrei, P. Eles, and Z. Peng. On-line thermal aware dynamic voltage scaling for energy optimization with frequency/temperature dependency consideration. In Design Automation Conference, 2009. DAC '09. 46th ACM/IEEE, pages 490–495, July 2009.

[5] V.N. Darera and L. Jenkins. Utilization bounds for rm scheduling on uniform multiprocessors. In Embedded and Real-Time Computing Systems and Applications, 2006. Proceedings of 12th IEEE International Conference on, pages 315–321, 0-0.

[6] M. Fan and G. Quan. Harmonic semi-partitioned scheduling for fixed-priority real-time tasks on multi-core platform. In Design, Automation Test in Europe Conference Exhibition (DATE), pages 503–508, March 2012.

[7] Q. Han, M. Fan, and G. Quan. Energy minimization for fault tolerant real-time applications on multiprocessor platforms using checkpointing. In Low Power Electronics and Design (ISLPED), 2013 IEEE International Symposium on, pages 76–81, September 2013.

[8] V. Hanumaiah and S. Vrudhula. Energy-efficient operation of multi-core processors by dvfs, task migration and active cooling. Computers (TC), IEEE Transactions on, pages 1–14, 2012.

[9] Henry. A comparison of intels 32nm and 22nm core i5 cpus: Power, voltage, temperature, and frequency. Intel Cor., pages http://blog.stuffedcow.net/2012/10/intel32nm–22nm–core–i5–comparison/, 2012.

[10] H. Huang and G. Quan. Leakage aware energy minimization for real-time systems under the maximum temperature constraint. In DATE, pages 1–6, 2011.

[11] H. Huang, G. Quan, J. Fan, and M. Qiu. Throughput maximization for periodic real-time systems under the maximal temperature constraint. In Design Automation Conference (DAC), 2011 48th ACM/EDAC/IEEE, pages 363–368, June 2011.

[12] ITRS. International Technology Roadmap for Semiconductors (2011 Edition). International SEMATECH, Austin, TX, http://public.itrs.net/.

[13] R. Jayaseelan and T. Mitra. Temperature aware task sequencing and voltage scaling. ICCAD, pages 618–623, 2008.

[14] S. Bell and J. Rosenblatt. Mathematical analysis for modeling, December 1998.

[15] G. Moore. Cramming more components onto integrated circuits. Electronics Magazine, 38(8):114–117, May 1965.

[16] G. Quan and V. Chaturvedi. Feasibility analysis for temperature-constraint hard real-time periodic tasks. Industrial Informatics, IEEE Transactions on, 6(3):329–339, 2010.

[17] J. Rabaey, A. Chandrakasan, and B. Nikolic. Digital Integrated Circuits: A Design Perspective. Englewood Cliffs, NJ: Prentice-Hall, 2003.

[18] S. Sharifi, R. Ayoub, and T.S. Rosing. Tempomp: Integrated prediction and management of temperature in heterogeneous mpsocs. In Design, Automation Test in Europe Conference Exhibition (DATE), 2012, pages 593–598, March 2012.

[19] K. Skadron, M.R. Stan, W. Huang, S. Velusamy, K. Sankaranarayanan, and D. Tarjan. Temperature-aware microarchitecture. ICSA, pages 2–13, 2003.

[20] I. Ukhov, M. Bao, P. Eles, and Z. Peng. Steady-state dynamic temperature analysis and reliability optimization for embedded multiprocessor systems. In Design Automation Conference, June 2012.

[21] D. Yeh, L.S. Peh, S. Borkar, J. Darringer, A. Agarwal, and W. Hwu. Thousand-core chips [roundtable]. Design Test of Computers, IEEE, 25(3):272–278, 2008.

[22] Y. Liu and Y. Huazhong. Temperature-aware leakage estimation using piecewise linear power models. IEICE transactions on electronics, 93(12):1679–1691, 2010.

[23] W. Wolf. Multiprocessor system-on-chip technology. Signal Processing Magazine, IEEE, 26(6):50–54, 2009.

[24] V. Agarwal, M.S. Hrishikesh, S. Keckler, and D. Burger. Clock rate versus ipc: the end of the road for conventional microarchitectures. In Computer Architecture, 2000. Proceedings of the 27th International Symposium on, pages 248–259, June 2000.

[25] M. Fan, R. Rong, S. Liu, and G. Quan. Energy calculation for periodic multi-core scheduling in system thermal steady state with consideration of leakage and temperature dependency. The Journal of Supercomputing, 71(7):2565–2584, 2015.

[26] M. Fan, V. Chaturvedi, S. Sha, and G. Quan. An analytical solution for multi-core energy calculation with consideration of leakage and temperature dependency, Low Power Electronics and Design (ISLPED), 2013 IEEE International Symposium on, Beijing, pages 353–358, 2013.

Chapter 5

Multi-Objective Real-Time Dispatching Problem in Electric Utilities: An Application to Emergency Service Routing

Vinícius Jacques Garcia, Daniel Bernardon,
Iochane Guimarães and Júlio Fonini

Additional information is available at the end of the chapter

http://dx.doi.org/10.5772/62849

Abstract

This chapter presents a novel application of real-time dispatching problem to electric utilities when multi-objective is involved. It is described how the problem related to emergency services in electric utilities is considered, with an aggregated objective function developed to handle the minimization of the waiting time, the total distance traveled, the sum of all delays related to already assigned orders, and the cost of non-assigned emergency orders. After that, actual cases have shown the effectiveness of the proposed model to be adopted in real-world applications either as a search for optimal solution or by applying a heuristic-based algorithm developed.

Keywords: multi-objective optimization, dispatching problem, real-time systems, dynamic vehicle routing, emergency orders

1. Introduction

Electric power distribution utilities are charged of managing customer attendance and maintenance procedures in their network [1]. The consideration of emergency scenarios makes the problem even more complex especially by assuming resource constraints (human and material) and strict regulation policies that establish targets and indices related to this context [2].

Considering that repair crews help to maintain the network under normal conditions, that is, all the customers with power supply and non-technical problems associated with the electric network, emergency orders are normally related to equipment failures, overload conditions, and interrupted conductors [3].

From this context, the most relevant aspect to be considered refers to the waiting time associated with the emergency orders, since the level of injury or danger of death imposes immediate response from the network operation centre (NOC). The decision-making problem involves a considerable amount of data and several aspects and criteria, all of them related to network and equipment operation procedures. This context is close to that one described by Ribeiro et al. [4]: "decision making is a process of selecting 'sufficiently good' alternatives or course of actions in a set of available possibilities, to attain one or several goals."

Such a decision-making process when referring to emergency services in electric utility generally involves not only the waiting time (also referred as response time [5]) for emergency orders but also two even important aspects: the total distance traveled and the sum of all delays related to already assigned orders. The former sounds really intuitive, because the minimization of the total distance traveled by all crews improves their productivity by aggregating more time in their workday to complete the assigned orders. The latter aspect is that one more specific: the consideration of multitasked maintenance crews. They are always charged of pre-established routes that include orders known a priori when a set or emergency orders come up. This criterion of minimizing the sum of all delays represents the desired trade-off between the planning and actual scenarios, in such a way that they could be as similar as possible [6].

This chapter proposes a multi-objective approach based on a mathematical model to handle emergency orders under real-time conditions. It comprises four criteria related to this problem: the minimization of the waiting time for emergency services, the total distance traveled, the sum of all delays related to already assigned orders, and the cost of non-assigned emergency orders.

2. Problem description

The electric NOC is charged of attending emergency calls for 24 hours a day and 7 days a week, all answered by maintenance teams. Since they involve critical situations such as lack of supply or even the possibility of injury to people, they are considered critical tasks that require immediate attention. In this context, a real-time system is desirable and appropriate to support engineers to find the available teams that can meet these pending emergency work order (EWO) as soon as possible, thus defining what is called as the Emergency Dispatching and Routing Problem (EDRP).

Considering the urgency of these orders, the EDRP's main function is to reduce the waiting time, defined as the sum of travel time and execution times of service orders scheduled to be executed before the pending EWOs. The definition of EDRP assumed in this work comprises the problem of decision to allocate pending EWOs to maintenance crews available, adopting as a criterion of choice to minimize the waiting time. The problem becomes even more challenging from the consideration that these crews are multitasking: they serve not only the EWOS but also commercial services (customer demand orders). This characteristic gives the optimization problem a unique importance due to the associated complexity.

Such a conclusion comes from the fact that the EDRP corresponds to a dynamic vehicle routing problem [7, 8], which can be clearly distinguish from the static vehicle routing problem [9, 10] by assuming that at least some inputs to the problem can change during the execution of the previously defined routes. Therefore, there is a concurrence between the resolution of the EDRP and the dynamic generation of new EWOs [7] and the EDRP involves not only a dispatching decision (to which available crew a certain EWO will be assigned) but also a further routing decision: in which position of the existing routing a certain EWO should be inserted.

Some particular discussions about attributes related to dynamic vehicle routing problem addressed in this work will be introduced next.

2.1. Dynamic vehicle routing attributes

Particularly in the EDRP defined in this work, over the several aspects that may point the differences between the static and the dynamic fashion of vehicle routing problem described by Psaraftis [7], four of them must be highly considered:

1. Time dimension: It is important to keep track of geographic location of all vehicles, since that locations will be used to reach new EWO when they are made known, which means that it is also need to keep track of how vehicle schedules evolve over the time;

2. Near-term decisions: In the dynamic context of the vehicle routing problem included in the EDRP, there is a trade-off between take decisions based on near-term information or wait more time to take a greater defined landscape in order to promote better choices; even assuming that future information may change and incurring on risk of taking "a restrict" policy, near-term events are assumed more relevant in the formulation of the EDRP;

3. Faster computational times: The dynamic and also the emergency situation involved in the EDRP both require faster calculations for obtaining candidate solutions when comparing to the static context, since in this last one may be acceptable to wait for dozens of minutes or even hours; this requirement is that one that entails the real-time behavior involved in this work;

4. Indefinite deferment mechanisms: A certain level of deferment is desired since it makes a role of counterbalancing the near-term vision assumed; however, one has to describe some mechanisms to avoid that some particular EWOs, due to their unfavorable geographical characteristics when compared to other ones, may be postponed indefinitely.

From these specific characteristics emerge a combinatorial problem to construct several routes in order to meet customer demand in the context of an electric power distribution utility in Brazil, specifically with concern to the occurrence of EWO and thus describing a dynamic problem.

The main challenge when attending emergency services with multitasking maintenance crews refers to the trade-off between static and dynamic scenarios. These crews may systematically change their a priori routes with commercial orders upon the occurrence of EWOs, remembering that the latter orders have precedence over the first ones.

From this consideration, two main course of action may be assumed in order to route pending EWOs: (1) the complete restructuring of existing routes and (2) only the insertion of EWOs in any position of existing routes. The first case relates to route all orders simultaneously, whether commercial or emergency, forgetting existing routes. The second case involves restricting the changes in the a priori route, allowing only the inclusion of EWOs in any position. The problem addressed in this paper considers these two cases.

The main issue involved in EDRP refers to the presence of several conflicting optimization criteria. The main one is the waiting time to perform the EWOs, representing a tentative to mitigate the risks to the security of the electricity distribution network.

Another important criterion, this with an economic impact, refers to reducing the cost of the routes as the time needed to complete them, involving both commercial orders and EWOS. One can note that, in this case, a conflict regarding the precedence of EWOS and total cost: the higher is the precedence of EWOS, the higher will be the cost of the routes.

The third and last aspect to be considered refers to minimizing the sum of all delays related to the previously assigned services, in order to maintain the desired trade-off between the planning and actual scenarios.

All these questions will be discussed in details in the next section and further explained with practical examples for actual instances. The following section presents a simple example of EDRP instance.

2.2. A simple dispatching solution

Herein, there is an aspect that must be mentioned: all the repair crews have workday that may be different, thus affecting their availability to serve emergency services. An example of a possible EWO dispatching is given in **Figure 1**, which describes just one EWO (E0) and three crews available: crew 1, namely C1, 21 min far from E0; crew 2, namely C2, 60 min far from E0; and crew 3, namely C3, 30 min far from E0. With this information, one must decide that E0 must be dispatched to C1 since it has the smaller travel time, which in this case also corresponds to the smaller response time.

Figure 1. Example of an EWO dispatching.

It is worth noting that the geographical position of each crew is permanently changing by assuming the dynamic behavior involved, always conducting to the consideration of a multi-depot vehicle routing. Another aspect is that each crew has its proper working hours. As depicted in **Figure 1**, taking this assumption and considering that C1 has 9:00 am as its initial work time, C2 has 7:00 am as its initial work time, and C3 has 8:00 am as its initial work time, the time when the EWO comes up plays an important and definitive role on deciding which vehicle must be assigned to. If this time is 9:30 am, the previous analysis is appropriated, but if we consider 8:00 am, the following approaching time for each vehicle must be calculated: Vehicle 1 only will reach the EWO at 9:21 am; vehicle 2 will reach the EWO at 9:00 am; vehicle 3 will reach the EWO at 8:30 am. These results suggest that vehicle 3 must be dispatched to execute E0.

The next section is devoted to present the mathematical programming formulation developed to the EDRP.

3. Mathematical programming formulation for EDRP

The EDRP description presented in the previous section corresponds to a multi-objective and multi-attribute vehicle routing problem [11], with the most important ones stated as follow, according to the taxonomy of Eksioglu et al. [10]:

1. Real-time solution method (1.2.4);
2. On-site service—waiting times (2.5.2);
3. Customers on node (3.2.1);

4. Geographical location of customers—both urban and rural zones (3.3.3);
5. Multiple origins (3.4.2);
6. Time window restrictions on vehicles (3.6.4);
7. Exactly n vehicles—equivalent to TSP (3.7.1);
8. Uncapacitated vehicles (3.8.2);
9. Deterministic travel time (3.10.1);
10. Travel time dependent transportation cost (3.11.1);
11. Partially dynamic (4.1.2).

With all these attributes assumed, a mathematical programming formulation may be stated in order to define how to treat these characteristics and also to allow a further resolution by exact methods, when possible.

The following subsections are devoted to describe the formulation developed: First, the set of parameters and variables are presented, followed by the objective functions definition; finally, the constraints are defined in blocks in such a way to give a better understanding of how the previously defined attributes are related to.

3.1. Parameters and variables

All the conditions and information necessary to have a solution for an EDRP instance are presented in three tables: **Tables 1–3**. The first one is devoted to describe general parameters, the second defines crew-related parameters, and the last one reports the service order-related parameters. In all tables, the first column ("PARAM") includes the parameter identification and the second one presents the corresponding description ("DESCRIPTION").

PARAM	**Description**
D_{ij}	Distance in hours between node i and node j
F	The set of all objective functions
W_i	Factor that weighs the objective function i, with $\sum_{i \in F} W_i = 1$

Table 1. General parameters.

PARAM	**Description**
CC	Cost per hour of any crew (in $/h)
$PRED_i$	The set of predecessors nodes of node i in the initial route: $i \in V_s \cup V_c \cup V_e$
R	The set of routes
RT_i	The initial route of node i

http://dx.doi.org/10.5772/62849

PARAM	**Description**
SEQ_i	The sequence number of node i, in the corresponding route
SUC_i	The set of successors nodes of node i in the initial route: $i \in V_s \cup V_c \cup V_e$
$T0_r$	The initial time of crew r
T_r	Time that the r crew should finalize its route
U	Maximum acceptable time to any crew finish its route
V_s	The set of starting nodes, corresponding to crew positions
V_t	The set of terminal nodes, corresponding to artificial nodes created to make easier the finishing route time calculations

Table 2. Crew-related parameters.

PARAM	**Description**
EC	Cost related to each non-assigned emergency order (in $)
OC_i	Cost of the service order i (in $/h)
$PRED_i$	The set of all predecessor nodes of node i
ST_i	Service time of order i (in hours)
$SUCi$	The set of all successor nodes of node i
TA_i	Expected arrival time for service order i on the initial route
TE_i	Time when emergency order i was generated
TS_i	Service time of order i, $i \in V \setminus V_s \setminus V_t$
V	The set of all programmed and emergency orders, including starting and terminal nodes: $V = V_c \cup V_e \cup V_s \cup V_t$
V_a	The set of all assigned service orders: $V_a = \{i \in V_c \cup V_e \mid RT_i \neq -1\}$
V_b	The set of orders which are in the first position on the initial routes: $V_b = \{i \in V_{ce} \mid SEQ_i = 1\}$
V_c	The set of programmed orders
V_{ce}	$V_{ce} = V_c \cup V_e$
V_e	The set of emergency orders
V_{en}	The set of emergency orders which are unassigned to route crews: $V_{en} = \{i \in V_e \mid RT_i = -1\}$
V_{ens}	$V_{ens} = V_{en} \cup V_s$
V_r	The set of all emergency orders that are already routed: $V_r = \{i \in V_e \mid RT_i = 1\}$
V_{sce}	$V_{sce} = V_s \cup V_c \cup V_e$

Table 3. Service order-related parameters.

After parameter decryption, the set of variables must be introduced. Since this formulation refers to a mixed integer programming model [12], it includes both discrete and continuous variables. In addition, the set of discrete variables have two distinct subsets: the first comprising nonnegative integer variables and the latter referring to binary variables.

It is worth noting that the set of decision variables includes four main attributes: **precedence** between service orders, **assignment** of orders to routes, and finally, **time** information of when repair crews arrive at service orders or when these crews complete their workdays. **Table 4** presents all the variable sets defined to the proposed formulation.

SET	**Description**
x_{ijr}	Binary variable indicating if the node i is preceding of node j on the route r: $x_{ijr}=1$ if it is true and $x_{ijr}=0$ otherwise
y_{ir}	Binary variable indicating if node i is included on the route r:$y_{ir}=1$ if it is true and $y_{ir}=0$ otherwise
s_i	Binary variable denoting the assignment of emergency order i to any available crew: $s_i=1$ if it is true and $s_i=0$ otherwise
t_i	Real variable indicating the arrival time on node i
u_i	Integer variable indicating the relative position of the node i

Table 4. Variable sets defined for the proposed formulation.

3.2. Objective functions

Following the preceding definition on Section 2, about the criteria involved in the multi-objective and real-time approach for service-order dispatching and routing, four objective functions are considered in this work: an objective function, Eq. (1), to denote the waiting time in hours involved in the solution proposed; an objective function, Eq. (2), to denote the total route cost, related to the sum of all travel times between any two nodes weighted by the hourly cost of the crews; an objective function, Eq. (3), to denote the number of hours related to the delay caused by the new assignment when compared to the initial routes; and finally, an objective function, Eq. (4), to denote the cost of non-assigned emergency orders.

It is worth noting that in all criteria, the unit remains the same: the number of financial units involved per hour ($/h).

$$Min \sum_{i\in V_e} OC_i t_i \tag{1}$$

$$Min \quad CC.\sum_{i\in V_{sce}} \sum_{j\in V_{ce}} \sum_{r\in R} D_{ij}.x_{ijr} \tag{2}$$

$$Min \quad \sum_{i\in V_a} OC_i.\max\{0;t_i - TA_i\} \tag{3}$$

$$Min \quad \sum_{i \in V_e} OC_i.(1 - s_i) \tag{4}$$

Since we are focus on a multi-objective approach, all the four criteria must be considered together in the optimization process. In this work, it is assumed an a priori approach to address the multi-objective problem [13], from the previous definition of all W_i factors before conducting the optimization process to dispatch and route. Eq. (5) presents the four criteria of Eqs. (1)–(4) weighted by corresponding W_i factors.

$$\begin{aligned} Min \quad & W_1.\sum_{i \in V_e} OC_i t_i + W_2.CC.\sum_{i \in V_{sce}} \sum_{j \in V_{ce}} \sum_{r \in R} D_{ij}.x_{ijr} + \\ & + W_3.\sum_{i \in V_a} OC_i.\max\{0; t_i - TA_i\} + W_4.\sum_{i \in V_e} OC_i.(1 - s_i) \end{aligned} \tag{5}$$

3.3. Basic constraints

After introducing all criteria put together with an unique objective function, there is a set of equations to define the constraints to be assumed in the formulation proposed. The first set of constraints are called just as "basic constraints," since they are related to the assignment of already routed orders or referring conditions as precedence and non-anomalous route construction: for instance, overlapping routes, service orders included in more than one route, etc.

$$y_{ir} = 1, \qquad \forall i \in V_{sce} \setminus V_{en}, \forall r \in R, r = RT_i \tag{6}$$

$$\sum_{i \in V_s} y_{ir} = 1, \qquad \forall r \in R \tag{7}$$

$$\sum_{i \in V_s} y_{ir} = 1, \qquad \forall r \in R \tag{8}$$

$$\sum_{i \in V_t} y_{ir} = 1, \qquad \forall r \in R \tag{9}$$

$$\sum_{r \in R} y_{ir} = 1 - s_i, \qquad \forall i \in V_{en} \tag{10}$$

$$\sum_{j \in V \setminus V_s, i \neq j} \sum_{r \in R} x_{ijr} = 1, \qquad \forall i \in V_s \tag{11}$$

$$\sum_{j \in V \setminus V_t, i \neq j} \sum_{r \in R} x_{jir} = 1 , \qquad \forall i \in V_t \tag{12}$$

$$\sum_{j \in V_s} \sum_{r \in R} x_{ijr} = 1 , \qquad \forall i \in V_t \tag{13}$$

$$\sum_{j \in V_{en} \cup V_t \cup SUC_i} \sum_{r \in R} x_{ijr} = 1 , \qquad \forall i \in V_a \tag{14}$$

$$\sum_{j \in V_{ens} \cup PRED_i} \sum_{r \in R} x_{jir} = 1 , \qquad \forall i \in V_a \tag{15}$$

$$\sum_{j \in V_{en} \cup V_t \cup V_a, i \neq j} \sum_{r \in R} x_{ijr} \leq 1 , \qquad \forall i \in V_{en} \tag{16}$$

$$\sum_{j \in V_{ens} \cup V_a, i \neq j} \sum_{r \in R} x_{jir} \leq 1 , \qquad \forall i \in V_{en} \tag{17}$$

$$\sum_{j \in V, i \neq j} x_{ijr} = y_{ir} , \qquad \forall i \in V, \forall r \in R \tag{18}$$

$$\sum_{j \in V, i \neq j} x_{jir} = y_{ir} , \qquad \forall i \in V, \forall r \in R \tag{19}$$

$$\sum_{j \in V_s} x_{ijr} = y_{ir} , \qquad \forall i \in V_t, \forall r \in R \tag{20}$$

$$x_{iir} = 0 , \qquad \forall i \in V, \forall r \in R \tag{21}$$

The assignment of all orders, with exception of the unassigned emergency ones (V_{en} set), is guaranteed by Eq. (6). Eq. (7) ensures that any order should be assigned to no more than one route and Eqs. (8) and (9) define the designation of all starting nodes and of all terminal nodes, respectively. Eq. (10) corresponds to the coupling constraints for variable sets y and s, which means that, for all unassigned emergency nodes, the value of s corresponding variable is equal to 1 if it remains unassigned, requiring y corresponding variable to take the value 0.

In Eq. (11), it is guaranteed that each starting node should have exactly one successor node in the set $V \setminus V_s$, whereas the Eq. (12) ensures that the terminal nodes must have exactly one predecessor node belonging to the set $V \setminus V_t$; Eq. (13) states that each terminal node should have exactly one starting node as its successor node. In this sense, with regarding to each assigned service order belonging to the set V_a, Eqs. (14) and (15) ensure exactly one successor and one predecessor node, respectively. With regarding to unassigned emergency nodes, Eqs. (16) and (17) ensure no more than one successor node and no more than one predecessor node, respectively.

Eqs. (18)–(20) correspond to the coupling constraints for variable sets x and y. If a certain node i is assigned to a route r ($y_{ir} = 1$), this node should have one successor and one predecessor node in this route, Eqs. (18) and (19), respectively. Eq. (20) requires that each terminal node should be predecessor node of exactly one starting one.

Finally, Eq. (21) forbids connections of a node to itself.

3.4. Subtour elimination constraints

In order to have crew routes without subtours, Miller–Tucker–Zemlin (MTZ) constraints [14, 15] are defined on Eqs. (22)–(25). These constraints arise from definition of extra integer variables for each node, in such a way to have defined the relative order of each one of these nodes in their corresponding routes. First, all the starting nodes (V_s set) are defined as the beginning of each route, Eq. (22), followed by definition of the remaining ones ($V \setminus V_s$ set) to be restricted on the range of [2, $|V|$], Eqs. (23) and (24). Eq. (25) corresponds to the coupling constraints for variable sets x and u, referring that if node j is successor of node i on the route r by defining $x_{ijr} = 1$, the following inequality holds: $u_i \leq u_j - 1$.

The last set of constraints, Eq. (26), refers to the assumption of the initial routes from the definition of parameter SEQ: if node j follows node i on initial routes, $u_i < u_j$.

$$u_i = 1, \qquad \forall i \in V_s \tag{22}$$

$$u_i \geq 2, \qquad \forall i \in V \setminus V_s \tag{23}$$

$$u_i \leq |V|, \qquad \forall i \in V \setminus V_s \tag{24}$$

$$u_i - u_j + |V| x_{ijr} \leq |V| - 1, \qquad \forall i, j \in V \setminus V_s, \forall r \in R \tag{25}$$

$$u_i < u_j, \qquad \forall i, j \in V_a, SEQ_i \leq SEQ_j \tag{26}$$

3.5. Arrival time constraints

Computing the waiting time for all nodes is only possible by defining the values for the variable set t, described in **Table 4** as the arrival time.

Since each crew has a starting node in the first position of its route, Eq. (27) defines that all nodes in the set V_s their arrival time is zero. The next set of constraints, Eq. (28), establishes properly how the arrival time is calculated by considering three main factors:

(1) the arrival time of the predecessor node i (t_i); (2) the service time at node i (TS_i); and (3) the traveled distance between the predecessor node i and the current node j (D_{ij}). By adopting the factor $-U$, one attempts to switch off the constraint whenever $x_{ijr}=0$, since $t_i + TS_i + D_{ij} << U$ and allowing $t_j=0$. For $x_{ijr}=1$, the following inequality holds: $t_j \geq t_i + TS_i + D_{ij}$.

$$t_i = 0, \qquad \forall i \in V_s \tag{27}$$

$$t_j \geq t_i + TS_i + D_{ij} - U(1 - x_{ijr}), \qquad \forall i \in V \setminus V_t, \forall j \in V \setminus V_s, \forall r \in R, i \neq j \tag{28}$$

3.6. Domain constraints

Eqs. (29)–(33) present the domain of variable sets x, y, s, t, and u. The linear programming model is defined by assuming the continuous variables t, after aggregating the discrete ones: x, y, s, and u. Only this last set is not binary, and it is worth noting that the set s is only defined for emergency nodes: V_e.

$$x_{ijr} \in \{0,1\}, \qquad \forall i,j \in V, \forall r \in R \tag{29}$$

$$y_{ir} \in \{0,1\}, \qquad \forall i \in V, \forall r \in R \tag{30}$$

$$s_i \in \{0,1\}, \qquad \forall i \in V_e \tag{31}$$

$$t_i \in R^+, \qquad \forall i \in V \tag{32}$$

$$u_i \in Z^+, \qquad \forall i \in V \tag{33}$$

4. Proposed algorithm

The composition of the objective function presented in the previous section was evaluated by testing the model performed with the IBM ILOG CPLEX 12.5 optimization environment. Even for small instances, read up some units outstanding emergency orders and a few dozen commercial orders in the schedule of teams, it was possible to obtain the optimal solution with adaptations in the model developed in practice to accurately resolution impediment for various reasons: (i) the dispatch issue emergency orders has combinatorial nature; (ii) the real-time response requirements is very important; and (iii) variability in the characteristics of dispatch problem instances is very significant.

Given this perspective, a heuristic approach to the EDRP is developed carefully observing the mathematical model described in Section 3. The heuristic algorithm corresponds to a search in variable neighborhood with multiple restarts, allowing versatility adjustments and easy adaptation to different dispatch scenarios and also relative efficiency as the numeric result.

The compromise was found with the algorithm which refers to the need for real-time response. This requirement may be relaxed in the case of a very large number of instances, such as in situations of extreme weather events that cause a very unusual number of EWOs. In these situations, what you want is to meet emergency orders as soon as possible, including completely passing over the planned orders. On the other hand, in more commonplace situations whether meet emergency orders as soon as possible but at the same time, minimizing the delay in the a priori routing planning with commercial orders.

The next sections describe both the decision support system architecture developed and the proposed heuristic algorithm to the EDRP described in Section 3.

4.1. Decision support system architecture

In order to deal with this dichotomy, the concept of dispatch scenarios was developed, exploiting basically the balance or imbalance between supply (availably of working hours) and demand (service time of pending emergency orders). In addition, the EDRP considered in this work should be able to handle real-time automatic dispatch of EWOs.

Assuming this entire context, a computational approach based on decision support systems [16] is proposed, since these systems provide concepts, definitions, and techniques that help decision makers in the decision process, especially by analyzing and furnishing alternatives of mathematical models in a reasonable time. The key idea involved is the proper use of techniques inspired by the mathematical model presented in Section 3, combined with efficient heuristics to furnish reasonable solutions bearing in mind the real-time requirements previously assumed [17]. Following these principles, it is proposed an architecture for the system as shown in **Figure 2**.

In order to provide real-time capabilities in the proposed computational system, the great representation of multi-core processors on most computers available suggests that this character may be exploited in parallelizable architectures. The first premise of the proposal is to divide the geographical of the electric utility into smaller areas that do not represent interconnection resources over a day, as if these areas were isolated from the point of view of the planning of calls in a day. For each one of these areas, there is a thread involving all the components of the architecture of **Figure 2**.

Another important constructive feature of the proposed architecture is to be event-driven [17], due to the component "Checking event queue." This queue contains all the operations related to the EDRP, whether logs or even actions to be taken: dispatch a given crew to attend a certain pending EWO.

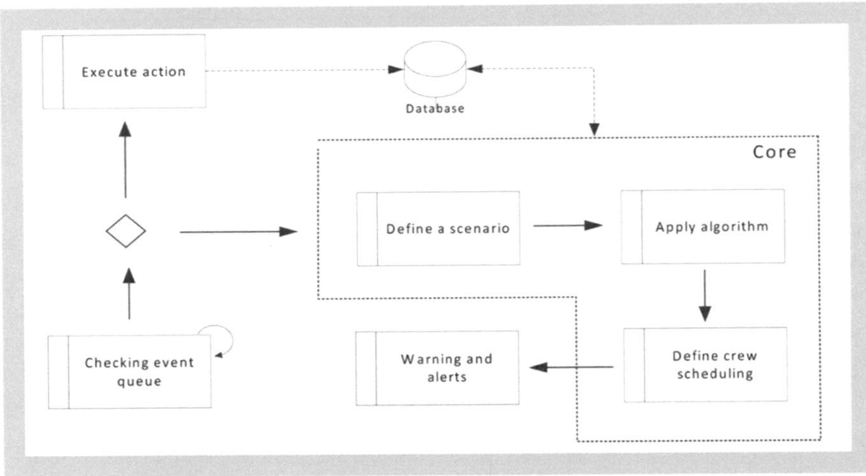

Figure 2. Proposed decision support system architecture.

Which is the best scenario? This answer is given by the component "Define a scenario," which evaluates how is the relationship between supply and demand, in such a way that supply refers to the remaining working time hours and demand refers to the service time of pending EWO. Whenever the required service time is much greater than the number of working time hours available, it is possible one is facing a situation of extreme climate event, thus requiring at least disregard the commercial demands or even add more working time hours for triggering extra repair crews. When low demand occurs, that is, the number of crews is greater than the number of pending EWO; the assignment problem emerges [18], and an exact solution for this problem is suitable as a lower bound to the original problem described in Section 3.

The next step after defining a scenario to the EDRP refers to execute the most appropriated algorithm to solve it, component "Apply algorithm." Afterwards, the component "Define crew scheduling" carries out final checking, since there may have been changes in the crews as non-communication or temporary unavailability. A report of the whole process is in charged of the component "Warning and alerts."

4.2. Proposed heuristic algorithm

The main reason for employing a "Variable Neighborhood Search"-based algorithm [19] for the EDRP refers to the possibilities of including adaptation in the optimization process based on the instance, even by applying several types of neighborhoods or even by applying neighborhood reduction strategies when the search space appears to be huge. These possibilities of adaptation are especially important when facing with real-time system approaches such as that proposed in this work.

Figure 3 presents the proposed algorithm developed to EDRP. There are three parameters: instance, with all the data entered in the mathematical model of Section 4.1.2, the number of permitted iterations (N), and the number of neighborhoods (T). The algorithm begins with a

http://dx.doi.org/10.5772/62849

constructive procedure in step 1, which systematically creates a solution for the EDRP by checking the gain promoted by each insertion of a pending EWO on the already constructed routes, taking into observation the aggregated objective function of Eq. (5). Since it is a greedy procedure, the best choice is assumed and the next pending EWO is evaluated until all of them are designated.

```
VariableNeighborhoodSearch ( Instance, N, T )
1.  sol = GreedyConstruction ( Instance );
2.  it = 1;
3.  While it < N do
4.      k = 1;
5.      While k < T do
6.          newsol = Shake(Instance, sol, k);
7.          end = 0;
8.          do
9.              neighborsol = GenerateNeighborSolution (Instance, newsol, k);
10.             If Evaluate(neighborsol) < Evaluate (newsol) Then
11.                 newsol = neighborsol;
12.             Else
13.                 end = 1;
14.         While end < 1;
15.         If Evaluate (newsol) < Evaluate (sol) Then
16.             sol = newsol;
17.             k = 1;
18.         Else
19.             k = k +1;
20.     it = it +1;
21.     If Restart( sol, newsol, it ) Then
22.         sol = GreedyConstruction ( Instance );
23. Return sol;
```

Figure 3. Proposed "Variable Neighborhood Search"-based algorithm.

The loop structure between steps 3 and 22 is relates to the algorithm itself that has a number of repetitions given by the parameter N. Steps 4–19 are equal to the search itself, where the variable k is the neighborhood considered: k = 1 is equivalent to insertion neighborhood, and k = 2 corresponds to the 2-opt neighborhood. Step 6 corresponds to a disturbance procedure applied to the current solution (sol), considering neighborhood defined by parameter k. This disturbance corresponds to changing the assignment of a given EWO or even changing the relative position in the corresponding route. From there, the repetition structure of the steps 8–14 is responsible for generating new neighbor solutions as they represent gains in the objective function (steps 10 and 11), which means lower values since the EDRP is defined for a minimization criterion—Eq. (5).

If the loop structure of steps 8–14 is over, it is checked if the solution generated by the search is better than the incumbent solution (sol), step 15. If so, one assumes the resulting solution search (newsol) as new incumbent and backup solution for the initial neighborhood (step 17). Otherwise, proceed to the next neighborhood (step 19) in an attempt to seek a minimum alternative and different location from the previous neighborhood.

The count of search iterations is performed in step 20, followed by the reset approach that is one of the advantages of this algorithm (steps 21 and 22). This process is performed by comparing the difference between the incumbent solution and the resulting solution search, along with the number of iterations. The actual reset (step 22) occurs only when the number of iterations indicates that the search has reached 50% of the effort and the search does not promote further improvement.

5. Computational results and analysis

Aiming to evaluate the developed algorithm presented in the previous section and also the associated computer system, two case studies were developed focusing on the variation in the cost of EWO, and the consequent impact in the dispatch defined.

The following are each of these studies and the exploited details:

- Case study 1 refers to the ratio of cost of emergency orders and travel time;
- Case Study 2 relates to the influence of the cost of an EWO on the sequence of orders existing commercial.

In addition, a set of instances of EDRP was used in order to evaluate the performance of the proposed methodology when observing the computation time required, that is, if the real-time requirement is guaranteed. In all cases, the time required was less than a minute, and most were <10 s. The processor used is an Intel Core i5-3230M, 2.6 GHz, running Windows 7 operating system. **Table 5** summarizes these results.

Instance	Time (s)	No. of crews	No. of commercial orders	No. of emergency orders
c16	0.213	1	7	1
c24_1248	0.288	1	7	6
e1	0.370	5	30	6
e4	0.455	9	30	6
e2	0.471	6	30	6
a1_3108	0.669	4	26	9
a1_2229	0.703	4	26	11
a1_2130	0.805	4	26	11
a1_1210	1.090	4	26	12
a1_2027	1.876	4	26	15
j2	8.643	8	0	49

Table 5. General results for the proposed algorithm.

5.1. Case study 1

This study explored the first and fundamental characteristic of a review of a dispatch solution: the impact of the cost of EWO on travel time associated with.

Table 6 presents 11 test cases that were developed with one team and two EWO. One can see that the O4863657 cost has not changed, just O4863663 has changed from $100.00/h in case 11 to $2.00/h in the case 0. Three last columns of **Table 6** represent the components of the objective function that is impacted in this case study: expected cost of emergencies, travel costs, and the overall cost.

Instance	*O4863657 cost*	*O4863663 cost*	*f emergency*	*f displacement*	*f global*
r11	100	100	81	61	142
r10	100	90	80	61	141
r9	100	80	78	61	139
r8	100	70	77	61	138
r7	100	60	76	61	137
r6	100	50	74	61	135
r5	100	40	73	61	134
r4	100	30	71	61	132
r3	100	20	70	61	131
r2	100	10	43	86	129
r1	100	5	39	86	125
r0	100	2	36	86	122

Table 6. Results for test case 1.

From **Figure 4**, one can note that for O4863663 cost values ≥$20/h, corresponding to test cases r3–r11, this order is always chosen to be in the first route position by promoting the smallest displacement. When O4863663 cost is reduced to <$20/h, the cost of waiting time becomes more representative than displacement cost, causing the advance of the order with the greatest cost (O4863657) in the corresponding route. In addition, one can see the evolution of these components of the objective function and also the evolution of the costs of each of the orders considered in the study: (i) "F Emergency" is the portion corresponding to the cost of waiting time for emergency orders; (ii) "f displacement time" is the cost of the displacement performed; (iii) "f global" is the sum of two parts.

The highlight in **Figure 4** is given to the time when there is a reversal in the route sequence due to the change in the O4863663 cost: The cost of waiting for EWO was above the travel cost up to the test case r3, after it, the most appropriate decision to reduce "f global" is to choose that sequence with less waiting time. The result of this transition on the route of the team is illustrated in **Figure 5**.

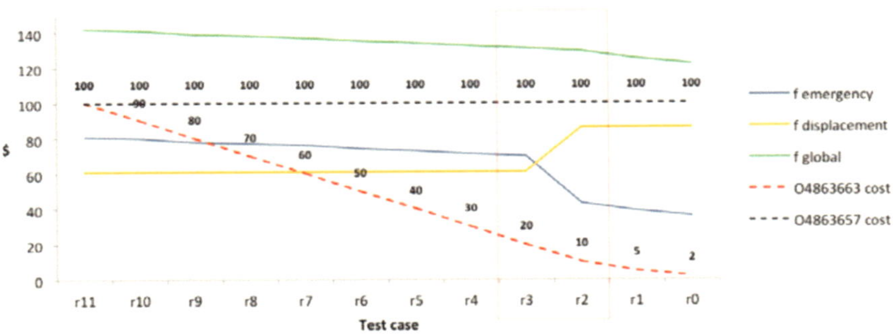

Figure 4. Results for all instances of case study 1.

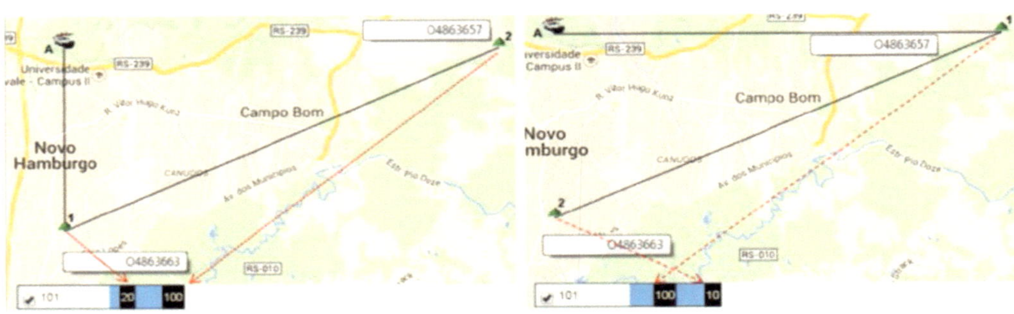

Figure 5. Analysis of the emergence of postponing on case study 1.

5.2. Case study 2

In this case study, it is verified the influence that EWO costs have on the relative position of these orders on the existing route.

Eight test cases were developed, always assuming only an emergency order and six commercial orders: two with priority 0 and 4 with priority 2.

Table 7 summarizes the results for each test case, and the columns contain the identification of test case, the cost of the E4354201 order, the expected cost of the emergency order ("f Emergency"), the delay cost on commercial orders ("f commercial"), the cost of displacement ("f displacement"), and the overall cost ("f global"), which equals the sum "f Emergency" + "f Commercial" + "f displacement". The cost E4354201 ranges from $24/h (test case "pr12") to $ 1/h ("pr5").

Instance	E4354201 cost	f emergency	f commercial	f displacement	f global
pr12	24	2.7	-209.8	33.1	-174.04
pr11	18	2.0	-209.8	33.1	-174.7
pr10	12	8.0	-219.5	35.1	-176.34
pr9	8	5.3	-219.5	35.1	-178.99
pr8	4	2.7	-219.5	35.1	-181.65
pr7	3	2.0	-219.5	35.1	-182.32
pr6	2	2.5	-229.6	43.7	-183.36
pr5	1	3.4	-232.0	43.1	-185.53

Table 7. Results for test case 2.

With the help of **Figure 6**, it is possible to identify the three areas highlighted in the chart that corresponds to changes in the route:

- First region: between transition from test case pr11 to test case pr10;
- Second region: between transition from test case pr7 to test case pr6;
- Third region: between transition from test case pr6 to test case pr5.

Transition costs of the first region causes the emergency order pass from the first to the second position on the route; second transition region makes the emergency order to be is only the third on the route; and finally, the last transition (third region) leads the emergency order to be in the last position of the route. Such events are highlighted in **Figure 6**, which illustrates the routes for test cases pr12, pr10, pr6, and pr5.

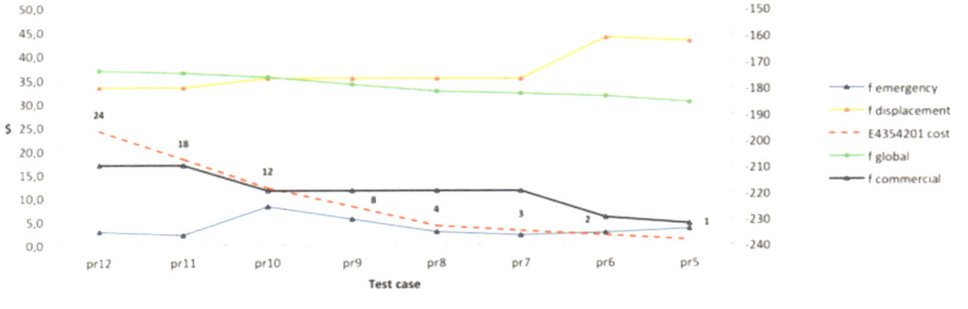

Figure 6. Analysis of the commercial orders delay on test case 2.

6. Conclusions

This work presents a heuristic approach to solve the emergency dispatching and routing problem, inspired by a newly developed mathematical formulation also presented. Some attributes of vehicle routing problem are addressed, particularly: the real-time solution; on-site service; multiple origins; time window restrictions on vehicles; and partially dynamic problem (**Figure 7**).

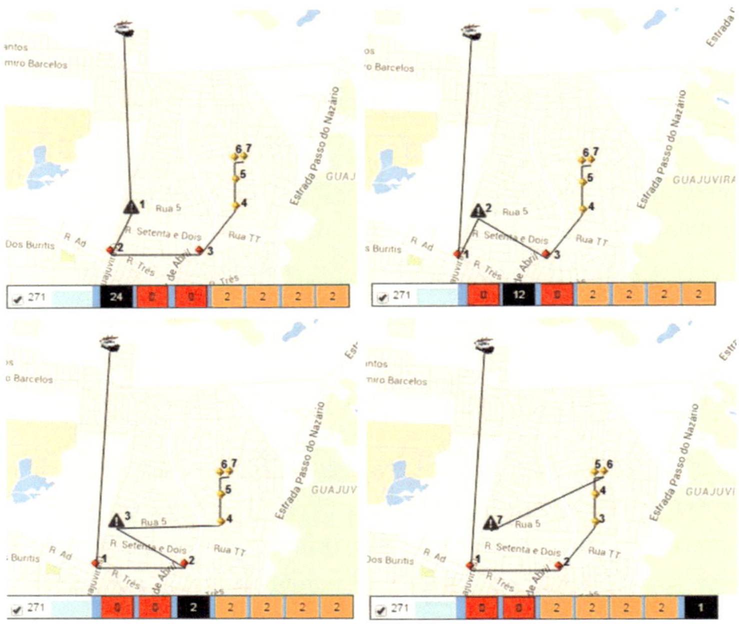

Figure 7. Analysis of the emergence of postponing on test case 1.

Several criteria and constraints are involved from that attributes assumed, basically considering the minimization of both the waiting time, travel times, the delay caused by the assignment of pending EWOs, and the cost of non-assigning them. The set of constraints include besides the general ones, those related to the partially dynamic problem addressed and the arrival time constraints due to the minimization of waiting time and to the assumption of on-site service.

The proposed methodology, traduced in a heuristic approach that carefully observes the mathematical programming formulation, comprises decision support system techniques deriving a specially architecture developed, with the important requirement to promote better efficiency on multi-processors systems in order to handle real-time conditions. Practical results based on actual cases show how suitable is the proposed system to be applied in real-time conditions and demonstrates the proper response to system parameters defined.

Acknowledgements

The authors would like to thank the technical and financial support of AES Sul Distribuidora Gaúcha de Energia SA.

Author details

Vinícius Jacques Garcia[1*], Daniel Bernardon[1], Iochane Guimarães[1] and Júlio Fonini[1,2]

*Address all correspondence to: viniciusjg@gmail.com

1 Federal University of Santa Maria, Santa Maria, RS, Brazil

2 AES Sul Power Utility, Porto Alegre, RS, Brazil

References

[1] Gonen T. Electric Power Distribution System Engineering. 2nd ed.: CRC Press, Bosa Roca; 2007. 834 p. ISBN 978–1420062007.

[2] Perrier N, Agard B, Baptiste P, Frayret J-M, Langevin A, Pellerin R, Riopel D, Trépanier M. A survey of models and algorithms for emergency response logistics in electric distribution systems. Computers & Operations Research. 2013; 40: 1895–1906.

[3] Murphy L, Wu FF. A Comprehensive Analysis of Distribution Automation Systems [Technical Report]. Berkeley: EECS Department, University of California; 1990. UCB/ERL M90/72.

[4] Ribeiro RA, Powell PL, Baldwin JF. Uncertainty in decision-making: An abductive perspective. Decision Support Systems. 1995; 13(2): 183–193.

[5] Ghiani G, Guerriero F, Laporte G, Musmanno R. Real-time vehicle routing: Solution concepts, algorithms and parallel computing strategies. European Journal of Operational Research. 2003; 151(1): 1–11.

[6] Pillac V, Gendreau M, Guéret C, Medaglia AL. A review of dynamic vehicle routing problems. European Journal of Operational Research. 2013; 225(1): 1–11.

[7] Psaraftis HN. Dynamic Vehicle Routing Problems. In: Golden BL, Assad, A editors. Vehicle Routing: Studies in Management Science and Systems. Amsterdam: Elsevier Science Publishers B V; 1988. pp. 223–248.

[8] Toth P, Vigo D. The vehicle routing problem. Society for Industrial & Applied Mathematics (SIAM); 2002.

[9] Laporte G. The vehicle routing problem: An overview of exact and approximate algorithms. European Journal of Operational Research. 1992; 59(3): 345–358.

[10] Eksioglu B, Vural AV, Reisman A. The vehicle routing problem: A taxonomic review. Computers & Industrial Engineering. 2009; 57(4): 1472–1483.

[11] Vidal T, Crainic TG, Gendreau M, Prins C. Heuristics for multi-attribute vehicle routing problems: A survey and synthesis. European Journal of Operational Research. 2013; 231: 1–21.

[12] Luenberger DG, Ye Y. Linear and Nonlinear Programming. 4th ed.: Springer, Switzerland; 2015. 546 p. ISBN 978–3319188416.

[13] Jozefowiez N, Semet F, Talbi E-G. Multi-objective vehicle routing problems. 2008; 189(2): 293–309.

[14] Miller C, Tucker AW, Zemlin RA. Integer programming formulations and traveling salesman problems. Journal of Association for Computing Machinery. 1960;7: 326–329.

[15] Bektas T, Gouveia L. Requiem for the Miller–Tucker–Zemlin subtour elimination constraints? European Journal of Operational Research. 2014; 236(3): 820–832.

[16] Shim JP, Warkentin M, Courtney JF, Power DJ, Sharda R, Carlsson C. Past, present, and future of decision support technology. Decision Support Systems. 2002; 33(2): 11–126.

[17] Pillac V, Guéret C, Medaglia AL. An event-driven optimization framework for dynamic vehicle routing. Decision Support Systems. 2012; 54(1): 414–423.

[18] Korte B, Vygen J. Combinatorial Optimization: Theory and Algorithms. 4th ed.: Berlin: Springer; 2008. 627p. ISBN 978–3540718437.

[19] Hansen P., Mladenović, N. Variable neighborhood search: Principles and applications. European Journal of Operational Research. 2001; 130(3): 449–467.

Chapter 6

Kalman Filtering and Its Real-Time Applications

Lim Chot Hun, Ong Lee Yeng, Lim Tien Sze and
Koo Voon Chet

Additional information is available at the end of the chapter

http://dx.doi.org/ 10.5772/62352

Abstract

Kalman filter was pioneered by Rudolf Emil Kalman in 1960, originally designed and developed to solve the navigation problem in Apollo Project. Since then, numerous applications were developed with the implementation of Kalman filter, such as applications in the fields of navigation and computer vision's object tracking. Kalman filter consists of two separate processes, namely the prediction process and the measurement process, which work in a recursive manner. Both processes are modeled by groups of equations in the state space model to achieve optimal estimation outputs. Prior knowledge on the state space model is needed, and it differs between different systems. In this chapter, the authors outlined and explained the fundamental Kalman filtering model in real-time discrete form and devised two real-time applications that implemented Kalman filter. The first application involved using vision camera to perform real-time image processing for vehicle tracking, whereas the second application discussed the real-time Global Positioning System (GPS)-aided Strapdown Inertial Navigation Unit (SINU) system implementation using Kalman filter. Detail descriptions, model derivations, and results are outlined in both applications.

Keywords: Kalman filter, real-time, navigation, vehicle tracking, GPS-aided-INS

1. Introduction

Kalman filter exists for the past 50 years. It was first introduced by Rudolf Emil Kalman in 1960 [1] and was implemented on the Apollo Project in 1961 to solve the space navigation problem [2]. Kalman filter is claimed to be an optimal estimator [1] due to its ability to optimally estimate the system's error covariance and use the prediction in a recursive manner to improve the system measurements from time to time. As such, Kalman filter was implemented as the estimator in various applications, such as in navigations [3, 4], image processing [5, 6], and finance [7].

One of the uniqueness in Kalman filter is that it consists of two distinct processes, namely, the prediction process and the measurement process. Both processes are combined and operated in a recursive manner to achieve optimal Kalman filtering process [8]. Another uniqueness of Kalman filter is the incorporation of prediction errors and measurement errors into the overall Kalman filtering process. It is common that each prediction and measurement process consists of errors in random nature. These errors or "noise" are normally being described using the stochastic process. On the other hand, a real-time application can be defined as an application or program that reacts or responses within a predefined time frame, where such predefined time frame is a quantified time using a physical clock [9]. From a real-time application's point of view, the real world's continuous time is turned into discrete time frame Δ. Different real-time applications have different Δ, which in turn defined the response time of the applications. The real-time application must react within the predefined time frame to provide an up-to-date response. Such real-time constraint forced the application to complete its routine within the time frame, else the output may not be accurately reflecting the current state of input [10].

Note that the realization of Kalman filter, in its recursive nature, can be described as a real-time implementation. In this book chapter, the authors will demonstrate two real-time Kalman filtering examples. The first example demonstrated the real-time Kalman filter implementation on vehicle tracking application using vision camera's image processing. A Kalman filtering model is established to estimate the positions and velocities of the moving vehicles and to provide tracking on the vehicles at a normally visible condition [11]. The second example demonstrated the Kalman filter implementation on the real-time Global Positioning System (GPS)-aided Strapdown Inertial Navigation Unit (SINU) System or GPS-aided INU system for Unmanned Aerial Vehicle (UAV) motion sensing. The results obtained from both experiments will be illustrated and discussed in this book chapter.

The outline of this chapter is as follows. Section 2 illustrates the generalized Kalman filter model from real-time system's point of view. Section 3 outlines the real-time vehicle tracking system using vision camera. The contents include the elaboration of image processing algorithms, illustration of the Kalman filtering model on the tracking system, result in acquisition, and discussions. Section 4 depicts the real-time GPS-aided SINU system for UAV motion sensing using Kalman filter. The contents included the derivation of Kalman filter for the GPS-aided SINU system, the offline and real-time implementation of the Kalman filter on the GPS-aided SINU system, results and discussions, and conclusion. Lastly, Section 5 concludes the chapter.

2. Kalman filter

Kalman filtering is a popular technique used to solve observer problems [12] in control engineering [13]. Numerous derivations of the Kalman filter model can be obtained from various researchers' works [3, 8, 12, 14, 15], where detailed elaborations and explanations of the Kalman filter, which included the derivation of the prerequisites such as the state space model and random variables, are outlined. Hence, in this chapter, the authors derived and explained the discrete real-time Kalman filter model from the implementation point of view to ensure readers can understand the idea of Kalman filter from the real-time implementation angle.

2.1. Discrete Kalman filter model

A typical Kalman filtering process is separated into two distinct processes, namely, the prediction process and the measurement process [14]. In general, the Kalman filter prediction model and the measurement model of a real-time system, expressed in discrete form, are as follows:

$$\boldsymbol{x}_k = \phi \boldsymbol{x}_{k-1} + \boldsymbol{Bu} + \boldsymbol{w}_k \tag{1}$$

$$z_k = \boldsymbol{Hx}_k + v_k \tag{2}$$

where x_k is the predicted output, z_k is the measurement output, ϕ denotes the state transition matrix, $\boldsymbol{B}$ is the control input matrix, and u is the optional control input matrix. H is the measurement transformation matrix, whereas w_k and v_k are the process noise matrix and measurement noise matrix, respectively. Both Equations (1) and (2) depict the general expression of the Kalman filtering process [14, 15]. In terms of real-time implementation, however, further elaborations are to be performed on Equations (1) and (2).

2.2. Kalman filter algorithm

The Kalman filtering algorithm starts from the prediction process by estimating the prediction state based on the derived state space equation. The state space equation, or state transition equation, may differ in different systems. From the implementation point of view, the expression of the prediction state, similar to Equation (1), is outlined as follows:

$$\tilde{\boldsymbol{x}}_k^- = \phi \tilde{\boldsymbol{x}}_{k-1} + \boldsymbol{Bu} \tag{3}$$

where $\tilde{\boldsymbol{x}}_k^-$ is defined as the *a priori* state estimated at the discrete instant *k*, and $\tilde{\boldsymbol{x}}_k$ is defined as the *a posteriori* state illustrated at the discrete instant *k* given the measurement z_k. Note that, from Equation (3), the *a priori* state $\tilde{x}_k^-$ can be elaborated as a hypothesized state predicted from the system's state transition equations, whereas the *a posteriori* state $\tilde{x}_k$ can be elaborated as the measured state obtained by the system's observation. By letting x_k be the true value of state measurement, the *a priori* prediction error $\boldsymbol{e}_k^-$ and *a posteriori* estimation error $\boldsymbol{e}_k$ can be expressed as:

$$e_k^- = x_k - \tilde{x}_k^- \tag{4}$$

$$e_k = x_k - \tilde{x}_k \tag{5}$$

From Equation (4), the *a priori* prediction error covariance can be expressed as:

$$P_k^- = E\left[e_k^- e_k^{-T}\right] = E\left[\left(x_k - \tilde{x}_k^-\right)\left(x_k - \tilde{x}_k^-\right)^T\right] \tag{6}$$

From Equation (6), substituting x_k. Equation (1) and $\tilde{x}_k^-$ with Equation (3) yielded:

$$\begin{aligned} P_k^- &= E\left[\left[\phi\left(x_{k-1} - \tilde{x}_{k-1}\right) + w_k\right] \cdot \left[\phi\left(x_{k-1} - \tilde{x}_{k-1}\right) + w_k\right]^T\right] \\ &= \phi \cdot E\left[\left(x_{k-1} - \tilde{x}_{k-1}\right) \cdot \left(x_{k-1} - \tilde{x}_{k-1}\right)^T\right] \cdot \phi^T + \phi \cdot E\left[\left(x_{k-1} - \tilde{x}_{k-1}\right) \cdot w_k^T\right] + \\ & E\left[w_k\left(x_{k-1} - \tilde{x}_{k-1}\right)^T\right] \cdot \phi^T + E\left[w_k w_k^T\right] \end{aligned} \tag{7}$$

Because the state estimation error and the process noise error are uncorrelated,

$$E\left[\left(x_{k-1} - \tilde{x}_{k-1}\right) \cdot w_k^T\right] = E\left[w_k\left(x_{k-1} - \tilde{x}_{k-1}\right)^T\right] = 0 \tag{8}$$

Therefore, Equation (7) can be simplified into:

$$\begin{aligned} P_k^- &= \phi \cdot E\left[\left(x_{k-1} - \tilde{x}_{k-1}\right) \cdot \left(x_{k-1} - \tilde{x}_{k-1}\right)^T\right] \cdot \phi^T \\ &+ E\left[w_k w_k^T\right] = \phi \cdot P_{k-1} \cdot \phi^T + \mathbf{Q}_k \end{aligned} \tag{9}$$

Equation (9) yielded an important step in the prediction process of the Kalman filtering algorithm in obtaining the *a priori* prediction error covariance using the system's state transition matrix ϕ, the *a posteriori* measurement error covariance from previous estimation P_{k-1} and the process noise covariance $\mathbf{Q}_k = E\left[w_k w_k^T\right]$. Hence, in summary, Equations (3) and (9) summarized the two most important equations in deriving the prediction process of the Kalman filter algorithm.

The next stage of the Kalman filtering algorithm is the measurement process. Equation (2) depicts the observation equation, or the actual measurement equation, of the system. The measurement output z_k is normally obtained from the system's measurement sensors or devices. From here, it is possible to express the *a posteriori* measurement $\tilde{x}_k$ as follows [16]:

$$\tilde{\boldsymbol{x}}_k = \tilde{\boldsymbol{x}}_k^- + \boldsymbol{K}_k\left(z_k - \boldsymbol{H}\tilde{\boldsymbol{x}}_k^-\right) \tag{10}$$

where $\boldsymbol{K}_k$ is the Kalman gain, and the term $\left(z_k - \boldsymbol{H}\tilde{x}_k^-\right)$ is commonly known as the measurement residual or innovation [14–16]. Substituting Equation (2) into Equation (10) yielded:

$$\tilde{\boldsymbol{x}}_k = \tilde{\boldsymbol{x}}_k^- + \boldsymbol{K}_k\left(\boldsymbol{H}\boldsymbol{x}_k + \boldsymbol{v}_k - \boldsymbol{H}\tilde{\boldsymbol{x}}_k^-\right) = \tilde{\boldsymbol{x}}_k^- + \boldsymbol{K}_k\boldsymbol{H}\left(\boldsymbol{x}_k - \tilde{\boldsymbol{x}}_k^-\right) + \boldsymbol{K}_k\boldsymbol{v}_k \tag{11}$$

Given the *a posteriori* measurement error covariance, with reference to Equation (5):

$$\boldsymbol{P}_k = E\left[\boldsymbol{e}_k\boldsymbol{e}_k^T\right] = E\left[\left(\boldsymbol{x}_k - \tilde{\boldsymbol{x}}_k\right)\left(\boldsymbol{x}_k - \tilde{\boldsymbol{x}}_k\right)^T\right] \tag{12}$$

Substituting Equation (11) into Equation (12) yielded:

$$\begin{aligned}
\boldsymbol{P}_k &= E\left[\left[\boldsymbol{x}_k - \tilde{\boldsymbol{x}}_k^- - \boldsymbol{K}_k\boldsymbol{H}\left(\boldsymbol{x}_k - \tilde{\boldsymbol{x}}_k^-\right) - \boldsymbol{K}_k\boldsymbol{v}_k\right]\cdot\left[\boldsymbol{x}_k - \tilde{\boldsymbol{x}}_k^- - \boldsymbol{K}_k\boldsymbol{H}\left(\boldsymbol{x}_k - \tilde{\boldsymbol{x}}_k^-\right) - \boldsymbol{K}_k\boldsymbol{v}_k\right]^T\right] \\
&= E\left[\left[(\boldsymbol{I} - \boldsymbol{K}_k\boldsymbol{H})\left(\boldsymbol{x}_k - \tilde{\boldsymbol{x}}_k^-\right) - \boldsymbol{K}_k\boldsymbol{v}_k\right]\cdot\left[(\boldsymbol{I} - \boldsymbol{K}_k\boldsymbol{H})\left(\boldsymbol{x}_k - \tilde{\boldsymbol{x}}_k^-\right) - \boldsymbol{K}_k\boldsymbol{v}_k\right]^T\right] \\
&= (\boldsymbol{I} - \boldsymbol{K}_k\boldsymbol{H})\cdot E\left[\left(\boldsymbol{x}_k - \tilde{\boldsymbol{x}}_k^-\right)\cdot\left(\boldsymbol{x}_k - \tilde{\boldsymbol{x}}_k^-\right)^T\right]\cdot(\boldsymbol{I} - \boldsymbol{K}_k\boldsymbol{H})^T + \boldsymbol{K}_k\cdot E\left[\boldsymbol{v}_k\cdot\boldsymbol{v}_k^T\right]\cdot\boldsymbol{K}_k^T - \\
&\quad (\boldsymbol{I} - \boldsymbol{K}_k\boldsymbol{H})\cdot E\left[\left(\boldsymbol{x}_k - \tilde{\boldsymbol{x}}_k^-\right)\cdot\left(\boldsymbol{K}_k\cdot\boldsymbol{v}_k\right)^T\right] - E\left[\left(\boldsymbol{K}_k\cdot\boldsymbol{v}_k\right)\left(\boldsymbol{x}_k - \tilde{\boldsymbol{x}}_k^-\right)^T\right]\cdot(\boldsymbol{I} - \boldsymbol{K}_k\boldsymbol{H})^T
\end{aligned} \tag{13}$$

Because the state estimation error and measurement noise error are uncorrelated,

$$E\left[\left(\boldsymbol{x}_k - \tilde{\boldsymbol{x}}_k^-\right)\cdot\left(\boldsymbol{K}_k\cdot\boldsymbol{v}_k\right)^T\right] = E\left[\left(\boldsymbol{K}_k\cdot\boldsymbol{v}_k\right)\left(\boldsymbol{x}_k - \tilde{\boldsymbol{x}}_k^-\right)^T\right] = 0 \tag{14}$$

Therefore, Equation (13) can be simplified into:

$$\begin{aligned}
\boldsymbol{P}_k &= (\boldsymbol{I} - \boldsymbol{K}_k\boldsymbol{H})\cdot E\left[\left(x_k - \tilde{x}_k^-\right)\cdot\left(x_k - \tilde{x}_k^-\right)^T\right]\cdot(\boldsymbol{I} - \boldsymbol{K}_k\boldsymbol{H})^T + \boldsymbol{K}_k\cdot E\left[v_k\cdot v_k^T\right]\cdot\boldsymbol{K}_k^T \\
&= (\boldsymbol{I} - \boldsymbol{K}_k\boldsymbol{H})\cdot\boldsymbol{P}_k^-\cdot(\boldsymbol{I} - \boldsymbol{K}_k\boldsymbol{H})^T + \boldsymbol{K}_k\cdot\boldsymbol{R}_k\cdot\boldsymbol{K}_k^T
\end{aligned} \tag{15}$$

Equation (15) depicts the error covariance update equation in the measurement process of the Kalman filtering algorithm. From Equation (15), one could obtain the optimal Kalman gain K_k

with minimal mean squared error, where the mean squared error is reflected by the *trace* of P_k [16], in which the *trace* is defined as the sum of the diagonal elements in the matrix. To do so, the error covariance update equation from Equation (15) can be rewritten as:

$$\boldsymbol{P}_k = \boldsymbol{P}_k^- - \boldsymbol{K}_k \cdot \boldsymbol{H} \cdot \boldsymbol{P}_k^- - \boldsymbol{P}_k^- \cdot \boldsymbol{H}^T \cdot \boldsymbol{K}_k^T + \boldsymbol{K}_k \cdot \left(\boldsymbol{H} \cdot \boldsymbol{P}_k^- \cdot \boldsymbol{H}^T + \boldsymbol{R}_k\right) \cdot \boldsymbol{K}_k^T \tag{16}$$

The mean squared error reflected by the *trace* of the error covariance P_k can be expressed as:

$$\begin{aligned} \mathbf{T}[\boldsymbol{P}_k] &= \mathbf{T}[\boldsymbol{P}_k^-] - \mathbf{T}[\boldsymbol{K}_k \cdot \boldsymbol{H} \cdot \boldsymbol{P}_k^-] - \mathbf{T}[\boldsymbol{P}_k^- \cdot \boldsymbol{H}^T \cdot \boldsymbol{K}_k^T] + \mathbf{T}[\boldsymbol{K}_k \cdot (\boldsymbol{H} \cdot \boldsymbol{P}_k^- \cdot \boldsymbol{H}^T + \boldsymbol{R}_k) \cdot \boldsymbol{K}_k^T] \\ &= \mathbf{T}[\boldsymbol{P}_k^-] - 2\mathbf{T}[\boldsymbol{K}_k \cdot \boldsymbol{H} \cdot \boldsymbol{P}_k^-] + \mathbf{T}[\boldsymbol{K}_k \cdot (\boldsymbol{H} \cdot \boldsymbol{P}_k^- \cdot \boldsymbol{H}^T + \boldsymbol{R}_k) \cdot \boldsymbol{K}_k^T] \end{aligned} \tag{17}$$

where $\mathbf{T}[\cdot]$ denote the *trace* of matrix and $\mathbf{T}[\boldsymbol{K}_k \cdot \boldsymbol{H} \cdot \boldsymbol{P}_k^-] = \mathbf{T}[\boldsymbol{P}_k^- \cdot \boldsymbol{H}^T \cdot \boldsymbol{K}_k^T]$, as the diagonals of both matrixes are identical. Performing the first derivative of Equation (17) with respect to Kalman gain K_k yielded:

$$\frac{d\mathbf{T}[\boldsymbol{P}_k]}{d\boldsymbol{K}_k} = -2\left[\boldsymbol{H} \cdot \boldsymbol{P}_k^-\right]^T + 2\boldsymbol{K}_k \cdot \boldsymbol{H} \cdot \boldsymbol{P}_k^- \cdot \boldsymbol{H}^T + 2\boldsymbol{K}_k \cdot \boldsymbol{R}_k = 0 \tag{18}$$

where $\frac{d\mathbf{T}[\mathbf{K}_k \cdot \mathbf{H} \cdot \mathbf{P}_k^-]}{d\mathbf{K}_k} = [\mathbf{H} \cdot \mathbf{P}_k^-]^T$ and $\frac{d\mathbf{T}[K_k \cdot (H \cdot P_k^- \cdot H^T + R_k) \cdot K_k^T]}{d K_k} = 2K_k \cdot (\boldsymbol{H} \cdot \boldsymbol{P}_k^- \cdot \boldsymbol{H}^T + \boldsymbol{R}_k)$. Rearranging Equation (18) yielded the optimal Kalman gain with minimal mean squared error, as follows:

$$\boldsymbol{K}_k = \boldsymbol{P}_k^- \cdot \boldsymbol{H}^T \cdot \left(\boldsymbol{H} \cdot \boldsymbol{P}_k^- \cdot \boldsymbol{H}^T + \boldsymbol{R}_k\right)^{-1} \tag{19}$$

Lastly, substituting Equation (19) into Equation (16) yielded:

$$\boldsymbol{P}_k = \boldsymbol{P}_k^- - \boldsymbol{P}_k^- \cdot \boldsymbol{H}^T \cdot \left(\boldsymbol{H} \cdot \boldsymbol{P}_k^- \cdot \boldsymbol{H}^T + \boldsymbol{R}_k\right)^{-1} \cdot \boldsymbol{H} \cdot \boldsymbol{P}_k^- = \left(\boldsymbol{I} - \boldsymbol{K}_k \cdot \boldsymbol{H}\right) \cdot \boldsymbol{P}_k^- \tag{20}$$

where Equation (20) is the simplified version of error covariance update equation expressed in terms of optimal Kalman gain obtained from Equation (19) and the *a priori* prediction error covariance obtained from Equation (9).

In summary, the Kalman filtering algorithm can be summarized and is shown in **Figure 1**. The prediction process, as shown in Figure 1, covers the prediction of *a priori* state and *a priori* error covariance. The measurement process, on the contrary, covers the calculation of optimal Kalman gain, updating the *a posteriori* estimation state and the *a posteriori* error covariance. Both processes run in a recursive manner, forming the well-known Kalman filtering algorithm.

http://dx.doi.org/ 10.5772/62352

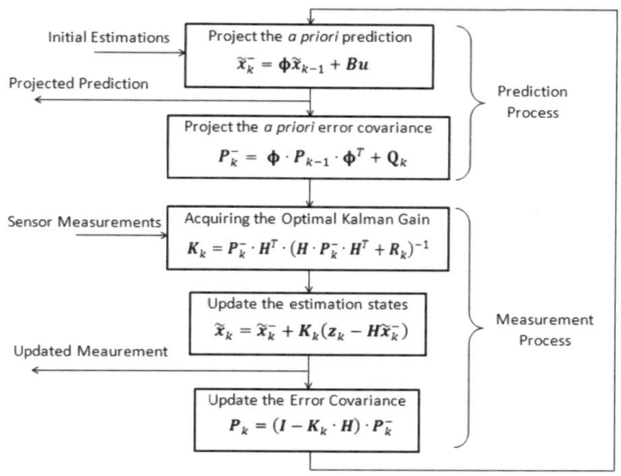

Figure 1. Block diagram of the Kalman filtering algorithm.

2.3. Real-time consideration of Kalman filter

Figure 1 depicts a typical Kalman filtering process algorithm in its recursive form. Notice from the block diagram that the algorithm processed each stage one by one and rewind back to the initial block for the next cycle of processing. From the real-time perspective, there are certain time critical events that need to be handled within a specific time frame. In this subsection, the time critical events are analyzed and discussed as part of the consideration of real-time Kalman filtering algorithm.

The pseudo code of the Kalman filtering algorithm is outlined in **Figure 2**. It is divided into three sections. The first section denotes the system initialization, and it is covered from steps 100 and 101. The second section is the prediction process section, covered from steps 200 to 202. The third and final section is the measurement process section, covered from steps 300 to 310. Note that the second and third sections run recursively.

```
100  System Initialization              /*Start up of System's models*/    } System Initialization
101  Load Initial Value                 /*Load pre-set initial value*/
200  Compute Prediction State x̃k⁻        /*Refer Eq. (3)*/                   } Prediction Process
201  Project the Prediction State x̃k⁻    /*Keep a record of current x̃k⁻*/
202  Compute Error Covariance Pk⁻       /*Refer Eq. (9)*/
300  if Measurement Sensors Ready                                           } Measurement Process
301       Read Measurements from Sensors   /*Obtain sensors reading*/
302       Pre-process Sensors Data         /*Convert data into zk*/
303  else
304       No Measurement
305  end if
306  Compute Kalman Gain Kk             /*Refer Eq. (19)*/
307  Compute Measurement State x̃k       /*Refer Eq. (10)*/
308  Project the Measurement State x̃k   /*Keep a record of current x̃k*/
309  Update Error Covariance Pk         /*Refer Eq. (20)*/
310  Goto 200
```

Figure 2. A typical Kalman filtering algorithm process pseudo code.

Figure 3 depicts the timing diagram of the real-time Kalman filtering algorithm based on the pseudo code illustrated in **Figure 2**. The following observations are obtained by examining **Figure 3**:

1. ΔT_{21} can be defined as the time required for Kalman filter prediction process from steps 200 to 202.

2. ΔT_{32} is defined as the time required for the measurement sensor's data preparation from steps 300 to 305. The time consists of reading the measurement data from the sensors and performs the preprocessing on the data as part of the measurement process preparation. Note that ΔT_{32} may be the most time-consuming factor in Kalman filtering process due to the preprocessing step 302. Depending on the application, the preprocessing of measurement data may require a substantial amount of processing power to complete.

3. ΔT_{43} depicts the time required for the measurement data computation process from steps 306 to 310. Three important parameters were computed within this time frame, namely, the optimal Kalman gain, the measurement states, and the error covariance measurements.

4. The total duration for a single iteration is ΔT_{41}, which is equal to ΔT_{21}+ΔT_{32}+ΔT_{43}. Note that ΔT_{41} shall not exceed Δ, where ΔT is defined as the fixed time-step of iteration. In most Kalman filter applications, ΔT is normally adopted as the sampling duration of incoming data. If the processing time for a single iteration exceeded Δ, then the next prediction will not be accurate.

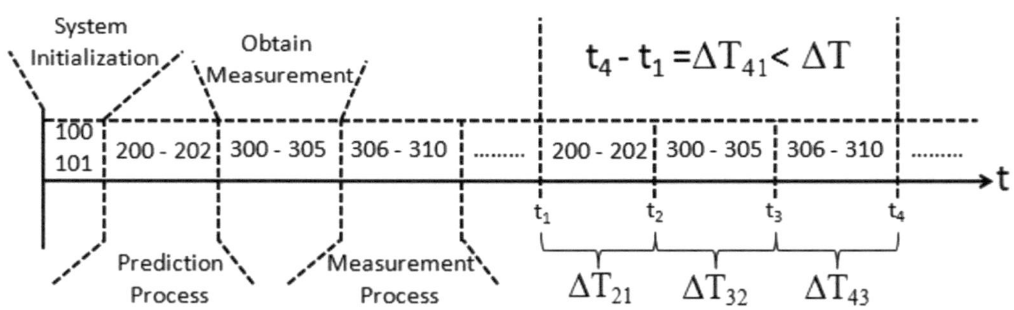

Figure 3. A typical timing diagram of real-time Kalman filtering algorithm process.

3. Vision-based real-time vehicle tracking system

A vision-based real-time vehicle tracking system used vision camera to achieve target tracking [17]. The number of tracked vehicle can be single or multiple. The detection and tracking of vehicles are done through the image processing of consecutive frames of video. Before tracking the vehicles across frames, target detection algorithm such as background subtraction is responsible for isolating the position of the moving vehicles in every frame. The tracking algorithm used the measurements from the detection stage to relate the moving vehicles from frame to frame. However, due to the limitation of performance in the target detection algorithm, it is not reliable to solely depending on the measurements computed from the detection stage. As such, Kalman filtering algorithm can be adopted to compensate the fluctuation and missing measurements whenever the detection stage fails. The missing measurements are predicted based on the center position and velocity of the detected vehicle. An experimental study was conducted on the real-time vehicle tracking at a road junction. The results showed that the Kalman filtering algorithm is capable of tracking the vehicles even with loss measurements appeared on the scene.

3.1. Preprocessing of vision-based vehicle tracking system

Traditionally, the road traffic monitoring is analyzed based on the data collected from the electronic sensor (i.e., loop detector) and manual observation by the human operator. The integration of multiple targets tracking algorithms in the vision-based vehicle tracking system offers an attractive alternative with additional potential to collect a variety of traffic parameters [18]. As illustrated in **Figure 4**, that the vehicle tracking process is the second processing stage in the existing vision-based traffic monitoring system. The performance of this stage greatly depends on the output from the first stage (i.e., the vehicle detection stage). The frames from the video input are recognized as image sequences and fed into the first stage of traffic monitoring system. Moving vehicles are segmented from the stationary background. Because a moving vehicle is formed by a sequence of images from the consecutive frames, the foreground images are matched and combined into its respective tracked objects.

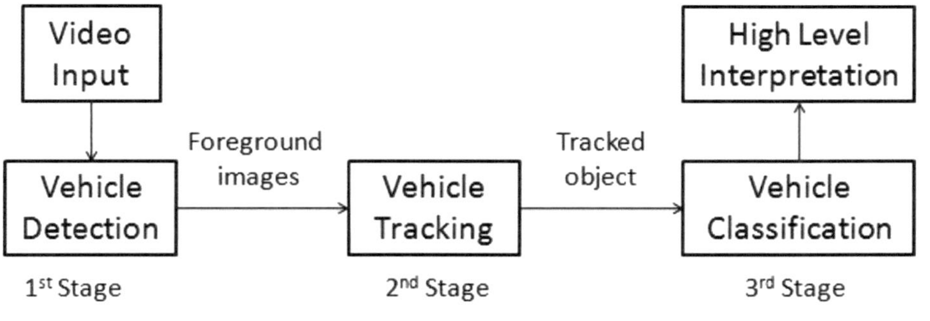

Figure 4. Processing stages of the vehicle monitoring system.

Background subtraction technique is the most widely used image processing algorithm for moving vehicle segmentation [19]. The basic idea of background subtraction algorithm is to subtract (in pixel-wise) all consecutive frames from an occupied background frame. As a result, this algorithm can be easily affected by sudden changes in background and illumination. Since then, numerous researches on updating the background image have been carried out to create a more adaptive background model. However, the contribution effort is still not able to perform vehicle segmentation perfectly, which indirectly affects the performance of vehicle tracking. This is where the Kalman filtering algorithm comes into the picture to improve the tracking performance.

3.2. Kalman filter model for vehicle tracking system

From the vehicle tracking system's point of view, the Kalman filter is to be designed to have the ability to predict the movement of vehicles in the future video frames. The prediction provides a suitable area for searching vehicles in the future frames. Consequently, it shortens the processing time by excluding the foreground images that is not located in the search area [14]. Besides, it also assists the tracking process in the situations where vehicles are temporarily lost due to failed detection.

In the common road traffic flow, vehicle movements can be sufficiently recorded with an optical sensor (i.e., camera) of 25 frames per second. This is because the changes in displacement of moving vehicles in x- and y-positions have been monitored to be small and do not show drastic changes, even at the road junction [20]. Kalman filter can be adopted for predicting the position of the vehicle, particularly during the loss of measurement detections. As discussed previously in Section 2.2, the Kalman filter is a recursive model between the prediction process and the measurement process. The prediction model of the vision-based vehicle tracking system, expressed in real-time discrete form, is outlined as follows:

$$\tilde{\mathbf{x}}_{n,k}^{-} = \left[\tilde{p}_{n,x,k}^{-} \ \tilde{p}_{n,y,k}^{-} \ \tilde{v}_{n,x,k}^{-} \ \tilde{v}_{n,y,k}^{-} \ \tilde{a}_{n,x,k}^{-} \ \tilde{a}_{n,y,k}^{-} \right]^{T} = \phi \cdot \mathbf{x}_{n,k-1} \tag{21}$$

with

$$\phi = \begin{bmatrix} 1 & 0 & \Delta T & 0 & (\Delta T)^2/2 & 0 \\ 0 & 1 & 0 & \Delta T & 0 & (\Delta T)^2/2 \\ 0 & 0 & 1 & 0 & \Delta T & 0 \\ 0 & 0 & 0 & 1 & 0 & \Delta T \\ 0 & 0 & 0 & 0 & 1 & 0 \\ 0 & 0 & 0 & 0 & 0 & 1 \end{bmatrix} \tag{22}$$

where $[\tilde{p}_{n,x,k}, \tilde{p}_{n,y,k}]$ denote the predicted vehicle location in pixels, $[\tilde{v}_{n,x,k}, \tilde{v}_{n,y,k}]$ denote the predicted velocities of the vehicle in pixels per second, $[\tilde{a}_{n,x,k}, \tilde{a}_{n,y,k}]$ denote the predicted vehicle acceleration, and ΔT and n are the sampling instant between image frames and the detected vehicle number, respectively. The predicted error covariance can be calculated as:

$$\boldsymbol{P}_k^{-} = \phi \cdot \boldsymbol{P}_{k-1} \cdot \phi^{T} + \mathbf{Q}_k = \phi \cdot \boldsymbol{P}_{k-1} \cdot \phi^{T} + \mathbf{Q}_k + E\left[\boldsymbol{w}_k \boldsymbol{w}_k^{T} \right] \tag{23}$$

where $\mathbf{Q}_k$ is assumed to be Gaussian noise of prediction process.

On the contrary, the measurement model of the vision-based vehicle tracking system, expressed in terms of real-time algorithm, is outlined as follows:

$$\mathbf{z}_{n,k} = \mathbf{H} \cdot \mathbf{x}_{n,k} = \begin{bmatrix} 1 & 0 & 0 & 0 & 0 & 0 \\ 0 & 1 & 0 & 0 & 0 & 0 \\ 0 & 0 & 1 & 0 & 0 & 0 \\ 0 & 0 & 0 & 1 & 0 & 0 \\ 0 & 0 & 0 & 0 & 1 & 0 \\ 0 & 0 & 0 & 0 & 0 & 1 \end{bmatrix} \cdot \begin{bmatrix} p_{n,x,k} \\ p_{n,y,k} \\ v_{n,x,k} \\ v_{n,y,k} \\ a_{n,x,k} \\ a_{n,y,k} \end{bmatrix} \tag{24}$$

where $[p_{n,x,k}, \ p_{n,y,k}]^T$ is the measured vehicle position in pixels, $[v_{n,x,k}, \ v_{n,y,k}]^T$ is the measured vehicle velocity in pixels per second, and $[a_{n,x,k}, \ a_{n,y,k}]^T$ is the measured vehicle acceleration in pixels per square second. The measured velocity and acceleration can be expressed as:

$$v_{n,x,k} = \left(p_{n,x,k} - p_{n,x,k-1}\right) / \Delta T \tag{25a}$$

$$v_{n,y,k} = \left(p_{n,y,k} - p_{n,y,k-1}\right) / \Delta T \tag{25b}$$

$$a_{n,x,k} = \left(p_{n,x,k} - 2p_{n,x,k-1} + p_{n,x,k-2}\right) / \left(\Delta T\right)^2 \tag{26a}$$

$$a_{n,y,k} = \left(p_{n,y,k} - 2p_{n,y,k-1} + p_{n,y,k-2}\right) / \left(\Delta T\right)^2 \tag{26b}$$

With Equations (24) to (26), the optimal Kalman gain can thus be derived using Equation (19) followed by the updates of the estimation state variables $\tilde{\mathbf{x}}_{n,k}$ using Equation (10) and the updates of error covariance P_k using Equation (20). Note that the measurement noise covariance matrix R_k is assumed to be Gaussian noise.

3.3. Experiments and results

An experimental study was carried out using the Kalman filtering model derived in Section 3.2 for real-time vehicle tracking. The experiment used the video stream captured from a static camera installed on a pedestrian bridge above the road, somewhere near the Multimedia University, Melaka, Malaysia. The Kalman filtering model is implemented with C++ programming language. The Open source Computer Vision (OpenCV) library [21] is used for the vehicle detection stage using the background subtraction method based on adaptive Gaussian mixture model in OpenCV. The tracking stage is demonstrated with the Kalman filtering algorithm for associating the foreground images with tracked vehicles from the previous frame.

Figure 5 depicts one of the image frames of the experiment. During the experiment, the tracking of vehicle number 8 (**Figure 5**, left) suffered lost detections due to the imperfection of background subtraction technique. **Figure 6** illustrates the tracking results comparison in terms of x- and y-positions in the image frames for the experiment. Note that there were lost detections in position of vehicle number 8 from frames 190 to 197, as shown in **Figure 6**. Notice that, despite the loss measurements of vehicle number 8, the Kalman filter algorithm can still provide adequate estimations to the vehicle's positions. Note that, although vehicle number 8 was not moving in a straight line, the tracking process was able to update the prediction according to the computed velocity and acceleration from the measurement model. This result shows that the Kalman filtering algorithm assures the continuous tracking of vehicles, although there are several lost measurements during the process.

Figure 5. Illustration of one of the image frames of Experiment 2.

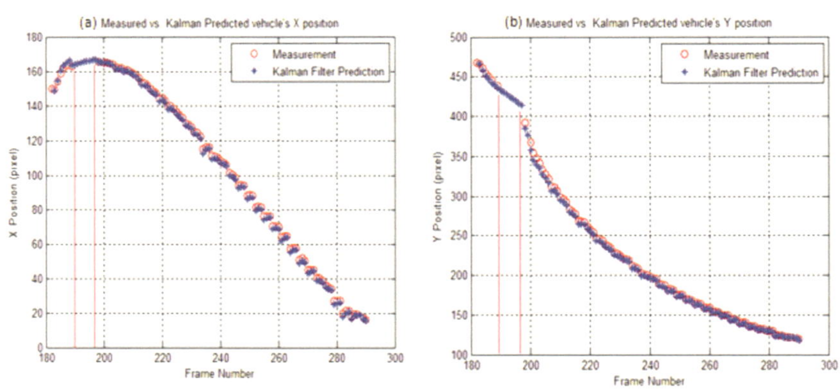

Figure 6. Comparison of vehicle number 8's tracking results for (a) x-position and (b) y-position in image frame.

3.4. Conclusion

This section demonstrated the experimental study of the Kalman filter model for multiple vehicle tracking. The model has incorporated the measurements of center positions of moving vehicles together with the computed velocity and acceleration from the displacement changes in the prediction phase. The tracking results show that the derived Kalman filter model is suitable for tracking multiple vehicles, although measurements are lost in a short period of time.

4. Real-time GPS-aided INU system

Inertial navigation system, which relied on inertial sensors [22] to operate, existed for the past few decades for navigation applications. The SINU is a low-cost inertial sensor developed to substitute the high-cost, high-performance inertial sensors. High-performance inertial sensors are commonly being controlled by government regulations, resulting in unattainable of the sensors in civilian applications. On the contrary, the low-cost, low-performance SINU sensors can be easily acquired, but its measurement data suffered from various errors [23] that jeopardized its accuracy. Due to this issue, the GPS data are adopted as an external reference source to minimize the SINU's errors through the implementation of the Kalman filter.

A typical SINU consists of three orthogonally aligned accelerometers and three orthogonally aligned gyroscopes that provide direct measurement on 3 degrees-of-freedom (DOF) accelerations and 3-DOF angular velocities. Some SINU consists of extra three orthogonally aligned magnetometers for true north measurement. These measurements, as discussed previously, are not accurate. To increase the SINU's accuracy, the GPS's position data obtained from dead reckoning technique is fused with the SINU data through the Kalman filtering algorithm. The system that used such fusion technique is commonly known as the GPS-aided SINU system, in which this fusion is known to retain the advantages of both SINU and GPS while discarding the disadvantages [4].

4.1. Inertial navigation equations

The GPS-aided SINU system is supposed to provide outputs in terms of position, velocity, and orientation. However, the direct outputs provided by the SINU are in terms of accelerations and angular velocities. Hence, the inertial navigation equations, or navigation equations, are formulated to describe the relationship between the GPS-aided SINU system's outputs in terms of the accelerations and angular velocities.

The general form of navigation equations can be derived as follows:

$$\tilde{\mathbf{x}}_k = \begin{bmatrix} \tilde{\mathbf{p}}_k^n \\ \tilde{\mathbf{v}}_k^n \\ \tilde{\mathbf{R}}_{b,k}^n \end{bmatrix} = \begin{bmatrix} \Delta T \cdot \mathbf{v}_{k-1}^n + \mathbf{p}_{k-1}^n \\ \Delta T \cdot \mathbf{R}_{b,k}^n \cdot \mathbf{s}_{k-1}^b + \mathbf{g}^n - 2\boldsymbol{\Omega}_{ie}^n \cdot \mathbf{v}_{k-1}^n + \mathbf{v}_{k-1}^n \\ \mathbf{R}_{b,k-1}^n \cdot e^{(\boldsymbol{\Omega}_{ib}^b - \boldsymbol{\Omega}_{in}^b)\cdot \Delta T} \end{bmatrix} \tag{27}$$

where ΔT represents the sampling time instant of the SINU sensor, $\mathbf{p}_k^n = [p_{x,k}^n \quad p_{y,k}^n \quad p_{z,k}^n]^T$ and $\mathbf{v}_k^n = [v_{x,k}^n \quad v_{y,k}^n \quad v_{z,k}^n]^T$ are the three-dimensional position and velocity in *navigation frame* (or *n-frame*), $\mathbf{R}_{b,k}^n$ represents the direct-cosine-matrix (DCM) that transforms *body frame* (or *b-frame*) to *n-frame*, $\mathbf{s}_k^b = [s_{x,k}^n \quad s_{y,k}^n \quad s_{z,k}^n]^T$ and $\mathbf{g}^n = [0 \quad 0 \quad -9.80665]^T$ represent the three-dimensional acceleration measurement (from the accelerometers) in *b-frame* and the gravitational force in *n-frame*, $\boldsymbol{\Omega}_{ie}^n$ is the skewed rotation rate matrix in *earth frame* [or *e-frame* with respect to *inertia-frame* (or *i-frame*)] projected to *n-frame*, $\boldsymbol{\Omega}_{ib}^b$ is the skew matrix of angular velocity measurement (from the gyroscopes) in *b-frame* with respect to *i-frame* projected to *b-frame*, and $\boldsymbol{\Omega}_{in}^b$ is the skewed transport rate matrix in *n-frame* with respect to *i-frame* projected to *b-frame*. Note that the definition of different *frames* can be found in [4].

4.2. Dynamic error model of inertial navigation equations

The navigation equations outlined in Equation (27) served as the ideal equations to calculate the position, velocity, and orientation based on the data measured from the SINU. However, as discussed earlier, the measurement data from the low-cost SINU contained various dynamic errors that were not reflected in Equation (27). Hence, perturbation process is applied on the navigation equations to acquire the dynamic error equations.

The dynamic error equations, expressed in continuous time, can be elaborated as:

$$\delta\dot{\mathbf{x}} = \begin{bmatrix} \delta\dot{\mathbf{p}}^n \\ \delta\dot{\mathbf{v}}^n \\ \dot{\boldsymbol{\varepsilon}}^n \end{bmatrix} = \begin{bmatrix} \mathbf{A}_{pp} \cdot \delta\mathbf{r}^n + \mathbf{A}_{pv} \cdot \delta\mathbf{v}^n \\ \mathbf{A}_{vp} \cdot \delta\mathbf{r}^n + \mathbf{A}_{vv} \cdot \delta\mathbf{v}^n + (\mathbf{s}^n \times)\boldsymbol{\varepsilon}^n + \mathbf{R}_b^n \cdot \delta\mathbf{s}^b \\ \mathbf{A}_{ep} \cdot \delta\mathbf{r}^n + \mathbf{A}_{ev} \cdot \delta\mathbf{v}^n - (\boldsymbol{\omega}_{in}^n \times)\boldsymbol{\varepsilon}^n - \mathbf{R}_b^n \cdot \delta\boldsymbol{\omega}_{ib}^b \end{bmatrix} \tag{28}$$

where $\mathbf{A}_{pp}$, $\mathbf{A}_{pv}$, $\mathbf{A}_{vp}$, $\mathbf{A}_{vv}$, $\mathbf{A}_{ep}$, and $\mathbf{A}_{ev}$ represent the Jacobians of position, velocity, and orientation error equations [24], respectively, with the subscripts p, v, and e representing the position, velocity, and orientation, respectively. A full description and elaboration of the Jacobians can be found in [24]. $\boldsymbol{\varepsilon}^n$ denotes the orientation errors, the $(* \times)$ operator represents the matrix's cross-product, $\mathbf{s}^n$ and $\boldsymbol{\omega}_{in}^n$ denote the three-dimensional acceleration measurement in *n-frame* and three-dimensional angular velocity measurement in *n-frame* with respect to *i-frame* projected in *n-frame*, $\delta\mathbf{s}^b$ and $\delta\boldsymbol{\omega}_{ib}^b$ denote the three-dimensional acceleration measurement errors in *b-frame* and three-dimensional angular velocity measurement error in *b-frame* with respect to *i-frame* projected in *b-frame*. Note that both $\delta\mathbf{s}^b$ and $\delta\boldsymbol{\omega}_{ib}^b$ are the random errors that reside in the SINU that causes the inaccuracy of the sensor [23].

Equation (28) can be expressed in the state space model as follows:

$$\delta\dot{\mathbf{x}} = \mathbf{A} \cdot \delta\mathbf{x} + \mathbf{B} \cdot \mathbf{u} \tag{29}$$

with

$$\mathbf{A} = \begin{bmatrix} \mathbf{A}_{pp} & \mathbf{A}_{pv} & 0_{3\times3} \\ \mathbf{A}_{vp} & \mathbf{A}_{vv} & (\mathbf{s}^n \times) \\ \mathbf{A}_{ep} & \mathbf{A}_{ev} & -(\boldsymbol{\omega}_{in}^n \times) \end{bmatrix}, \quad \mathbf{B} = \begin{bmatrix} 0_{3\times3} & 0_{3\times3} \\ \mathbf{R}_b^n & 0_{3\times3} \\ 0_{3\times3} & -\mathbf{R}_b^n \end{bmatrix}, \quad \delta\mathbf{x} = \begin{bmatrix} \delta\mathbf{r}^n \\ \delta\mathbf{v}^n \\ \boldsymbol{\varepsilon}^n \end{bmatrix}, \quad \mathbf{u} = \begin{bmatrix} \delta\mathbf{s}^b \\ \delta\boldsymbol{\omega}_{ib}^b \end{bmatrix} \tag{30}$$

where $\mathbf{0}_{3\times3}$ is a three-by-three zero matrix. It should be noted that the error matrix u in Equation (30b) can be modeled using the Gauss-Markov model or through the Allan variance analysis [23].

4.3. Kalman filtering model of GPS-aided SINU

The Kalman filter prediction stage of GPS-aided SINU system used the state space model of the dynamic error equations of the SINU to predict the errors. For real-time implementation, the dynamic error equations stated in Equation (29) are to be transformed into its discrete form as follows:

$$\delta\tilde{\mathbf{x}}_k = \Phi \cdot \delta\mathbf{x}_{\mathbf{k-1}} + \mathbf{w}_{k-1} \tag{31}$$

where $\boldsymbol{\Phi}$ denotes the transition matrix approximated to:

$$\boldsymbol{\Phi} = \mathbf{I}_{9\times9} + \mathbf{A} \cdot \Delta T = \begin{bmatrix} \mathbf{I}_{3\times3} + \mathbf{A}_{pp} \cdot \Delta T & \mathbf{A}_{pv} \cdot \Delta T & 0_{3\times3} \\ \mathbf{A}_{vp} \cdot \Delta T & \mathbf{I}_{3\times3} + \mathbf{A}_{vv} \cdot \Delta T & (\mathbf{s}^n \times) \cdot \Delta T \\ \mathbf{A}_{ep} \cdot \Delta T & \mathbf{A}_{ev} \cdot \Delta T & \mathbf{I}_{3\times3} - (\boldsymbol{\omega}_{in}^n \times) \cdot \Delta T \end{bmatrix} \tag{32}$$

and $\mathbf{w}_{k-1}$ is the error covariance matrix expressed as:

$$E\left[\mathbf{w}_k \cdot \mathbf{w}_i^T\right] = \begin{cases} \mathbf{Q}_k, & i = k \\ 0, & i \neq k \end{cases} \tag{33}$$

where $\mathbf{Q}_k$ represents the process noise covariance.

The observation equations of the dynamic errors, on the contrary, can be modeled as follows:

$$\mathbf{z_k} = \mathbf{H}_k \cdot \delta\mathbf{x}_k + \mathbf{e}_k \tag{34}$$

with

$$\delta\mathbf{x}_k = \begin{pmatrix} \tilde{\mathbf{p}}_k^n - \mathbf{p}_{GPS,j}^n \\ \tilde{\mathbf{v}}_k^n - \mathbf{v}_{GPS,j}^n \\ \tilde{\vartheta}_k^n - \vartheta_{MEAS,k}^n \end{pmatrix} \tag{35}$$

where $\tilde{\mathbf{p}}_k^n$, $\tilde{\mathbf{v}}_k^n$ and $\tilde{\vartheta}_k^n$ denote the three-dimensional position, velocity, and orientation vectors calculated from the navigation equations, expressed in *n-frame*. On the contrary, $\mathbf{p}_{GPS,j}^n$, $\mathbf{v}_{GPS,j}^n$ and $\vartheta_{MEAS,k}^n$ denote the three-dimensional position, velocity, and orientation vectors obtained from sensors measurement. The variables with subscript GPS indicate the parameters obtained from GPS measurements, whereas the orientation vector $\vartheta\tilde{}_k^n$ can be obtained from the DCM of $\tilde{\mathbf{R}}_{b,k}^n$ [25]. Meanwhile, the orientation measurement vector $\vartheta_{MEAS,j}^n$ is derived as:

$$\vartheta_{MEAS,k}^n = \begin{pmatrix} \phi_{MAG,k}^n \\ \theta_{MAG,k}^n \\ \psi_{MAG,k}^n \end{pmatrix} = \begin{pmatrix} -\mathrm{Atan2}\left(s_{y,k}^n, \sqrt{\left(s_{x,k}^n\right)^2 + \left(s_{z,k}^n\right)^2} \right) \\ -\mathrm{Atan2}\left(s_{x,k}^n, \sqrt{\left(s_{y,k}^n\right)^2 + \left(s_{z,k}^n\right)^2} \right) \\ -\mathrm{Atan2}\left(\psi_1, \psi_2\right) \end{pmatrix} \tag{36}$$

with

$$\begin{aligned} \psi_1 = {} & m_x^n cos\left(\theta_{MAG,k}^n\right) + m_y^n sin\left(\phi_{MAG,k}^n\right) sin\left(\theta_{MAG,k}^n\right) \\ & -m_z^n cos\left(\phi_{MAG,k}^n\right) cos\left(\theta_{MAG,k}^n\right) \end{aligned} \tag{37a}$$

$$\psi_1 = m_y^n cos\left(\phi_{MAG,k}^n\right) + m_z^n sin\left(\phi_{MAG,k}^n\right) \tag{37b}$$

where Equations (36) and (37) represent the orientation measurement vectors. Note that the vector $\begin{bmatrix} m_x^n & m_y^n & m_z^n \end{bmatrix}^T$ refers to the three-dimensional magnetic field strength in *n-frame* obtained from the magnetometers, and the operator atan2 represents the four-quadrant inverse tangent function.

http://dx.doi.org/ 10.5772/62352

Notice from Equation (35) that there are two different discrete instants described by subscripts j and k. These two different subscripts described two different discrete instants, with subscript k depicts the SINU's discrete instant, whereas subscript j depicts the GPS's discrete instant. In most cases, the SINU's sampling rate is much faster than the GPS's sampling rate. This creates phenomena in GPS-aided SINU system's Kalman filtering process that the filter will need to predict a multiple number of predictions before obtaining a measurement from GPS to correct the errors. **Figure 7** illustrates the time operation diagram of the matching of 5 Hz GPS data with the 40 Hz SINU data.

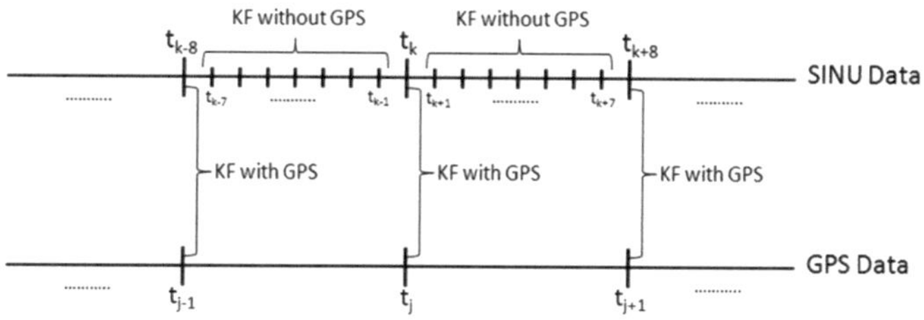

Figure 7. Real-time operational diagram of the GPS-aided SINU system.

4.4. GPS-aided SINU system design and its real-time implementation

Figure 8 delineates the operational block diagram of the design of GPS-aided SINU system. As shown in **Figure 8**, that the SINU consists of three-dimensional accelerometers, gyroscopes, and magnetometers that output three-dimensional accelerations, angular velocities, and magnetic field strengths, respectively. The sampling rate of the SINU is 40 Hz. By combining these data with the GPS data (5 Hz) through the Kalman filtering model, the system is able to compute the estimated position, velocity, and orientation errors, which could be used to improve the overall estimations.

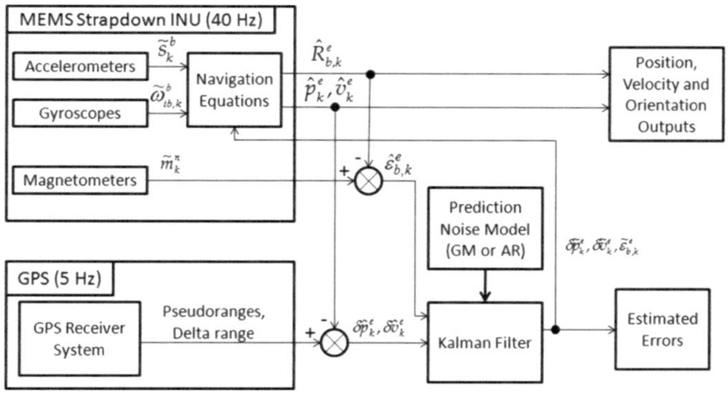

Figure 8. GPS-aided SINU system operational block diagram.

Offline field experiment using a moving car was carried out to verify the performance of the GPS-aided SINU system before real-time implementation. The Kalman filtering process is carried out in offline mode to verify the performance of the developed system. Note that, in the experiment, the SINU and GPS data rate are 40 and 5 Hz, respectively. The data obtained from the offline experiment was fed into the Kalman filtering model to obtain the offline measurements. To test the performance of the proposed GPS-aided SINU system, the same set of offline data was also fed into a conventional GPS-aided SINU system with no magnetometers. The result obtained from the conventional GPS-aided SINU system without magnetometers is compared to the result obtained from the proposed GPS-aided SINU system with magnetometers to verify the performance of the proposed system. From the results of the offline experiment, there is an average difference computed to be 2.84 m between the navigation paths of GPS-aided SINU system with and without magnetometers. The mean difference between the navigation paths of GPS measurements and the GPS-aided SINU system with magnetometers is computed to be ′0.173 m. On the contrary, the mean difference between the navigation paths of GPS measurements and the GPS-aided SINU system without magnetometers is calculated to be ′2.67 m, much higher than the mean difference from the previous calculation. Such results indicate that the proposed system work well in offline mode.

With the success offline implementation on the moving car, the system is now ready for real-time implementation. Both the GPS module and the SINU are connected to an embedded high-performance computer (HPC) through RS-232 for data acquisition and real-time processing. The embedded HPC used in the system come with an Intel Core™ 2 Duo Processor E7500, 4 GB DDR2 RAM, 40 GB hard drive integrated into Zotac Nforce 9300-ITX motherboard. Similar to the previous setting, the SINU's data rate is 40 Hz, which is relatively faster than the GPS data rate of 5 Hz. During the data acquisition stage, the embedded HPC acquired one set of SINU data every 25 ms (equivalent to 40 Hz). On the contrary, the embedded computer acquired one full GPS data every 0.2 s (equivalent to 5 Hz). Hence, it is obvious that there is a mismatch of GPS data to SINU data. As shown in **Figure 7**, when both GPS and SINU data are updated with the newest measurements, the real-time processing system will proceed with the Kalman filtering process to provide a new update on the error prediction. At the instances where newest GPS data were not available, the real-time system will compute the error prediction solely depending on the previous error prediction obtained from the Kalman filtering process and the newest SINU measurements.

A graphical user interface (GUI) is developed using Visual Basic software (from Microsoft Corporation) for the real-time implementation. A total of 31 variables will be saved into the solid-state hard disk continuously in binary file format. The first nine variables represent the raw data from the SINU, which serves the inputs of the GPS-aided SINU system. The subsequent 15 variables represent the computed three-dimensional position, velocity, orientation, acceleration errors, and orientation errors, which serve as the outputs of the GPS-aided SINU system. The last seven variables are the GPS data. **Figure 9** shows the GUI layout and the real-time experimental results of the developed real-time GPS SINU system. **Figure 9** (top left) indicates the serial ports setting for the SINU and the GPS. An"Operation Start"button is located beneath the serial ports frame. An *X*-*Y* graph is used to display both the real-time GPS path in green color line and the real-time SINU's navigation path in red color line. A group of real-time parameters could be found below the *X*-*Y* graph. These parameters included the real-time updated position, velocity, orientation, and GPS information. The incoming raw SINU data are displayed at the bottom of the GUI. Note that the position plots shown in **Figure 9** *X*-*Y* graph are the results from one of the field experiments conducted in Kampung Seri Pantai, Mersing, Malaysia. In this experiment, the GPS-aided SINU system is installed inside an UAV for motion sensing. The navigation path of the UAV, in GPS data, is shown using the Google Earth in Figure 10. The duration of the experiments was approximately 50 min. The recorded average flight speed was 145 km/h.

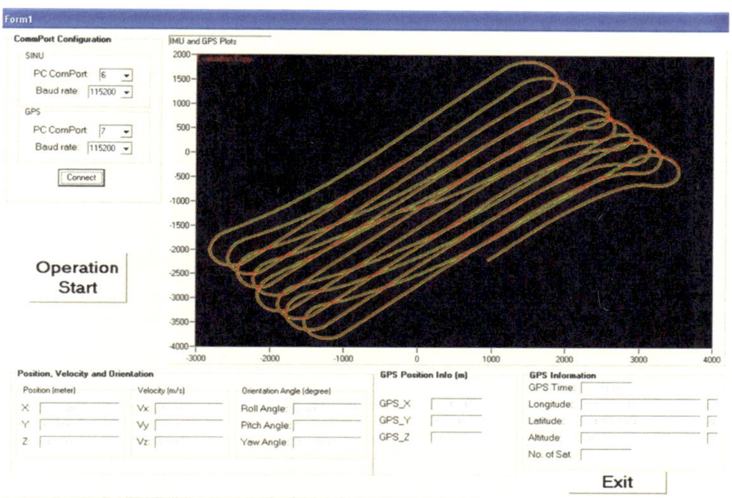

Figure 9. GUI of the real-time GPS-aided SINU system and its field experiment result.

Figure 10. Navigation path of the real-time GPS-aided SINU system experiment on a UAV in Google Earth.

Figures 11 and **12** illustrate the results obtained from the real-time experiment, with **Figure 11** depicting the real-time velocity plot and **Figure 12** depicting the real-time orientation plot. The motion sensing results are compared to the UAV's onboard Piccolo II Autopilot Navigation System [26] outputs. Note that the Piccolo II Autopilot Navigation System is a high-performance, commercial-grade navigation system for UAV autopilot. The mean square differences of position, velocity, and orientation were computed between the developed system and the Piccolo II system and the comparison results are outlined in **Table 1**. Such results indicate that the low-cost GPS-aided SINU system achieved a comparable, adequate performance when compared to a high-performance, high-cost system.

	Mean square difference
Position (m)	0.3081
Velocity (m/s)	0.0077
Orientation (°)	2.5930

Table 1. Mean square difference of position, velocity, and orientation estimation between the proposed GPS-aided SINU system's output with Piccolo II's output.

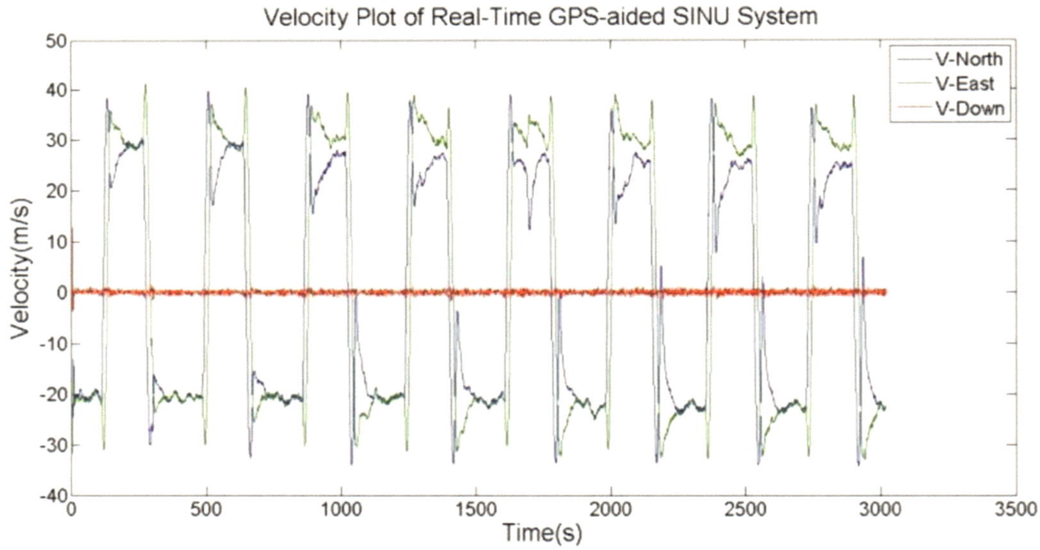

Figure 11. Real-time GPS-aided SINU system velocity plot.

http://dx.doi.org/10.5772/62352

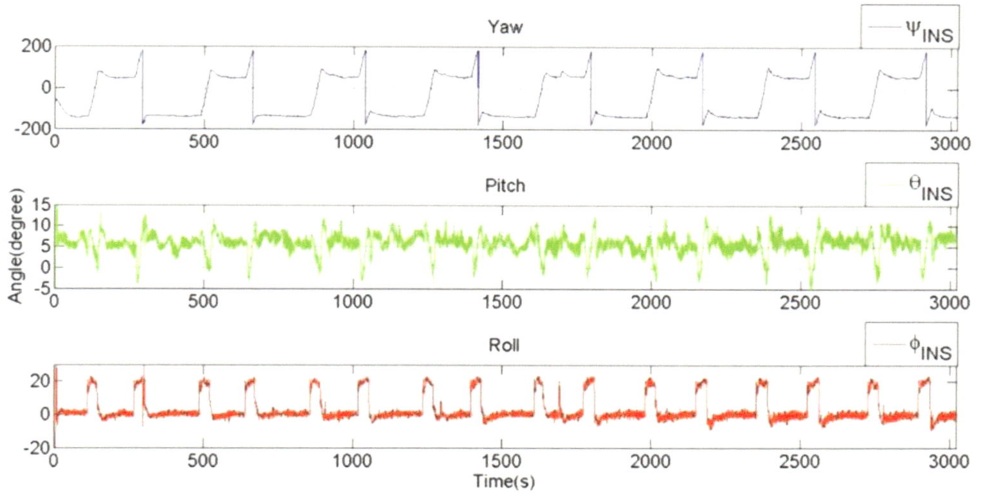

Figure 12. Real-time GPS-aided SINU system orientation plot.

5. Conclusion

This chapter illustrated the real-time implementation of Kalman filter in two applications, namely, the vision-based vehicle tracking system and the GPS-aided SINU system. The Kalman filtering algorithm was derived with the consideration of real-time element. Detail illustrations on deriving the Kalman filtering models for the vision-based vehicle tracking system and the GPS-aided SINU system were outlined and discussed. Both implementations were put on real-time experiments, and the results from both implementations were recorded and analyzed. The results show that the real-time Kalman filtering algorithms work well in the applications.

Author details

Lim Chot Hun[1*], Ong Lee Yeng[2], Lim Tien Sze[1] and Koo Voon Chet[1]

*Address all correspondence to: chlim@mmu.edu.my

1 Faculty of Engineering & Technology, Multimedia University, Melaka, Malaysia

2 Faculty of Information Science & Technology, Multimedia University, Melaka, Malaysia

References

[1] Kalman, R. E. A new approach to linear filtering and prediction problems. Trans ASME J Basic Eng. 1960;82(Series D):35–45.

[2] Grewal, M. S., Andrews, A. P. Applications of Kalman filtering in aerospace 1960 to the present [historical perspectives]. IEEE Control Syst Mag. 2010;30(3):69–78. DOI: 10.1109/MCS.2010.936465

[3] Barczyk, M., Lynch, A. F. Invariant observer design for a helicopter UAV aided inertial navigation system. IEEE Trans Control Syst Technol. 2013;21(2):791–806. DOI: 10.1109/TCST.2012.2195495

[4] Chot, H. L., Tien, S. L., Voon, C. K. Design and development of a real-time GPS-aided SINU system. Int J Adv Robot Syst. 2012;9:1–9. DOI: 10.5772/52681

[5] Salti, S., Lanza, A., Di Stefano, L. Synergistic change detection and tracking. IEEE Trans Circuits Syst Video Technol. 2015;25(4):609–622. DOI: 10.1109/TCSVT.2014.2355695

[6] Bresson, G., Feraud, T., Aufrere, R., Checchin, P., Chapuis, R. Real-time monocular SLAM with low memory requirements. IEEE Trans Intell Transport Syst. 2015;16(4): 1827–1839. DOI: 10.1109/TITS.2014.2376780

[7] Racicot, F.-E., Theoret, R. Forecasting stochastic volatility using the Kalman filter: an application to Canadian interest rates and price-earnings ratio. IEB Int J Finance. 2010;1:28–47.

[8] Faragher, R. Understanding the basis of the Kalman filter via a simple and intuitive derivation. IEEE Signal Process Mag. 2012;29(5):128–132. DOI: 10.1109/MSP.2012.2203621

[9] Mall, R. Real-Time Systems: Theory and Practice. 1st ed. Prentice-Hall; 2009. 242 p. ISBN: 81-317-0069-0.

[10] Kopetz, H. Real-Time Systems: Design Principles for Distributed Embedded Applications. 2nd ed. Springer; 2011. 376 p. DOI: 10.1007/978-1-4419-8237-7.

[11] Ong L. Y., Lau, S. H., Koo, V. C., Lim, C. H. An experimental study on vision-based multiple target tracking. Int J Microwave Opt Technol. 2014;9(1):134–138.

[12] Janiszewski, D. Extended Kalman Filter Based Speed Sensorless PMSM Control with Load Reconstruction, Kalman Filter, Vedran Kordic (Ed.), ISBN: 978-953-307-094-0, InTech.

[13] Ogata, K. Modern Control Engineering. 5th ed. Prentice-Hall; 2010.

[14] Welch, G., Bishop, G. An Introduction to the Kalman filter. Department of Computer Science, University of North Carolina, Chapel Hill, Tech. Rep. TR95041; 2000.

[15] Galleani, L., Tavella, P. Time and the Kalman Filter. IEEE Control Syst. 2010;30(2):44–65. DOI: 10.1109/MCS.2009.935568.

[16] Lacey, T. Tutorial: The Kalman filter. Computer vision. Available at: http://web.mit.edu/kirtley/kirtley/binlustuff/literature/control/Kalman%20filter.pdf.

[17] Goo, J., Aggarwal, J. K., Gokmen, M. Tracking and segmentation of highway vehicles in cluttered and crowded scenes. IEEE Workshop on Applications of Computer Vision (IEEE WACV); 2008.

[18] Huang, C. L., Liao, W. C. A vision-based vehicle identification system. Proceedings of the 17th International Conference on Pattern Recognition (ICPR 2004), 2004; 4: 364–367.

[19] Jie, Y., Wang, J. Q., Lu, H. Q. A hierarchical approach for background modeling and moving objects detection. Int J Control Automation Control. 2010;8:940–947.

[20] Aydos, C., Bernhard, H., William, U. Kalman filter process models for urban vehicle tracking. 12th International IEEE Conference on Intelligent Transportation Systems; 2009; 1–8.

[21] Open Source Computer Vision. Available at: http://opencv.org. Accessed 12 April 2013.

[22] Barbour, N., Schmidt, G. Inertial sensor technology trends. IEEE Sensors J. 2001;1(4): 332–339.

[23] Lim, C. H., Tan, W. Q., Lim, T. S., Koo, V. C. Practical approach in estimating inertial navigation unit's errors. IEICE Electron Express. 9(8):772–778.

[24] Kong, X. Y. Inertial navigation system algorithms for low cost IMU. Ph.D. thesis, The University of Sydney, August 27, 2000.

[25] David, H. T., John, L. W. Strapdown Inertial Navigation Technology. 2nd ed. The Institution of Electrical Engineering and Technology, United Kingdom; 2004.

[26] Cloud Cap Technology. Piccolo Autopilots.Available at: http://www.cloudcap-tech.com/piccolo_system.shtm. Accessed 15 December 2015.

Chapter 7

A Real-Time Bilateral Teleoperation Control System over Imperfect Network

Truong Quang Dinh, Jong Il Yoon,
Cheolkeun Ha and James Marco

Additional information is available at the end of the chapter

http://dx.doi.org/10.5772/63033

Abstract

Functionality and performance of modern machines are directly affected by the implementation of real-time control systems. Especially in networked teleoperation applications, force feedback control and networked control are two of the most important factors, which determine the performance of the whole system. In force feedback control, generally it is necessary but difficult and expensive to attach sensors (force/torque/pressure sensors) to detect the environment information in order to drive properly the feedback force. In networked control, there always exist inevitable random time-varying delays and packet dropouts, which may degrade the system performance and, even worse, cause the system instability. Therefore in this chapter, a study on a real-time bilateral teleoperation control system (BTCS) over an imperfect network is discussed. First, current technologies for teleoperation as well as BTCSs are briefly reviewed. Second, an advanced concept for designing a bilateral teleoperation networked control (BTNCS) system is proposed, and the working principle is clearly explained. Third, an approach to develop a force-sensorless feedback control (FSFC) is proposed to simplify the sensor requirement in designing the BTNCS, while the correct sense of interaction between the slave and the environment can be ensured. Fourth, a robust-adaptive networked control (RANC)-based master controller is introduced to deal with control of the slave over the network containing both time delays and information loss. Case studies are carried out to evaluate the applicability of the suggested methodology.

Keywords: bilateral teleoperation, real-time, network, control, feedback, classification

1. Introduction

Teleoperation, which allows a human operator to interact with the environment remotely, extends humans' sensing, decision making, and operation beyond direct physical contact. Since its introduction in the late 1940s, teleoperation systems have been deployed worldwide in numerous domains ranging from space exploration, underwater operation, and hazardous assignment to micro-assembly, and minimally invasive surgery.

In common, control schemes for teleoperation systems can be classified as either compliance control or bilateral control. In the compliance control [1, 2], the contact force sensed by the slave device is not reflected back to the operator, but is used for the compliance control of the slave device. On the contrary, in the bilateral control [3–5], the contact force is reflected back to the operator. The operator is able to achieve physical perception of interactions at the remote site similar to as directly working at this site. Consequently, it improves the accuracy and safety in teleoperation. Thus, the bilateral control has drawn a lot of attention.

Figure 1 shows a generic configuration of a bilateral teleoperation system which includes five components: operator, master, communication network, slave, and environment. The master is capable of acquiring information about the desired manipulation actions and assigning the tasks to the slave. It normally consists of an input component, such as a joystick, console, or tactile device, and a force-reflecting mechanism (FRM) to exert the reflected forces on the human operator. The slave is a robotic device that takes the place of the human operator to carry out the required tasks at the remote environment. It is usually equipped with sensors to acquire information about the task process to feed back to the master.

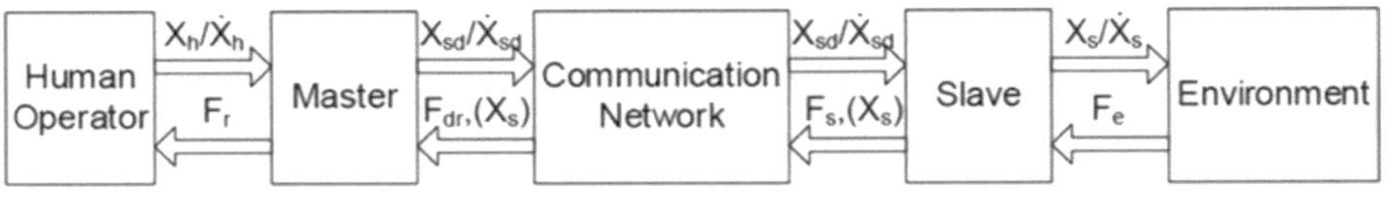

Figure 1. Generic configuration of a bilateral teleoperation system.

There are two common control architectures of bilateral teleoperation systems: position–position and position–force architectures. In the first approach, the master position is passed to the slave device, and the slave position is passed back to the master side. The reflected force applied to the operator is derived from the position difference between the two devices and, therefore, this approach is not desirable in cases of free motion. In contrast, the position–force approach uses directly the force measured at the remote site rather than the position error. In this architecture, the contact force, sensed by a force/torque sensor mounted on the slave device, is scaled by a force-reflecting gain (FRG), and this scaled force is reflected back to the operator via the master device. This method then provides the operator a better perception of tasks execution at the remote site.

In order to derive sufficiently the FRG, two important tasks are required: first, to detect the environment and, second, to determine the contact force at the slave site. Many studies have been carried out to optimize the FRG [4, 5]. Although the reported algorithms showed some remarkable results, there remain some drawbacks such as how to determine the FRG appropriately with unknown environments; and especially, it is difficult and expensive to attach proper sensors (force/torque/pressure sensors) to detect the loading conditions. Additionally, the use of these kinds of sensors is cost-ineffective and difficult to be installed in practice. Especially, it is easy to be damaged when the system operates under hazard conditions. Incorporation of teleoperation and force feedback requires bidirectional information exchange between the master and slave via the network. In contrast to the advantages such as cost saving, power consumption, easy implementation, and maintenance, a networked control system (NCS) leads to two major problems, inevitable random time-varying delays and packet dropouts because of restrictions imposed by the transmission data rate and channel bandwidth. Due to sensitivity of bilateral teleoperation systems to time delays and packet dropouts, even a small time delay can destabilize the system [6].

Disregarding the packet loss problem, numerous methods have been proposed [7–9] to minimize the bad effect of time delay. Herein, the controllers were designed based on the assumptions that time delay was constant [7], bounded [8], or had a probability distribution function [9]. Moreover, these assumptions just considered that the time delay in the closed control loops was less than one sampling period while in practice, it is random and irregular. To compensate large and uncertain delays, other studies suggested adaptive control schemes using variable sampling periods, which were based on neural networks (NNs) or prediction theories [10–12]. Although the performances were improved, there were requirements on acquiring the real delay data for the training processes, which were not appropriately discussed.

To adapt with NCSs compromising not only time delays but also packet dropouts, many important methodologies, such as state feedback control [13], robust control [14–16], predictive and model-based predictive control [17, 18], were proposed. By using these techniques, the NCS performances were remarkably improved over the traditional methods. However in most studies, time delays and packet dropouts were assumed to be priorly known and bounded to design the controllers. The sampling period was always fixed in these studies and, subsequently, limited the control performances. Furthermore, computation delay normally at the master side is also one important factor affecting directly the system performance. Recently, an advanced robust variable sampling period control approach has been developed for nonlinear systems containing both the kinds of delays and packet dropouts [19–21]. The applicability of this method was proved through real-time experiments.

Therefore to fully overcome the above-mentioned problems, a simple and cost-effective real-time bilateral teleoperation networked control system (BTNCS) is introduced in this chapter. The advanced concept for designing a bilateral master-slave teleoperation networked control system is proposed, and the working principle is clearly addressed. Next, an approach to develop a force-sensorless feedback control (FSFC) is proposed to simplify the sensor requirement in designing the BTNCS while the correct sense of interaction between the slave and the environment can be ensured. To deal with the networked control of the slave, a robust-adaptive networked control (RANC)-based master controller is suggested to compensate for the problems of time delays and information loss. Case studies are carried out to evaluate the applicability of the suggested methodology.

2. Bilateral teleoperation networked control system

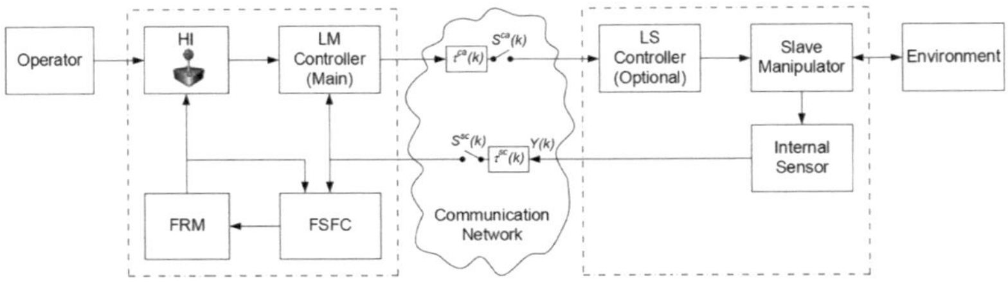

Figure 2. Proposed architecture of the BTNCS.

Without loss of generality, the architecture of the BTNCS is suggested in **Figure 2**. The design for this BTNCS should address the following issues:

- The local master (LM) controller functions as the main control unit of the system to ensure that the slave manipulator could execute robustly and accurately the tasks given by the operator via a human interface (HI), disregarding the impacts of networked communication problems and environments. The local slave (LS) controller is, therefore, an optional design. It can be just a buffer or a zero-order holder (ZOH) to receive the control input derived by the LM controller and distribute sequentially to the manipulator.
- There is no force/pressure/torque sensor to be attached at the manipulator end to minimize the cost and risks. Only an internal sensor, as displacement sensor, is used to monitor the manipulator trajectory and send back to the LM controller to form a closed control loop.
- The interaction between the manipulator and environment is, therefore, estimated by the FSFC module at the master side. Here, the FSFC should consist of two parts: first, an environmental interaction (EI) estimator to detect the environment characteristics as well as to derive properly a reflecting force required to be applied to a physical device in the HI module (as a joystick); second, an FRM controller to drive the FRM to generate the desired reflecting force.
- The FRM is suggested to be constructed using pneumatic rotary actuators. This use brings some advantages over the traditional design with DC electric motors. Compared with an electric motor, a pneumatic actuator provides a higher ratio of force-mass, and can produce larger reflected force without using any reduction mechanism, such as gearbox. In addition, with the pneumatic solution, the FRM is able to work under safe conditions without damage from the operator.
- Due to having different control modules and other functions at the master side, computation delays τ^{com} need to be taken into account when designing the LM controller.

- The communication network has unavoidable delays, τ^{ca} and τ^{sc}, and packet dropouts, represented by "virtual" switches, S^{ca} and S^{sc}, in the forward and backward channels, respectively. S^{ca} (S^{sc}) is opened (or 1) when a packet loss event exits.

The following are attempted to address the two important issues in designing the BTNCS which are the FSFC and the LM controller.

3. Force-sensorless feedback control

3.1. Design of FSFC

As stated in Section 2, the FSFC compromises the two main modules: EI estimator and FRM controller. The FRM controller can be selected as a typical feedback controller in which the reference input is the desired reflecting force sent from the environment classifier and the feedback signal can be the force/torque/pressure at the physical device of the HI module.

The EI estimator is suggested as in **Figure 3**. This estimator with two inputs and one output contains four blocks: Learning Vector Quantitative Neural Network (LVQNN) classifier, slave dynamics, environment dynamics, and fuzzy-based FRG tuner. Without loss of generative, the interactive environment can be represented by two factors: damping c_e and stiffness k_e. Thus, The LVQNN classifier is firstly designed with two inputs and two outputs to classify the environment. The two inputs are the command and response from the slave while the two outputs are predicted values of the environment damping and stiffness, $\hat{c}_e$ and $\hat{k}_e$, respectively. Next, these predicted values are fed into both the environment dynamics and fuzzy-based FRG tuner. Synchronously, the slave command is also input to the slave dynamics. The interaction between the slave dynamics and environment dynamics—loading force—is, therefore, estimated and denoted as $\hat{F}_e$. Meanwhile, the fuzzy-based FRG tuner is designed with two inputs, $\hat{c}_e$ and $\hat{k}_e$, and one output which is value of the FRG. Finally, the desired reflected force, F_{dr}, is derived from the estimated loading force and the FRG.

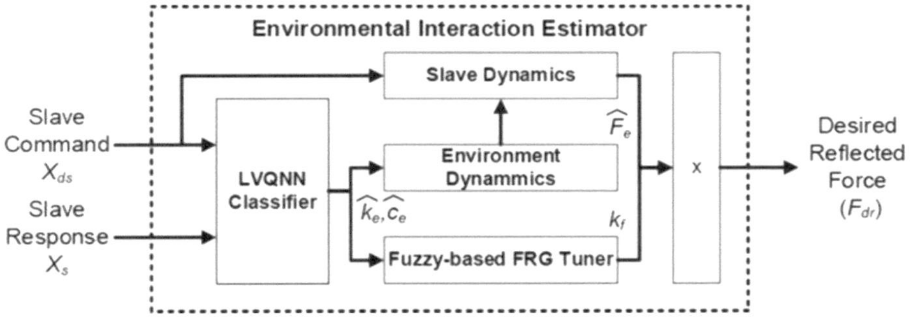

Figure 3. Configuration of the proposed environmental interaction estimator.

3.2. LVQNN classifier

3.2.1. Learning vector quantitative Neural Network

NN is one of the powerful artificial intelligent techniques that emulates the activity of biological NNs in the human brain. LVQNN is a hybrid network which uses advantages of competitive learning and bases on Kohonen self-organizing map or Kohonen feature map to form the classification [22].

Figure 4 shows a generic structure of an LVQNN with four layers: one input layer with m nodes, first hidden layer named competitive layer with S_1 nodes, second hidden layer named linear layer with S_2 nodes, and one output layer with n nodes (in this case, $S_2 \equiv n$).

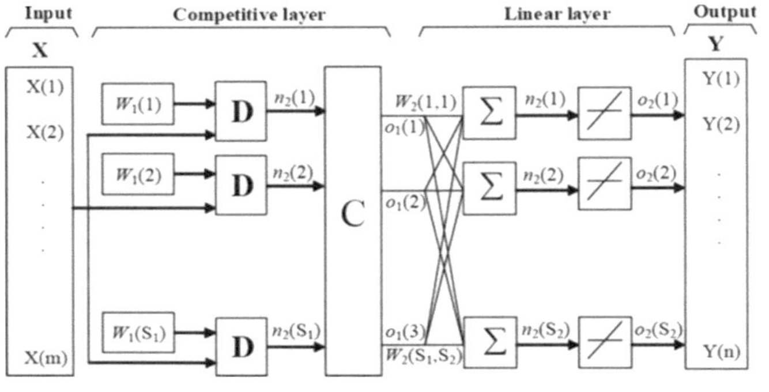

Figure 4. Structure of the LVQNN.

The core of the LVQNN is based on the nearest-neighbor method by calculating the Euclidean distance weight function, D, for each node, n_j, in the competitive layer as in the following:

$$n_j = D(X, W_1(j)) = \sqrt{\sum_{i=1}^{m} \left(X(i) - W_1(j,i)\right)^2}, \; j = 1,..,S_1 \tag{1}$$

where X is the input vector; $W_1(j,i)$ is the weight of node j^{th} in the competitive layer corresponding to element i^{th} of the input vector.

Next, the Euclidean distances are fed into function C which is a competitive transfer function. This function returns an output vector o_1, with 1, where each net input vector has its maximum value, and 0 elsewhere. This vector is then input to the linear layer to derive an output vector o_2, where each element corresponded to each node of the output layer and computed as

$$Y(k) = o_2(k) = k_W(k) n_2(k) = k_W(k) \sum_{j=1}^{S_1} W_2(k,j) o_1(j), \; k = 1,..,n, (n \equiv S_2) \tag{2}$$

http://dx.doi.org/10.5772/63033

where $W_2(k,j)$ is the weight of node k^{th} in the linear layer corresponding to element j^{th} of the competitive output vector; $k_W(k)$ is linearized gain of node k^{th} in the linear layer.

In the learning process, the weights of LVQNN are updated by the well-known Kohonen rule, which is shown in the following equation:

$$\begin{cases} W_1^{t+1}(j) = W_1^t(j) + \mu\left(X - W_1^t(j)\right) \text{ IF: } X \text{ is classified correctly} \\ W_1^{t+1}(j) = W_1^t(j) - \mu\left(X - W_1^t(j)\right) \text{ IF: } X \text{ is classified incorrectly} \end{cases}, j = 1,..,S_1 \tag{3}$$

where μ is the learning ratio with positive and decreasing with respect to the number of training iterations ($n_{iteration}$), $\mu = n_{iteration}^{-1}$.

3.2.2. Design of LVQNN classifier

Here, the LVQNN classifier is designed and implemented into the FSFC to distinguish different working environments at the slave side in an online manner. To enhance the given task with the limited number of input information, the input vector of the classifier is constructed as a vector of current and several historical values of four signals: the slave driving command, $\{X_{ds}^{(0)}, X_{ds}^{(-1)}, \ldots, X_{ds}^{(-g)}\}$, slave response, $\{X_s^{(0)}, X_s^{(-1)}, \ldots, X_s^{(-p)}\}$, and their derivatives, $\{dX_{ds}^{(0)}, dX_{ds}^{(-1)}, \ldots, dX_{ds}^{(-h)}\}$and $\{dX_s^{(0)}, dX_s^{(-1)}, \ldots, dX_s^{(-q)}\}$, respectively, while the final outputs are the environment damping and stiffness, $\hat{c}_e$ and $\hat{k}_e$.

For applications to classify the environment which is varied with both the damping and stiffness values, the output from the classifier should be the mix of classes with different ratios. In order to enhance this task, a so-called smooth switching algorithm is proposed here. The environment class is, therefore, determined by the smooth combination of the current class detected by the LVQNN (Y) and the previous class using a forgetting factor, λ

$$class(t) = \lambda \times class(t-1) + (1-\lambda) \times Y(t) \tag{4}$$

Similarly, the estimated values of the damping coefficient and stiffness are produced by

$$\begin{cases} \hat{c}_e(t) = \lambda \times \hat{c}_e\big|_{class(t-1)} + (1-\lambda) \times \hat{c}_e\big|_{Y(t)} \\ \hat{k}_e(t) = \lambda \times \hat{k}_e\big|_{class(t-1)} + (1-\lambda) \times \hat{k}_e\big|_{Y(t)} \end{cases} \tag{5}$$

Additionally, in order to avoid influences of noises on the classification performance, the forgetting factor is online tuned with respect to the changing speed of the classifier outputs:

Step 1: Set the initial value for the forgetting factor, λ=0.5; define a small positive threshold, $0<\gamma_1<\gamma_2$, for the classifier output changing speed, v_Y, which is defined by the number of sampling periods when Y continuously changes.

Step 2: For each step, check v_Y and update λ by comparing v_Y with γ using the following rule:

+ If $v_Y = 0$, Then $\lambda(t+1) = \lambda(t)$;

+ Else If $(v_Y > \gamma_2)$, Then $\lambda(t+1) = \lambda(t+1)/2$ and reset $v_Y = 0$;

+ Else If $(v_Y \geq \gamma_1) \& (v_Y(t) \leq \gamma_2)$, Then $\lambda(t+1) = \lambda(t+1) \times 2$ and reset $v_Y = 0$;

+ Otherwise, $\lambda(t+1) = \lambda(t)$.

3.2.3. An illustrative example

3.2.3.1. Test rig setup

To evaluate the effectiveness of the LVQNN classifier, an experimental system has been designed as in **Figure 5**. One joystick with one Degree of freedom (DOF) is used to generate driving commands for the slave. An FRM which employs a valve-driven mini pneumatic rotary actuator and two bias springs is attached to the opposite side of the joystick handle. The slave employs an asymmetrically pneumatic cylinder as its manipulator. The displacement of the cylinder rod is sensed by a linear variable displacement transducer (LVDT). The interaction between the master and slave is enhanced by the communication module which can perform either wire-by-wire or wireless protocol. To generate environmental conditions for the slave manipulator, compression springs with different stiffness values are installed in serial with the cylinder rod. An air compressor is used to supply the pressurized air for both the FRM and the slave. A compatible PC and a multifunction data acquisition device are employed to perform the communication between the PC and master. The system specifications are listed in **Table 1**.

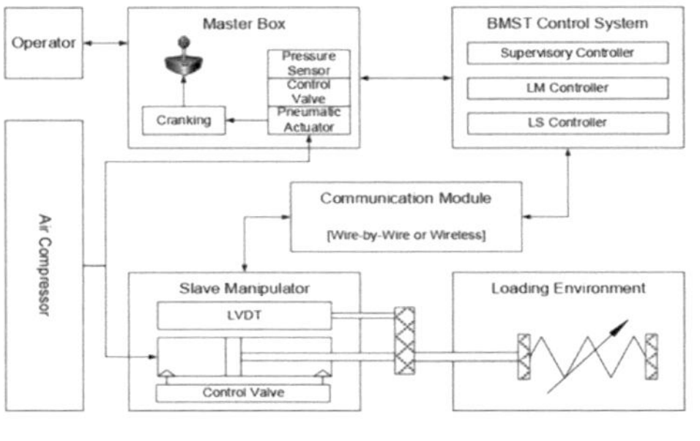

Figure 5. Design layout for the experimental BMST system.

http://dx.doi.org/10.5772/63033

Parts	Type	Component characteristics
Rotary actuator	CRB1BW15 90-D	Max. torque: 0.9 Nm
Pressure sensors	SDE1-D10-G2-W18	Pressure range: 0–10 bar
Pneumatic cylinder	CDC-20	Stroke: 100 mm, bore: 20 mm, rod: 8 mm
Servo valves	MPYE-5-1/4-010B	Control voltage range: 0–10 VDC
LVDT	Novotechnik TR100	Measurement range: 0–100 mm
Springs	Case 1, Case 2, Case 3	Randomly selected

Table 1. Specifications of the system components.

Input number	Number of nodes in the hidden layer				
	20	**25**	**30**	**35**	**40**
20	80.35	80.50	81.48	82.17	81.29
24	81.14	81.19	82.26	81.48	82.78
28	80.61	80.03	81.66	81.12	81.69
32	75.34	80.64	85.64	81.00	81.80
36	81.03	81.58	81.93	81.85	80.49
40	79.30	80.98	80.90	80.13	80.22
	Goodness of fit [%]				

Table 2. Learning success rate of the LVQNN classifier [%].

3.2.3.2. *LVQNN classifier training and verification*

In order to train the network, the prior task is acquiring the target data. Real-time teleoperation experiments without force feedback concept were performed on the test rig. Both the three springs mentioned in Table 1 were used to generate the environmental conditions. For each condition, a trajectory for the slave manipulator was randomly given by the operator. The slave information, including the valve driving command and cylinder rod displacement, with respect to each spring was acquired with a sampling period of 0.02 s.

Next, each of the acquired slave data sets was used to perform the input vector, while the correspondingly selected spring was used as the target output class (1, 2, or 3). To investigate performance of the LVQNN classifier with respect to different structures, several trainings were performed with the selected data set by varying the number of inputs from 20 to 40, and the number of hidden neurons was changed from 20 to 40. After the training process, the results (goodness of fit [%]) of the LVQNN are analyzed in **Table 2**. It shows that the most suitable LVQNN structure was realized with 32 nodes in the input vector and 30 nodes in the competitive layer. The learning success rate in this case was highest with 85.64 [%].

Real-time teleoperation experiments were performed in order to investigate the ability of the LVQNN classifier in practice. Other three experiments with the three loading conditions were carried out with the same cylinder trajectories given from the master using an open-loop control. The classification results were then achieved as displayed in **Figure 6–8**. The results imply that the proposed classifier could online detect well the loading conditions and, therefore, is capable of producing precisely decisions on the environment characteristics.

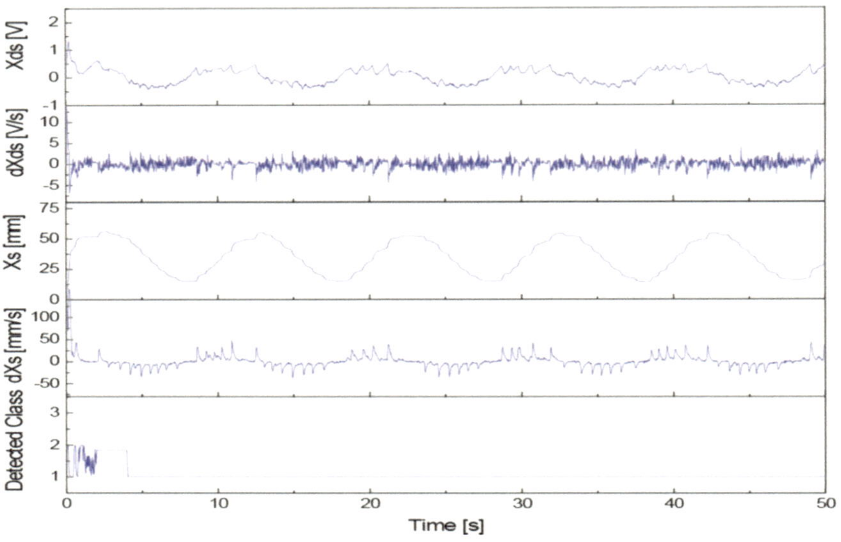

Figure 6. Real-time classification of the optimized LVQNN with respect to spring case 1.

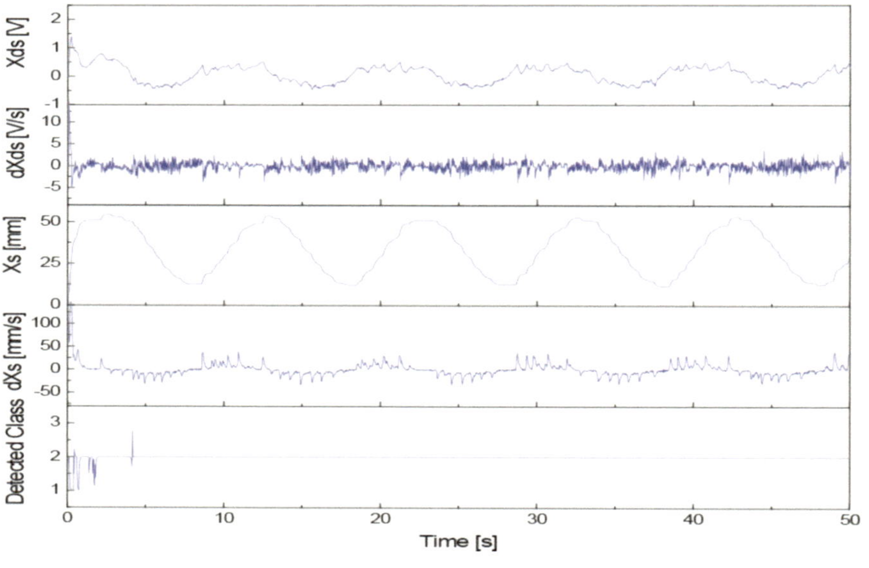

Figure 7. Real-time classification of the optimized LVQNN with respect to spring case 2.

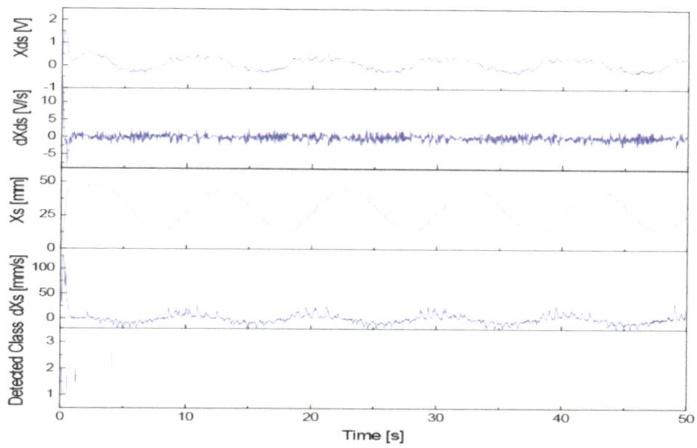

Figure 8. Classification performance of the optimized LVQNN with respect to spring case 3.

4. Robust-adaptive networked control

4.1. Problem and RANC design concept

In this section, the RANC approach for a generic system is introduced to support the design of the LM controller. Consider a discrete-time plant [20, 21]:

$$\begin{cases} x_{k+1} = Ax_k + Bu_k + Ed_k \\ y_k = Cx_k \end{cases} \tag{6}$$

where $x_k \in R^n$is the state vector, $u_k \in R^m$is the control input, $y_k \in R^p$is the controlled output, $d_k \in R^d$is the environment impact, and A, B, C and E are matrices with appropriate dimensions.

The RANC-based LM controller in **Figure 2** is then designed based on the following issues [20, 21]:

- Both the actuators and controller are event-driven.
- The sensors are time-driven with variable sampling period T. For step $(k+1)^{th}$, this sampling period T_{k+1} is online optimized depending on the total system time delay τ_{k+1} to make sure:

$$\begin{cases} \tau_{k+1} = \tau_{k+1}^{com} + \tau_{k+1}^{ca} + \tau_{k+1}^{sc} \\ T_{k+1} \geq \tau_{k+1} > 0 \end{cases} \tag{7}$$

- Sets of continuous packet dropouts $\{p_d\}$ are online detected and bounded by $\bar{p}_{k+1}$:

$$\bar{p}_{k+1} = \sup(p_d), 1 \le d < k+1 \tag{8}$$

Using the results in references [20, 21], the configuration of an NSC using the proposed RANC controller is clarified in **Figure 9**. Herein, the RANC mainly consists of five modules: Time Delay and Packet Detector (TDPD), Time Delay Predictor (TDP), Variable Sampling Period Adjuster (VSPA), Quantitative Feedback Theory (QFT), and Robust State Feedback Controller (RSFC). The TDPD module is firstly used to detect the network problems at the current state. This information is then sent to the TDP to perform one-step-ahead prediction of system delays which are the inputs of the VSPA to adjust effectively the sampling period. The two modules, QFT and RSFC, are employed to construct the so-called hybrid controller to compensate for the influences of delays and packet dropouts. A smart switch (SSW) is employed to switch the hybrid controller to QFT or RSFC based on the outputs of the TDPD detector and the TDP predictor with rule:

- The QFT is selected (SSW = 0) once there is no packet loss and all delay components are less than their pre-defined threshold values: ($\lceil * \rceil$is ceiling function to return the nearest integer)

$$\bar{\tau}_{QFT}^{com} = \left\lceil \tau_k^{com} \right\rceil, \bar{\tau}_{QFT}^{ca} = \left\lceil \tau_k^{ca} \right\rceil, \bar{\tau}_{QFT}^{sc} = \left\lceil \tau_k^{sc} \right\rceil, \bar{\tau}_{QFT} = \left\lceil \tau_k \right\rceil, \forall k \tag{9}$$

- Otherwise, the RSFC is chosen (SSW = 1).

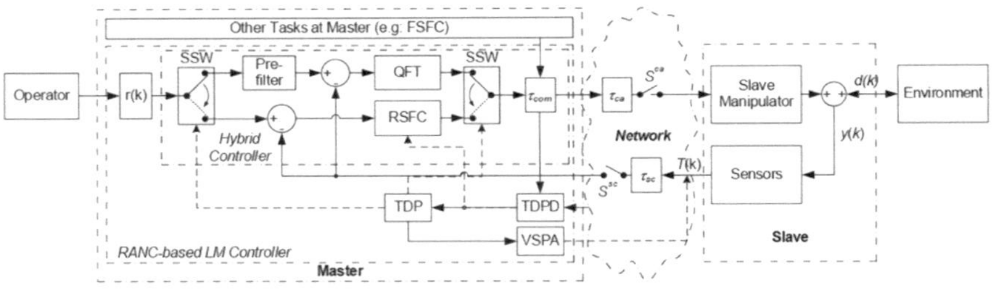

Figure 9. Configuration of networked LM controller using the RANC approach.

4.2. Design of RANC components

4.2.1. Design of VSPA

By using the TDPD and TDP, the sampling period for the coming step ($k+1$) is defined as

$$\begin{aligned} &T_{k+1} = \lceil T_{new} / T_0 \rceil T_0 = k_T T_0,\ k_T = \lceil T_{new} / T_0 \rceil = 1, 2, \ldots \\ &T_{new} = \max(T_0, \hat{\tau}_{k+1}^{com} + \hat{\tau}_{k+1}^{ca} + \hat{\tau}_{k+1}^{sa}) = \max(T_0, \hat{\tau}_{k+1}), T_0 >= 0.1T_p,\ (T_0 \text{is initial sampling period}) \end{aligned} \tag{10}$$

http://dx.doi.org/10.5772/63033

where $\hat{\tau}_{k+1}^{com}$, $\hat{\tau}_{k+1}^{ca}$ and $\hat{\tau}_{k+1}^{sa}$ are the delays estimated by the TDP.

4.2.2. Design of TDPD

To measure accurately time delays and packet dropouts, the TDPD employs a micro-control unit (MCU) with proper logic. Here, PIC18F4620 MCU from microchip equipped with a 4 MHz oscillator is suggested to be used [19]. The real-time measurement accuracy of 50μs[19] which is suitable for this application. For each step k^{th}, the TDPD enhances the following tasks:

- Derive the real working time using the MCU, t_k.
- For a command u_k sent from the controller to the plant, a time stamp is encapsulated into this packet to detect the forward delay, τ_k^{ca}, and packet dropouts if having, p_k^{ca}.
- For the signals sent from the sensors to the controller, they are combined with time stamps to detect the delay, τ_k^{sc}, and packet dropouts if having, p_k^{sc}.
- The total number of continuous packet dropouts is then determined as:

$$p_k = S_k^{ca} p_k^{ca} + S_k^{sc} p_k^{sc} \tag{11}$$

- Depend on the time stamps to detect the computation delay at the controller side, τ_k^{com}.

4.2.3. Design of TDP

The TDP based on a so-called adaptive gray model with single-variable first-order, AGM (1,1) to estimate the system delays in the coming step, $\hat{\tau}_{k+1}^{com}$, $\hat{\tau}_{k+1}^{ca}$, and $\hat{\tau}_{k+1}^{sa}$. The AGM (1,1) prediction procedure is as follows:

Step 1: For an object with a data sequence
$\{y_{Object}(t_{O1}), y_{Object}(t_{O2}), \ldots, y_{Object}(t_{Om})\}$ $(m \geq 4)$, the raw input gray sequence representing for the object data is derived as

$$y_{raw}^{(0)} = \left\{y_{raw}^{(0)}(t_1), y_{raw}^{(0)}(t_2), \ldots, y_{raw}^{(0)}(t_n)\right\};\ \Delta t_k = t_k - t_{k-1};\ k = 2,..,n \geq 4; \tag{12}$$

Note: Eq. (12) is obtained from Eq. (14) if condition (13) satisfies; otherwise, it is obtained from Eq. (15).

$$\begin{aligned}&\Delta t_{Oi} / T_{\text{TDP}} < 2;\ \Delta t_{Oi} = t_{Oi} - t_{O(i-1)};\ \forall i \in [2,\ldots,m];T_{\text{TDP}} \text{ is the prediction sampling period}\\&\Delta t_{O1} = t_{O1} - t_{Olast};t_{Olast} : \text{time of previous value of } y_{Object}(t_{O1})\end{aligned} \tag{13}$$

$$y_{raw}^{(0)}(t_k) = y_{Object}(t_i);\ t_k = t_{Oi};\ k = 1,...,n;\ n = m \tag{14}$$

$$\begin{aligned} & y_{raw}^{(0)}(t_1) = y_{Object}(t_1);\ t_k = t_{k-1} + T_{\text{TDP}} \\ & y_{raw}^{(0)}(t_k) = Sa_i + Sb_i(t_k - t_{Oi})^1 + Sc_i(t_k - t_{Oi})^2 + Sd_i(t_k - t_{Oi})^3 \\ & t_{Oi} \le t_k \le t_{O(i+1)};k = 2,...,n;\ n = \lfloor (t_{Om} - t_1)/T_{TDP} \rfloor;i = 1,...,m-1 \end{aligned} \tag{15}$$

where $\{Sa_i, Sb_i, Sc_i, Sd_i\}$ $(i=1, \ldots, m-1)$is a $[4 \times m - 1]$ coefficient matrix of the spline function going through the object data set $\{(t_1, y_{Object}(t_1)), \ldots, (t_m, y_{Object}(t_m))\}$.

Theorem 1: There always exist two non-negative additive factors, c_1 and c_2, to convert any raw sequence (12) to a gray sequence which satisfies both the gray checking conditions.

Proof: The proof of this theorem can be found in reference [19].

Thus from (12), the gray sequence is derived using *Theorem* 1:

$$y^{(0)} = \left\{y^{(0)}(t_1), y^{(0)}(t_2),..., y^{(0)}(t_n)\right\} > 0;\ y^{(0)}(t_k) = y_{raw}^{(0)}(t_k) + c_1 + c_2;\ k = 1,...,n \tag{16}$$

Step 2: Use the 1-AGO to obtain a new series $y^{(1)}$ from $y^{(0)}$:

$$y^{(1)}(t_k) = \sum_{i=1}^{k} y^{(0)}(t_i) \times \Delta t_k = \sum_{i=1}^{k} \left(y_{raw}(t_i) + c_1 + c_2\right) \times \Delta t_k \tag{17}$$

Step 3: Create the background series $z^{(1)}$ from $y^{(1)}$ by the following general algorithm:

$$z^{(1)}(t_k) = \alpha(t_k) y^{(1)}(t_k) + (1 - \alpha(t_k)) y^{(1)}(t_{k-1});k = 2,...,n \tag{18}$$

$$\alpha(t_k) = \beta\alpha_{aver} + (1-\beta)\alpha_{adapt}(t_k) \tag{19}$$

$$\alpha_{adapt}(t_k) = \begin{cases} 1, \text{ IF}: s(t_k) \ge \sum\limits_{i=1}^{k+1} \Delta t_i / \sum\limits_{i=1}^{n} \Delta t_i \\ s, \text{ IF}: \sum\limits_{i=1}^{k-1} \Delta t_i / \sum\limits_{i=1}^{n} \Delta t_i < s(t_k) < \sum\limits_{i=1}^{k+1} \Delta t_i / \sum\limits_{i=1}^{n} \Delta t_i \\ 0, \text{ IF}: s(t_k) \le \sum\limits_{i=1}^{k-1} \Delta t_i / \sum\limits_{i=1}^{n} \Delta t_i \end{cases} \tag{20}$$

$$s(t_k) = \log\left(y^{(0)}(t_k) / y^{(0)}(t_1)\right) / \log\left(y^{(0)}(t_n) / y^{(0)}(t_1)\right) \tag{21}$$

where α_{aver} is the average weight and set as 0.5 [23, 24]; β is a momentum rate within range [0, 1] and tuned by a Lyaponov-based SISO fuzzy mechanism (LFM) in order to guarantee a robust prediction performance (see the proof of this theory in reference [20])

Step 4: Establish the gray differential equation:

$$y^{(0)}(t_k) + az^{(1)}(t_k) = b \tag{22}$$

$$\hat{\beta}_{ab} = \begin{bmatrix} \hat{a} & \hat{b} \end{bmatrix}^T = \left(B^T B\right)^{-1} B^T Y; B = \begin{bmatrix} -z^{(1)}(t_2) & 1 \\ -z^{(1)}(t_3) & 1 \\ \vdots & \vdots \\ -z^{(1)}(t_n) & 1 \end{bmatrix}, Y = \begin{bmatrix} y^{(0)}(t_2) \\ y^{(0)}(t_3) \\ \vdots \\ y^{(0)}(t_n) \end{bmatrix} \tag{23}$$

Step 5: Setup the AGM (1,1) prediction as follows:

$$\hat{y}^{(0)}(t_k) = \left(\hat{b} - \hat{a}y^{(1)}(t_{k-1})\right) / \left(1 + \alpha(t_k)\hat{a}\Delta t_k\right) = \frac{\hat{b} - \hat{a}y^{(0)}(t_1)\Delta t_1}{1 + \alpha(t_2)\hat{a}\Delta t_2} \prod_{i=3}^{k} \frac{1 + \left(\alpha(t_{i-1}) - 1\right)\hat{a}\Delta t_{i-1}}{1 + \alpha(t_i)\hat{a}\Delta t_i} \tag{24}$$

Step 6: Perform the predicted value of y at step $(n + p)^{\text{th}}$:

$$\hat{y}_{raw}^{(0)}(t_{n+p}) = \frac{\hat{b} - \hat{a}y^{(0)}(t_1)\Delta t_1}{1 + \alpha(t_2)\hat{a}\Delta t_2} \prod_{i=3}^{n+p} \frac{1 + \left(\alpha(t_{i-1}) - 1\right)\hat{a}\Delta t_{i-1}}{1 + \alpha(t_i)\hat{a}\Delta t_i} - c_1 - c_2 \tag{25}$$

where p is the step size of the grey predictor. In this case, $p = 1$.

4.2.4. Design of QFT controller

Denotes the transfer functions of the plant and the controller in the NCS as $G_p(s)$ and $G_c(s)$, respectively. The closed-loop transfer function from input $R(s)$ to output $Y(s)$ including delays can be expressed as

$$T^{\text{NCS}}(s) = \frac{Y(s)}{R(s)} = \frac{G_c(s)G_p(s)e^{-(\tau_{com} + \tau_{ca})s}}{1 + G_c(s)G_p(s)e^{-\tau s}} \tag{26}$$

And the open-loop transfer function is then derived as

$$L^{\text{NCS}}(s) = G_c(s)G_p(s)e^{-\tau s} \tag{27}$$

Next, the procedure to design this robust controller can be expressed as follows [25, 26]:

Step 1: The QFT controller should be designed on how the tracking signal meets the acceptable variation range with respect to a reference (for each value of ?i of interest)

$$T_l^{\mathrm{NCS}}(j\omega_i) \le \left|T^{\mathrm{NCS}}(j\omega_i)\right| \le T_u^{\mathrm{NCS}}(j\omega_i) \tag{28}$$

Step 2: Establish bounds for robust stability of the closed-loop system

$$\left|T^{\mathrm{NCS}}(j\omega)\right| \le M = 1.4,\ \omega \ge 0 \tag{29}$$

Step 3: A sensitivity function is defined as

$$S(j\omega) = \left(1 + L^{\mathrm{NCS}}(j\omega)\right)^{-1},\ \omega \ge 0 \tag{30}$$

Establish bounds for noise and disturbance rejection of the closed-loop system

$$\left|1 + L(j\omega)\right|_{\max}^{-1} \le M_D(\omega),\ M_D > 1\left(M_{\mathrm{dB}} > 0\mathrm{dB}\right), \omega \ge 0 \tag{31}$$

Step 4: Define a working frequency range of the NCS.

Step 5: Bases on the nominal plant to design the controller, $G_{QFT}(s)$, with initial poles and zeros.

Step 6: Use the loop-shaping method to refine the controller designed in Step 5. The principle to guarantee a robust control performance is the loop gain value is always on or above the boundaries defined by constraints (28)–(31) and, is to the right or on the robustness forbidden region for any critical frequency within the range defined in Step 4.

Step 7: The controller resulted from Step 6 could ensure that the variation in magnitude of $T^{\mathrm{NCS}}(s)$ (26) is satisfied at the desired constraints. However, it does not guarantee that the magnitude of $T^{\mathrm{NCS}}(s)$ actually lies between the given bounds $T_l^{\mathrm{NCS}}(j\omega_i)$ and $T_u^{\mathrm{NCS}}(j\omega_i)$for the whole frequency range. Therefore, a pre-filter $F_{QFT}(s)$ is necessary to be designed and placed in front of the controller to compensate for this problem.

4.2.5. Design of RSFC

The RSFC is designed to deal with the NCS in cases that the delays are greater than the threshold values defined in Eq. (9), and/or there exists packet dropouts. To simplify the analysis, it can be assumed that $r_k = 0$ (**Figure 9**) during the system modeling and RSFC design. The system discrete form for step $(k + 1)^{\mathrm{th}}$ can be expressed through the following three cases:

Case 1: There is no packet loss in network transmission during both current period and previous period:

$$x_{k+1} = A_k^0 x_k + B_k^0 u_k + B_{k-1}^1 u_{k-1} + Ed_k \tag{32}$$

where $A_k^0 = e^{AT_k}$, $B_k^0 = \int_0^{T_k-\tau_k} e^{At} B\mathrm{d}t$, $B_k^1 = \int_{T_k-\tau_k}^{T_k} e^{At} B\mathrm{d}t$.

Case 2: There exists i packet dropouts up to step k^{th}:

$$x_{k+1} = A_k^0 x_k + B_{k-i}^2 u_{k-i} + Ed_k \tag{33}$$

where $B_k^2 = \int_0^{T_k} e^{At} B\mathrm{d}t$.

Case 3: There were p_d continuous packet dropouts just passed up to step $(k-1)^{\text{th}}$:

$$x_{k+1} = A_k^0 x_k + B_k^0 u_k + B_{k-p_d-1}^1 u_{k-p_d-1} + Ed_k \tag{34}$$

Since, the general discrete form of the system can be established as

$$x_{k+1} = A_k^0 x_k + B_k^0 \delta_k^0 u_k + \sum_{j=1}^{2} \sum_{i=1}^{\bar{p}_{k+1}} B_{k-i}^j \delta_{k-i}^j u_{k-i} + Ed_k \tag{35}$$

where δ^l is an activation function:

$$\delta^l = \begin{cases} 1, & \text{If subsystem } l \text{ is activated}, l = \{0,1,2\} \\ 0, & \text{Otherwise.} \end{cases} \tag{36}$$

In case of no delays, the control rule is designed as

$$u_k = Kx_k \tag{37}$$

Then, Eq. (35) can be re-written in the following form:

$$x_{k+1} = \left(A_k^0 + B_k^0 \delta_k^0 K\right) x_k + \sum_{i=1}^{\bar{p}_{k+1}} \left(\sum_{j=1}^{2} B_{k-i}^j \delta_{k-i}^j \right) K x_{k-i} + E d_k \tag{38}$$

or

$$X_{k+1} = \Phi_k X_k + \Phi_E d_k \tag{39}$$

where $X_k = \left[x_k^T \quad x_{k-1}^T \quad \cdots \quad x_{k-\bar{p}_{k+1}}^T\right]^T$, $\Phi_k = \begin{bmatrix} \begin{bmatrix} A_k^* & B_{1k}^* & \cdots & B_{(\bar{p}_{k+1}-1)k}^* \end{bmatrix} & B_{\bar{p}_{k+1}k}^* \\ I_{\bar{p}_{k+1} \times \bar{p}_{k+1}} & 0 \end{bmatrix}$,

$$\Phi_E = \begin{bmatrix} E & 0 & \cdots & 0 \end{bmatrix}^T, A_k^* = A_k^0 + B_k^0 \delta_k^0 K, B_{ik}^* = K \sum_{j=1}^{2} B_{k-i}^j \delta_{k-i}^j.$$

Theorem 2: For given constants $\xi_i^j > 0$, if there exist positive definite matrices $P_i^* > 0$, $K_1 > 0$, $K_2 > 0$, $i \in [0, 1, \ldots, \bar{p}_{k+1}]$, $j = \{0, 1, 2\}$ such that following inequalities:

$$\begin{bmatrix} \xi_i^{-2} P_i^* & K_1^* \Phi_A^T + K_2^{*T} \Phi_B^T \\ \Phi_A K_1^{*T} + \Phi_B K_2^* & K_1^* + K_1^{*T} - P_i^* \end{bmatrix} > 0 \tag{40}$$

hold, then the NCS (39) is exponentially stable with a positive decay rate by using the RSFC control gain derived by

$$K_{\mathrm{RSFC}} = K_2 K_1^{-T} \tag{41}$$

with $K_1^* = diag[\{K_1\}]$, $K_2^* = diag[\{K_2\}]$, $K_{\mathrm{RSFC}}^* = diag[\{K_{\mathrm{RSFC}}\}]$

$$\Phi_A = \begin{bmatrix} \begin{bmatrix} A_k^0 & \cdots & 0 \end{bmatrix} & 0 \\ I & 0 \end{bmatrix}, \Phi_B = \begin{bmatrix} \begin{bmatrix} B_k^0 \delta_k^0 & \cdots & \sum_{j=1}^{2} B_{k-\bar{p}_{k+1}+1}^j \delta_{k-\bar{p}_{k+1}+1}^j \end{bmatrix} & \sum_{j=1}^{2} B_{k-\bar{p}_{k+1}}^j \delta_{k-\bar{p}_{k+1}}^j \\ 0 & 0 \end{bmatrix}.$$

Proof: The proof of this theorem can be found in reference [20].

http://dx.doi.org/10.5772/63033

4.3. An illustrative example

4.3.1. Networked control system setup

To validate the RANC applicability, a simple networked control system was set up based on the configuration in **Figure 9**. Here, the main controller was built in an experimental PC equipped with the MCU (presented in Section 4.2.2) The network module includes one coordinator and one router employed the ZigBee protocol [19]. The multifunction card was used to perform the communications with the TDPD module and the network. The control objective is speed tracking control of a servomotor system via the setup network. Here, the servomotor system was *RE*-max series manufactured by Maxon Corporation. The transfer function from the input to output of this system can be expressed as [20]

$$G_p(s) = \frac{32300}{0.001s^2 + 20.93s + 493.4} \tag{42}$$

To evaluate the capability of the proposed RANC, a comparative study of the RANC with three existing approaches, a QFT-based robust controller (QFTRC), a static state feedback controller (SSFC), and a hybrid QFT–SSFC as shown in **Table 3**, has been investigated. To make control challenges, disturbance loads and computation delays were randomly generated. Here, the loads were created by putting the system into a varied magnetic field which affected on the motor shaft. Meanwhile, an arbitrary matrix-based complex calculating procedure representing a complex application was added to the controller at the PC side.

Control method	Main control modules					Functions	
	QFT	SFC		SSW-based TDPD–TDP	VSPA based TDP	Delay compensation	Packet loss compensation
		Fixed gain	Dynamic gain				
QFTRC	√					√	
SSFC		√				√	√
QFT–SSFC	√	√		√		√	√
RANC	√		√	√	√	√	√

Table 3. Specifications of the compared controllers.

Based on Section 4.2.4, QFT delay bounds were defined as
$\bar{\tau}_{QFT}^{com}$ =0.02*s*, $\bar{\tau}_{QFT}^{ca}$ =0.03, $\bar{\tau}_{QFT}^{sc}$ =0.03and, the QFT controller was designed as

$$G_{QFT}(s) = \frac{30.5387s^2 + 56684.6s + 3328880}{10^{-8}s^3 + 0.002852s^2 + 180.2s + 1260000}$$
$$F_{QFT}(s) = 426.65/(s + 400) \quad (43)$$

Based on Section 4.2.5 and by setting the initial bounds for the total delay and packet dropouts as: $\bar{\tau}_0$=0.1s>$\bar{\tau}_{QFT}$, $\bar{p}_0$=2; the initial RSFC gain was computed as K_{RSFC}^0=[0.3796 0.2642].

The initial sampling period of the RANC was selected as 10 ms, while that of the other controllers must be fixed to 0.15 s to cover all the delays.

4.3.2. Real-time experiments

In this section, real-time speed tracking of a servomotor system over the setup network has been investigated in which the reference speed was selected as 10 rad/s. The experiments using the comparative controllers were carried out and, consequently, the results were displaced in **Figure 10**. An analysis on the control performances using four evaluation criteria, *PO* (percent overshoot), *ST* (settling time), *SSE* (steady state error) and *MSE* (mean square error), is then performed as demonstrated in **Table 4**.

Controller	**Step responses**			
	PO [%]	**ST [s]**	**SSE [%]**	**MSE [rad/s]^2**
QFTRC	2.6	1.0	13.9	1.23
SSFC	8.67	2.1	6.18	1.87
QFT–SSFC	2.07	1.35	5.88	1.35
RANC	0.2	0.8	1.58	0.63

Table 4. Comparison of NCS performances using different controllers.

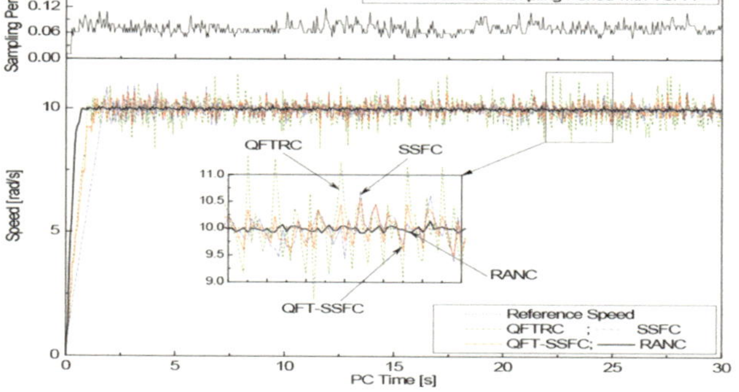

Figure 10. Step speed performances using different controllers.

From **Figure 10** and **Table 4**, it is clear that the worst-case performance was with the QFTRC. It is because the QFTRC was designed for an NCS in which the delays are bounded by constraint (9) and there is no packet dropout. Hence when facing with the networked servo-motor including both the large delays and packet dropouts, the controller could not guarantee the robust tracking (*SSE* was 13.9%). In case of using the SSFC for which the control gain was designed for the worst network conditions (large delays and highest number of continuous packet dropouts), *SSE* was remarkably reduced to 6.18%. However due to this fixed control gain use, the system response was much slower than that of the QFTRC. Additionally, due to lack of disturbance rejection capability, the SSFC could not ensure a smooth tracking (PO = 8.67% and ST = 2.1s). The QFT--SSFC, by taking advantages of both the QFT and SSFC, could improve the tracking result. Nonetheless, the QFT–SSFC with fixed control gains and fixed sampling period restricted the system adaptability to the sharp variations of network problems and disturbances (*SSE* was slightly reduced to 5.88%).

The best tracking result was achieved by using the RANC (see **Figure 10** and **Table 4**). It comes as no surprise because the RANC possesses all the advantages of the QFT and state feedback designs and, the high adaptability to the system changes by using the adaptive control gains and adaptive sampling period. **Figure 11** demonstrates the delay and packet dropout detection and prediction results of the TDPD and TDP modules, respectively. During the operation, these were supported by the VSPA and hybrid QFT–RSFC modules to regulate properly the sampling period and control gains.

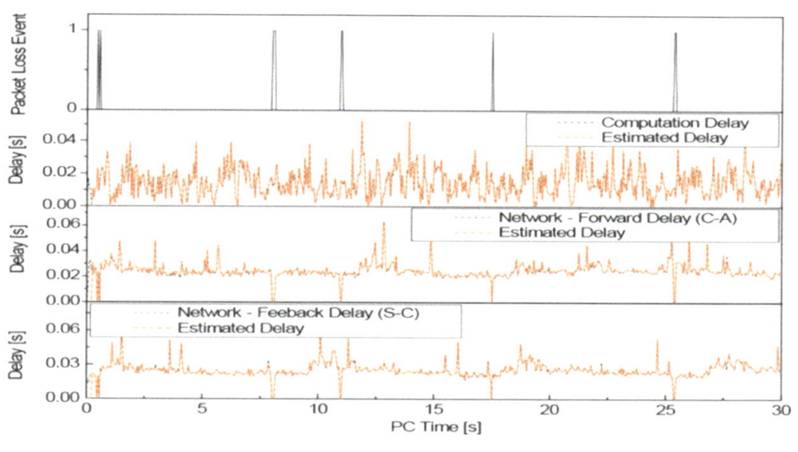

Figure 11. Step speed case: performances of TDPD and TDP.

5. Conclusions

In summary, an advanced bilateral teleoperation NCS has been introduced. In addition, the two important issues in designing the BTNCS system, FSFC and RANC, have been clearly addressed. The LVQNN-based FSFC shows the safe and cost-effective solution in controlling the FRM while the RANC-based LM controller is a feasible choice to drive the slave manipulator over the network with delay and packet loss problems.

The effectiveness of the LVQNN classifier as well as the RANC controller has been confirmed through the two case studies and analysis. One of our future research topics would be the full design of the proposed BTNCS to investigate the applicability of this method in a practical application such as remote construction equipment.

Author details

Truong Quang Dinh[1*], Jong Il Yoon[2], Cheolkeun Ha[3] and James Marco[1]

*Address all correspondence to: q.dinh@warwick.ac.uk

1 WMG, University of Warwick, United Kingdom

2 Korea Construction Equipment Technology Institute, Korea

3 School of Mechanical Engineering, University of Ulsan, Korea

References

[1] Park W.I, Kwon S.C, Lee H.D, Kim, J (2012) Real-time thumb-tip force predictions from noninvasive biosignals and biomechanical models. Int. J. Prec. Eng. Man. 13(9): 1679–1688.

[2] Jung K.M, Chu B.S, Park S.S, Hong D.H (2013) An implementation of a teleoperation system for robotic beam assembly in construction. Int. J. Prec. Eng. Man. 14(3): 351–358.

[3] Shafiqul I, Peter X.L, Abdulmotaleb E.S (2014) New stability and tracking criteria for a class of bilateral teleoperation systems. Inf. Sci. 278: 868–882.

[4] Kuchenbecker J.K, Niemeyer G (2006) Induced master motion in force-reflecting teleoperation. ASME J. Dyn. Sys. Meas. Control 128(4): pp. 800–810.

[5] Polushin I.G, Liu P.X, Lung C.H (2012) Stability of bilateral teleoperators with generalized projection-based force reflection algorithms. Automatica 48: 1005-1016.

[6] Sun D, Naghdy F, Du H (2014) Application of wave-variable control to bilateral teleoperation systems: A survey. Annu. Rev. Control 38: 12–31

[7] Zhang W, Branicky M.S, Phillips S.M (2001) Stability of networked control systems. IEEE Control Syst. Mag. 2: 84–99.

http://dx.doi.org/10.5772/63033

[8] Hua C.C, Liu X.P (2013) A new coordinated slave torque feedback control algorithm for network-based teleoperation systems. IEEE/ASME Trans. Mechatronics 18(2): 764–774.

[9] Yang F, Wang Z, Hung Y.S, Mahbub G (2006) H∞ control for networked control systems with random communication delays. IEEE Trans. Autom. Control 51(3): 511–518.

[10] Yi J.Q, Wang Q. D, Zhao B, Wen J.T (2007) BP neural network prediction-based variable-period sampling approach for networked control systems. Appl. Math. Comput. 185: 976–988.

[11] Chien L.L, Pau L.H (2010) Design the remote control system with the time-delay estimator and the adaptive Smith predictor. IEEE Trans. Ind. Informat. 6(1): 73–80.

[12] Daniel L.E, Mario E.M (2012) Variable sampling approach to mitigate instability in networked control systems with delays. IEEE Trans. Neural Netw. Learn. Syst. 23(1): 119–126.

[13] Li H, Sun Z, Chow M.-Y, Sun F (2011) Gain-scheduling-based state feedback integral control for networked control systems. IEEE Trans. Ind. Electron. 58(6): 2465–2472.

[14] Shi Y, Huang J, Yu B (2013) Robust tracking control of networked control systems: Application to a networked DC motor. IEEE Trans. Ind. Electron. 60(12): 5864–5874.

[15] Gao H, Chen T, Lam J (2008) A new delay system approach to network-based control. Automatica 44(1): 39–52.

[16] Gao H, Chen T (2008) Network-based H∞ output tracking control. IEEE Trans. Autom. Control 53(3): 655–667.

[17] Yang R, Liu G.-P, Shi P, Thomas C, Basin M.V (2014) Predictive output feedback control for networked control systems. IEEE Trans. Ind. Electron. 61(1): 512–520.

[18] Pang Z.-H, Liu G.-P, Zhou D, Chen M (2014) Output tracking control for networked systems: A model-based prediction approach. IEEE Trans. Ind. Electron. 61(9): 4867–4877.

[19] Truong D.Q, Ahn K.K, Trung N.T (2013) Design of an advanced time delay measurement and a smart adaptive unequal interval grey predictor for real-time nonlinear control systems. IEEE Trans. Ind. Electron. 60(10): 4574–4589.

[20] Truong D.Q, Ahn K.K (2015) Robust variable sampling period control for networked control systems. IEEE Trans. Ind. Electron. 62(9): 5630–5643.

[21] Truong D.Q, Lee S, Liem D.T, Ahn K.K (2015) Robust tracking control of networked control systems included uncertainties. Proceedings of 2015 IEEE International Conference on Advanced Intelligent Mechatronics (AIM): 1049–1054.

[22] Schneider P, Biehl M, Hammer B (2009) Adaptive relevance matrices in learning vector quantization. Neural Comput. 21(12): 3532–3561.

[23] Deng J.L (1982) Control problem of grey system. Syst. Control Lett. 1(5): 288-294.

[24] Truong D.Q, Ahn K.K (2009) Force control for hydraulic load simulator using self-tuning grey predictor—fuzzy PID. Mechatronics 19(2): 233-246.

[25] Truong D.Q, Ahn K.K (2009) Self tuning of quantitative feedback theory for force control of an electro-hydraulic test machine. Control Eng. Pract. 17(11): 1291–1306.

[26] Ahn K.K, Truong D.Q, Nam D.N.C, Yoon J.I, Yokota S (2010) Position control of polymer metal composite actuator using quantitative feedback theory. Sens. Actuat. A Phys. 159(2): 204–212.

Chapter 8

Wireless Real-Time Monitoring System for the Implementation of Intelligent Control in Subways

Alessandro Carbonari, Massimo Vaccarini,
Mikko Valta and Maddalena Nurchis

Additional information is available at the end of the chapter

http://dx.doi.org/10.5772/62679

Abstract

This chapter looks into the technical features of state-of-the-art wireless sensors networks for environmental monitoring. Technology advances in low-power and wireless devices have made the deployment of those networks more and more affordable. In addition, wireless sensor networks have become more flexible and adaptable to a wide range of situations. Hence, a framework for their correct implementation will be provided. Then, one specific application about real-time environmental monitoring in support of a model-based predictive control system installed in a metro station will be described. In these applications, filtering, resampling, and post-processing functions must be developed, in order to convert raw data into a dataset arranged in the right format, so that it can inform the algorithms of the control system about the current state of the domain under control. Finally, the whole architecture of the model-based predictive control and its final performances will be reported.

Keywords: Environmental monitoring, Real-time control, Wireless sensor networks, Performance evaluation, Network design

1. Introduction

One of the most critical components in an advanced real-time control system is the implementation of a real-time monitoring network. Indeed, real-time monitoring is in charge of measuring the actual state of the domain that is controlled. The features and requirements of the network depend on the type of control that is implemented and on its architecture. In this chapter, we will focus on the importance of wireless sensor-based environmental networks (WSNs) targeted to real-time control of complex buildings. Then, we will show what role they play in the implementation of a model-based predictive control (MPC) system, that is one of the most advanced approaches presently considered.

To this purpose, the basic characteristics of MPC will be clarified and some of the most popular applications will be described in Section 2. Section 3 will report on the technical features of typical WSNs for environmental monitoring and will sum up its background. The purpose of Section 4 is analyzing the whole architecture of real-time environmental monitoring systems. Hence, it will argue typical constraints, requirements, technical issues, choice criteria that are helpful for designing and installing such systems in harsh environments. For the sake of clarity, this chapter will refer to the real case of an MPC system applied to the "Passeig de Gràcia" (PdG) subway station in Barcelona, which was the topic of an EU funded 3-year research project. In that same section, all the issues connected with real-time data management will be faced, including pre-processing (i.e. filtering and re-sampling) and post-processing functions (e.g., more complex procedures that convert pre-processed data into a format that can be interoperable with the controller unit of the MPC system). Finally, the most important information about the MPC system integrated in the PdG station and the benefits obtained thanks to the MPC will be discussed in Section 5. Conclusions and references will terminate this chapter.

2. Model-based predictive control systems

2.1. State-of-the-art and applications

Efforts to reduce the energy consumption of public buildings and spaces have recently been receiving increasing concern. Energy savings define a clear objective: to minimize energy consumption, while maintaining acceptable comfort levels in the presence of uncertainties. Thus, uncertainty must be explicitly considered by including adaptation capabilities in order to adjust the control strategy to changing conditions. Comfort and H&S requirements define operative constraints that can be either hard or soft: this implies that constraints must be explicitly considered in the control strategy. These constraints can be satisfied only if a suitable and robust sensor network is deployed in the controlled spaces.

Among the hard control approaches, MPC [1–3] is one of the most promising techniques for HVAC systems because of its ability to integrate disturbance rejection, constraint handling, and dynamic control and energy conservation strategies into controller formulation. In fact, for complex constrained multi-variable control problems, MPC has become the accepted standard in the process industries [4].

MPC computes the optimal control policy by minimizing a proper cost function subject to certain constraints on input, output, or state variables. Its success is largely due to its unique ability to optimally control either linear or nonlinear MIMO processes using a predictive model and explicitly considering constraint in its formulation. Explicit consideration of uncertainty is discussed in a number of contributions [5–8] and can be achieved using stochastic models and by minimizing the probability of constraint violation. Due to these reasons, MPC has been successfully implemented in various researches on buildings over the last years. A review of the representative studies about MPC can be found in [9], which also exploits the Building Controls Virtual Test Bed (BCVTB) for running a building energy simulation with real-time Building Energy Management System (BEMS) data as inputs.

In subways applications, as far as metro operators are concerned, they suffer from the high-energy consumption of their facilities. While the lighting, ventilation, and vertical transport systems are crucial for the safety and comfort of passengers, they represent the most of the non-traction energy required in underground stations. Hence, as shown in [10], the intelligent control of these subsystems can significantly reduce their energy consumption without impacting the passenger comfort or safety or requiring expensive refurbishment of existing equipment.

Differently from the buildings above ground, the environmental conditions (temperature and humidity) are quite stable in underground spaces and, usually, there is no need for heating in winter but just for cooling in summer. Since no air-conditioning plant is usually installed in underground spaces, the air change becomes a key requirement that must be guaranteed by means of mechanical ventilation that compensates for lacks of natural ventilation. Therefore, in this domain, both the natural and the forced air flows are relevant and produce thermal effects that cannot be neglected. Nevertheless, it has to be remarked that a specific norm about air change in underground spaces has not been drawn up yet.

Underground stations are also characterized by a large number of output variables (temperature, air exchange, CO_2 and PM_{10} concentrations in platform and energy consumption of actuators) but by a small number of input variables (usually just one fan): this reduces the controllability and the possibility of simplifying the control task by coupled sub-problems decomposition. The decomposition into simpler (eventually coupled) sub-problems, in fact, is possible when different output variables are mainly affected by different control inputs: since usually the control input is just the speed of the station fan for controlling many output comfort and air-quality variables, there is no chance for decomposition. Therefore, the problem is handled with a cost function formed by a weighted sum of conflicting objectives and subject to appropriate constraints, while the control task is faced through an optimization problem.

This severe controllability issue means that a whole building control strategy, such as MPC, is much more effective.

Model predictive control, in fact, may be used to enhance BEMSs so that they can improve their control performances getting close to optimal behavior [11].

2.2. The control architecture

The overall control scheme is depicted in **Figure 1**. The energy manager is in charge of enabling or disabling controller functionalities. A supervisory subsystem is in charge of checking the correct operation of each subsystem and alerting the energy manager in the case of failures, faults, or constraint violations. It is also in charge of detecting unreliable sensory data and to switch to a safe control policy (the original one) when needed. A set of software proxies, one for each sensor or external data or actuator, acts as middle-ware, thus making information available to and from the control system independently from the specific hardware or external service adopted. A monitoring subsystem (see Section 4) collects information about station status (via the sensor network detailed in Section 3), and predictions about disturbance factors that affect the dynamic behavior, such as external uncontrolled fan (i.e., not controlled fans), people, trains, and weather.

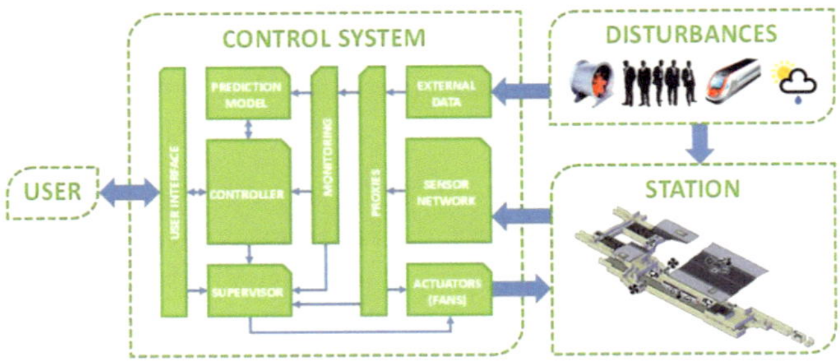

Figure 1. Typical architecture of an MPC.

The disturbances have to be measured and, if possible, predicted by a model that provides the future behavior of non-controllable factors. For trains and external fans, the station operator can always provide schedules that may be reasonably used as a measure or prediction. Any slight variation from the schedule can be addressed by the disturbance rejection capability of the feedback control scheme (**Figure 1**). When available, these schedules or the status of trains and external fans can be accessed in real time through the SCADA system already installed in the station, thus improving the reliability of the measures of these disturbances. A large-scale simulation study performed in [12] showed a potential for the energy savings and/or improvements in thermal indoor environment when using the weather forecasts in a predictive control strategy compared to a simple rule-based control, despite the uncertainty in the weather forecasts. Therefore, weather forecasts and local weather stations are used to improve control performance. As shown in [13], a large part of the energy savings potential can be captured by taking into account also for instantaneous occupancy information.

This information is then processed and made available for use by the controller subsystem (Section 5.1). The prediction model (described in following Section 5.2), fed with all the available information, is used to carry out a scenario analysis and to select what control policy ensures the best predicted performance in terms of energy consumption and comfort. The corresponding optimal solution is applied to the station as control action, and the process is repeated at each control step.

In this framework, as for each control system, the sensor network that will be described in the next section is of paramount importance, since it determines the ability of the system to reject disturbances and unpredictable events.

http://dx.doi.org/10.5772/62679

3. Environmental monitoring networks

3.1. Typical architecture of an WSN-based environmental monitoring system

In the last decades, we have witnessed a significant evolution of environmental monitoring systems. This wide category embraces a considerable range of application scenarios—from public surveillance to industrial automation. The first monitoring systems were mainly based on high-precision sensors; hence, the cost and complexity for deploying such systems is typically higher and the efficiency lower than most current solutions. Nowadays, the terrific advances in low-power devices and wireless technologies have driven an evolution toward wireless sensor networks (WSN)-based monitoring approaches. Typically, a set of sensor nodes is deployed over an area, each of them including a set of sensing units as well as one or more wireless interfaces. In many cases, off-the-shelf sensor nodes are used, providing a trade-off between the cost and complexity of network deployment and maintenance, and the accuracy of the measurements.

Although each application scenario imposes its own requirements, there exist some common rules when deploying a wireless sensor network for monitoring purpose. A set of sensor nodes is deployed over the area of interest, and one or more entity is added for collecting the data. Usually, there is at least one central sink gathering sensor measurements, either periodically or after a "long" monitoring time interval, which could be defined for instance as one entire day or 1 month, depending on the time requirements of the application. A real-time monitoring application normally imposes stricter time requirements (e.g., collect measurements every 2 min). In fact, in many practical deployments sensor nodes are divided in subsets (e.g., based on location) and a hierarchical architecture is employed. In addition, it is very common to deploy also a set of gateways, each collecting measurements from a subset of the sensor nodes, so as to improve scalability and reliability of the system. A gateway is normally a device that is not limited in power and storage, but in some cases, it could be one of the low-power devices taking also the role of collection point.

Concerning the communication point of view, there has been a great deal of effort in defining new standards, algorithms, and protocols for WSN connectivity, strongly motivated by the high potential of using those networks in several different application scenarios. Hence, nowadays a considerable number of solutions are employed in real deployment to provide robust connectivity. Although many technologies and mechanisms exist, a complete description of all of them is out of the scope; hence, we briefly mention some of those that are more related with our area of interest.

In fact, physical and media access control layers are most commonly implemented according to the IEEE 802.15.4 standard, which is designed for low-power and low-data-rate devices using short-range transmission. The maximum data rate is 250 kbits/s, and range is typically few tens of meters. As the standard is intended for low data rate, the packet size is limited to 127 bytes. The standard allows three frequency bands (868, 915, and 2450 MHz). Commercially, available devices typically work on 2.4 GHz band. IEEE 802.15.4 defines three topologies that may be used by the upper layer protocols: star, mesh and cluster tree. Typically, the radio listening and transmitting power consumptions are in the order of few tens of milli-watts, and idle and sleep modes consume significantly less.

Many communication mechanisms are based on 802.15.4 standard. 6LoWPAN (IETF working group) is an adaption layer allowing IPv6 traffic transmitted through 802.15.4 network, which apply packet restructuring due to the very limited size of 802.15.4 packets. One of the most widely used approaches is the ZigBee stack, which defines various layers on top of 802.15.4 and specifies three possible roles for nodes. The coordinator and the router are fully functional devices, while an end device cannot route packets. On the other hand, WiFi typically is not used by sensor devices, due to the high power need, but it is often used for connecting gateway(s) to the Internet, or to a central server receiving all the collected data.

In the next section, we briefly discuss some of the existing solutions for WSNs used in the context of environmental monitoring, highlighting the most common approaches and technologies employed, whenever disclosed.

3.2. State-of-the-art of WSN-based environmental monitoring systems

The class of WSNs deployed for environmental monitoring purpose is relatively wide, thus including a large set of different technologies, environments, architectures, and applications. Let us summarize them based on a simple taxonomy, by first distinguishing between outdoor and indoor.

In the former case, it is possible to identify two main sub-classes, depending on the location where sensors are placed—under the ground or over a surface. If the signal is transmitted over the air, the transmission propagation is significantly different, thus the communication distance significantly wider, allowing longer-range transmissions also compared to the indoor case, since less obstacles are typically present in this case. The most typical use case is the monitoring of a field or farm, aimed to obtain environmental measures data, number of animals within an area or any moving object, for detecting intruders. In urban areas, the most common objectives are surveillance and traffic or road surface monitoring. In [14], the authors describe a WSN for monitoring a potatoes crop. More than 100 TinyOS-based sensing nodes were sensing the environment and sending data to one gateway, connected to a central server through Wi-Fi. Barrenetxea et al. [15] reports the case of a similar deployment of 16 nodes on a rock glacier in Switzerland, but GPRS was used instead of Wi-Fi. In collaboration with biologists, authors of [16] deployed a IEEE802.15.4-based WSN for capturing the habitat of foxes, whereas [17] capture the distribution of seabirds on an island through a network of 150 TinyOS-based sensors organized in one single-hop and one multi-hop network, both connected to a central gateway through their own gateway.

If the sensors are placed below the ground surface, the goal is the monitoring of the status of the ground, either for complementing the monitoring above the ground (e.g., for intelligent irrigation), or for more specific objectives, such as landslide monitoring for earthquake prediction. A fundamental issue is the modeling of the underground communication channel, in order to properly design the network and avoid burying and un-burying sensors many times, which is complicated and time-consuming [18]. The architecture is usually less structured, and based on the characteristics of the soil, typically obtained in a pre-deployment phase, with one or more gateways over the ground surface [19].

Concerning indoor scenarios, we can further split this class into two sub-categories: subway (i.e., underground transportation systems) and building (e.g., office, museum). Both of them may experience a significant impact of the human presence, as well as carried wireless-equipped devices, on the signal propagation [20]. Usually, building hosting offices, museums or malls, are regularly structured, and sensors are installed for surveillance in the offices of a company, or inside other public place such as a museum. In [21], a 16-nodes WSN is deployed over the three floors of a medieval tower, in order to monitor and detect potentially dangerous vibrations. One sink collecting all data was placed at the top floor where access to the external Wi-Fi network was available. Peralta et al. [22] describe a preliminary testbed and lessons learnt from a deployment in a museum in Portugal.

On the other hand, the environment of subways is proven to be more harsh, mainly due to high-speed train crossing the area of interest, and the (building) structure, which can seriously affect the signal propagation and quality of a link between two adjacent nodes, due to tunnels, stairs, and substantial use of metal and concrete materials [23]. The typical motivation for deploying a WSN for underground transportation system monitoring is safety and energy saving [24]. Several interesting results and practical guidelines are reported in [25], which describes two deployments in two underground railway stations, one in Prague and one London. Before the actual deployment, accurate measurements were performed in order to model the propagation of the signal within the tunnels of interest and properly plan the network design. The evaluation suggested the centre of the tunnel as the best place for placing the receiver and transmitter's antennas, which turn out to be not practical in real deployment, confirming the gap between ideal installation design, and feasibility in real settings.

4. Wireless real-time environmental monitoring systems

4.1. Requirements, constraints, and challenges

One of the most peculiar issues of a WSN is the lifetime of the system. Typically, environmental monitoring needs a network stable and reliable for months or years, whereas employing sensor nodes implies significantly lower time ranges. Moreover, several reasons can lead to node failure or reboot, causing unexpected network behavior and loss of data, all these events potentially requiring access to the (failed) node for re-configuring or re-charging it. However, the cost and potentially high distance make it unfeasible to operate on the network continuously, implying the need for self-configuration and self-maintenance feature implementation. In addition, several mechanisms can be employed not only for energy harvesting, but also for reducing the energy consumption associated with sensing and/or transmission: MAC duty cycle, data aggregation, data prediction [24, 26].

One of the main challenges of a *wireless* network is the communication reliability, as the wireless channel is intrinsically unstable and requires a maximum distance and certain physical conditions to be verified in order to guarantee data delivery (e.g., obstacles among nodes might undermine the connectivity). On the other hand, wireless links provide the flexibility to easily and gradually deploy a network, reducing the need and cost for maintenance and facilitating incremental deployment (e.g., through self-organizing and self-healing properties).

Real-time monitoring implies that the measurements taken from the sensors have to be delivered over a *short-time* interval. Although the duration depends on the specific application, data must be delivered quickly, thus an off-line data gathering method is not suitable. For all the above reasons, the system must be robust in terms of failure and reliable in terms of connectivity. When deploying a network for real-time monitoring, a certain level of redundancy is usually desired, so that some sensor nodes can mitigate the effect of a failure or lack of others, not only for sensing the environment, but also to guarantee forwarding of other nodes' measurements to the central sink [25].

The wide range of possible application scenarios make it unfeasible to identify a widely recognized "best" strategy, although a set of general rules can be inferred. The location of sensor nodes must ensure coverage of the entire area under monitoring, both from a sensing and a connectivity point of view. Regarding the former, the actual coverage depends on the application and the monitoring area, where some sub-areas might be excluded and some others might require higher sensor density (e.g., tunnel). As for the latter, it is essential to guarantee that there are not isolated nodes at any time during the period of monitoring, and that all of them are able to reach the data collection entity. In practical terms, (at least) one routing path to the sink and/or gateway must be available and known at each sensor node. Several implications can be deduced: (1) each node must be located so as to be within the transmission range of at least another node of the network; (2) routing path(s) must be acquired from each sensor and dynamically updated whenever needed (e.g., after failure); (3) if duty cycle is performed, it must be designed so as to guarantee that awake periods of nodes belonging to a routing path overlap enough to guarantee proper transmission/reception. In addition to it, each specific (category of) environment imposes physical constraints on where nodes can be located, the propagation of the signal and the network design.

To conclude this discussion, let us focus on the constraints and challenges typically related to subway environments, and the real deployment under study. Several real deployments evaluation have demonstrated the special care needed before the actual installation [25], highlighting the importance of performing accurate measurements of the signal power under different conditions, as the structure of underground transportation systems typically exacerbate some issues, such as the multi-path fading.

4.2. The case study: design choices and criteria

In this section, we describe a real-world use case of an environmental monitoring system deployed in the context of the EU-funded SEAM4US (Sustainable Energy mAnageMent for Underground Stations) project, aimed to energy management optimization. The main role of the sensor network is to track in real-time both environmental and energy measures of interest, an intelligent control system (Section 2). The WSN was installed in the "Passeig de Gracia"

http://dx.doi.org/10.5772/62679

(PdG) subway station in Barcelona, one of the most crowded in the city, connecting three important railway lines and having on average more than fifty trains per hour.

The monitoring platform is in charge of gathering data from sensors, re-arranging and post-processing them into a database, and forwarding clean, time aligned measurements to the intelligent control unit that is in charge of applying optimum control policies for energy savings. PdG metro station is a harsh environment for wireless sensor placement, operation and communication, as many station areas are located far from each other, many obstacles can severely affect the signal propagation, and it is a highly dynamic scenario due to passengers and trains crossing the station every day. The station area is rambling, thus connecting all nodes directly to the gateway was neither feasible nor efficient. For that reason, the network architecture was done in such a way to provide multi-hop paths from all nodes to the gateway.

Several sensor nodes were installed inside the metro station, each of them sensing a specific set of environmental aspects under investigation. One of the most important design choices was to deploy a wireless network, as the need for wiring all the nodes can easily limit the installation options. For similar reasons, most of the sensor nodes are battery powered, whereas all the sensor gateways have power supply, in order to guarantee continuous operation. The position of sensors was decided according to the specific requirements for modeling and controlling the system. Due to the limitation mentioned above, it is often necessary to choose a trade-off between requisites from monitoring, wireless communication, and building structure.

Regarding the values transmitted, they should typically be estimated as the average value out of a set of measurements, thus sensors should be typically installed in several locations scattered around the station. Then, a calibration process was applied to estimate at what extent measurements were affected by their sub-optimal locations and, when feasible, correction factors were applied.

Routing plays a key role to ensure correct data delivery. To allow multi-hop communication and adapt to the variable condition, we implemented a dynamic routing protocol to achieve flexibility and quicker setup. Indeed, the protocol periodically exchanges a very restricted amount of information, taking advantage of other control packets, so that routing information are updated frequently, but the amount of additional control traffic is very low. The actual ad-hoc routing procedure, involving more control packet to be exchanged, is used only in case of missing information. The routing algorithm takes both link quality and hop-count into account, in order to better capture the quality of each available path.

Each sensor acquires its settings from the gateway after reboots and error conditions, and it stores some previous measurements. This approach significantly helped to avoid data loss in case of unexpected events, such as sudden worsening of signal quality in the station. Concerning the energy consumption, using cheap battery instead of more expensive energy harvesters allowed us to achieve a battery lifetime that was enough for the project requirements.

Data reliability was strengthened by implementing a mechanism that periodically verifies the data received at the gateway server and requests data re-transmission in case of missing values.

In practice, real-time monitoring is stricter in terms of delay requirements; hence, the mechanism parameters must be tuned according to the specific requirements. During the modeling and testing time, the design of the monitoring network turned out to be redundant both in terms of measurements collected and in terms of available adjacent nodes for routing, due to some changes in terms of requirements. Clearly, in this kind of harsh environment, redundancy is often needed or desired, as it contributes to increase the reliability of the system.

4.3. Implementation and system performance

The system consists of the central SEAM4US server, various gateway servers, gateway nodes, and sensor nodes. Gateway servers are Linux servers (FitPCs) connected to the gateway node. The gateway and sensor nodes are implemented on the processing and communication board by Redwire LLC called Econotag, with an additional 32 KHz oscillator and one of the four sensor boards specifically designed to fulfill the requirements of the project. **Table 1** lists all of them, reporting the specific environmental aspects measured through every board. In addition, **Figure 2** illustrates how the WSN is installed within the station, also showing that the network is divided in four sub-networks from the communication point of view (SN2, SN3, SN4, SN5), whereas SN1 includes only the weather station.

Type	Probes	Sensor IDs
Sensor Board 1	-Air pressure -Air temperature -Surface temperature -High-speed anemometer	1, 3, 4, 5, 6, 7, 8, 10, 11, 12, 13, 14, 15, 16, 17, 18, 20, 21, 22, 23, 24, 25, 27, 28, 29, 30, 31, 32, 33, 34, 57
Sensor Board 2	-Air pressure -Relative humidity -CO2 -PM10	26, 35
Sensor Board 3	-Air temperature -Surface temperature -Low-speed anemometer -Differential pressure	9, 56
Weather Station	-Solar radiation -CO2 -PM10	55

Table 1. List of sensors deployed within PdG station.

http://dx.doi.org/10.5772/62679

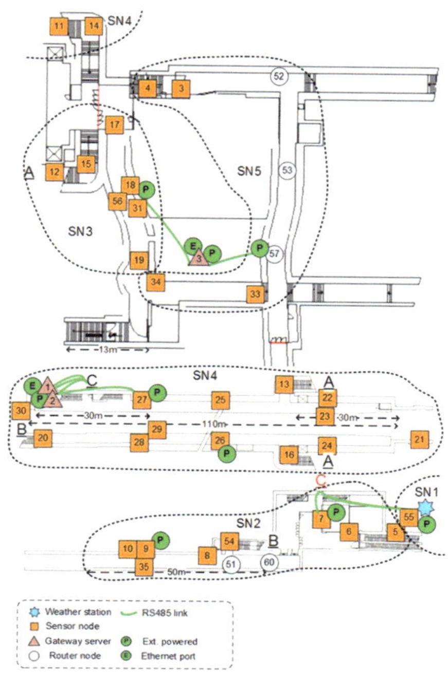

Figure 2. WSN deployment within PdG station.

We installed Contiki OS as an operating system to the nodes. We made various additions to OS, such as routing and control protocol, to make it more suitable to our needs. Concerning power saving, we implemented an energy efficient MAC protocol that combines R-MAC [27] and ContikiMAC [28], leading to a cross-layer mechanism able to allow nodes to stay in sleep mode most of the time, according to the application's data sampling and delay requirements [29]. This way, we are able to achieve battery replacement periods of many years, as shown from the estimation in **Figure 3**, which was satisfactory for this use case.

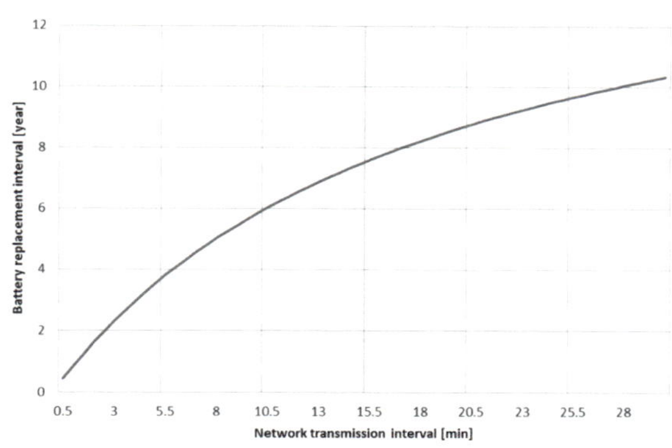

Figure 3. Battery replacement period plotted over network transmission interval.

The requirement in terms of data delivery can be summarized by specifying the maximum allowed packet loss (PL) as 20%. In fact, the system was able to satisfy the requirement as the average packet delivery ratio over the entire network during the evaluation period was 13%. An interesting finding is that in this kind of environment, sub-networks can show significant differences in terms of performance compared to other more homogeneous scenarios. For a quick look at this aspect, in **Table 2**, we reported the values of some performance indicators observed during a period of 1 week, both the average value over the entire network and the average for each sub-network: the PL, the number of hops to the gateway (NH), and the number of available routing paths to the gateway (NP).

Average	PL	NH	NP
TOT	13%	2.04	17.34
SN2	7%	2.19	16.8
SN3	24%	2.3	4.25
SN4	5%	1.9	31
SN5	35%	1.77	1.6

Table 2. Performance indicators observed during one week.

The total average is not the average of the values shown below, since each sub-network has different number of nodes. The sub-network SN4 is the one that cover the tunnel where on average one train every minute passes, implying that it is located in a very dynamic environment mainly due to passengers and trains crossing. As you can see from **Table 2**, SN4 is the sub-network with the lowest PL and the higher number of available paths. Indeed, we could observe that the number and position of sensor nodes in SN4 was sufficient to ensure many multi-hop alternative paths for each node, despite the challenging condition. On the other hand, SN5 has the highest PL, mainly because each node has very limited alternative paths to reach the gateway, and renovation areas surround or partially cover this area, limiting communication and worsening channel condition. Hence, we can say that in harsh environments it is important that every node has some alternative paths to reach the central server, as this redundancy contributes to reduce the PL.

4.4. Architecture of the monitoring sub-system

A fundamental issue in the implementation of MPC is the interface between the model used to drive the control logics and the data gathered by means of the sensor network. Models used in the MPC control loop are based on a somewhat idealized representation of the environment: clean data, perfect time alignment, direct measures of all the necessary physical quantities, etc. Of course, this is not the case in real systems [30]. Therefore, specific modules must be developed to recover a data flow from the sensor network that is suitable for feeding the model predictions: the monitoring subsystem (**Figure 4**).

http://dx.doi.org/10.5772/62679

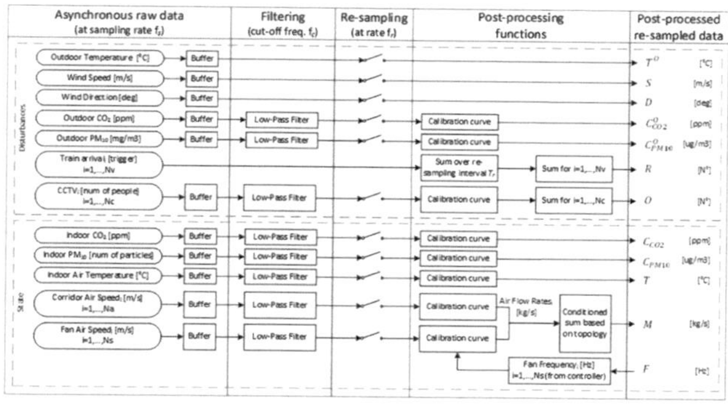

Figure 4. Raw data pre-processing, filtering and resampling.

The main task of the monitoring subsystem is to act as an interface between the model used to drive the control logics and the data gathered by means of the WSN described in Section 3. Indeed, the control model accepts as inputs synchronized clean data, complete records at regular time intervals. However, this is never the case of raw data sent by a WSN. For that reason, the monitoring subsystem was made up of a set of units developed to recover a data flow from the WSN and convert them into a suitable form for feeding the control model computations. Summarizing, three main steps are accomplished by this component:

- filtering in order to reduce the aliasing and the noise of raw data;
- re-sampling to perform time alignment;
- post-processing (i.e., unit conversion, calibration, estimation of indirect measurements).

In this sub-section, filtering and re-sampling will be described, whereas post-processing will be the object of the next subsection.

Raw data are asynchronously acquired by the sensor network with sampling frequency f_s (subject to some drift due to network latency); therefore, they have to be aligned in time before entering the controller. This task is carried out by a re-sampling centralized process that, at a fixed rate f_r, captures the updated value for each sensor and stores it. In order to avoid aliasing, according to Shannon's theorem [31], this process requires input data to be low-pass filtered with a cut-off frequency greater than half the re-sampling frequency $f_c \leq f_r/2$.

Filtering is used to smooth data; however, it introduces a delay that, when too long, could make the information useless for control purposes. The delay introduced by the filter depends on filter order, type and cutoff frequency (i.e., frequency at −3 dB of attenuation) with respect to sampling frequency f_s. An IIR filter type was selected and used as the best compromise between complexity, selectivity, and phase shift. Once the cutoff frequency is given, the filter parameter can be computed as

$$a = e^{-2\pi f_c} / f_s \tag{1}$$

and a filter recursive form for implementation is

$$y_n = (1-a) \cdot x_n - a \cdot y_{n-1} \tag{2}$$

A sampling frequency f_s must be established in order to avoid, or limit, aliasing noise in the digital signal. Again, according to Shannon's theorem, this is done based on the spectrum occupancy band of the continuous signal to be sampled. In order to determine the spectrum occupancy of each sensor type, a data collection campaign was performed in the real station. Data were acquired for a whole week with a high sampling rate in order to obtain an over-sampled dataset. The sampling rate was 1 min for temperatures, wind speed, and wind direction and 10 s for air speed and concentration of pollutants. The sampled data were then re-sampled and aligned in time every 10 s. A Welch mean-square spectrum was then estimated and analyzed. Defining B_{-20dB} as the frequency at which power attenuation is at least −20 dB between the amplitude of the lower harmonics in the spectrum and the amplitude of the spectral components beyond spectrum occupancy band B_{-20dB} itself, its value can be graphically determined from the spectrum plots.

Shannon's theorem states that, given a signal with occupancy band B, in order to keep all the original information in the sampled signal and to avoid aliasing, the sampling interval must be $f_s > 2B$. In our case, the sensors are much more reactive than the system dynamics and much of the original information contain noise that can be removed by post-process filtering with cut-off frequency $f_c \ll f_s$. Thus, a small amount of aliasing can be tolerated if it falls in the part of the spectrum that is cut by the post-process low-pass filter, that is, when $f_c < B$, a less restrictive relation can be applied: $f_s > B + f_c$. In other words, it is necessary to have $f_s > f_s^L$, where:

$$f_s^L = \begin{cases} B + f_c, when\, f_c < B \\ 2B, otherwise \end{cases} \tag{3}$$

The cut-off frequency for post-process low-pass filter f_c and the re-sampling frequency f_r are chosen so that reasonable values for raw sampling frequency f_s and residual aliasing are achieved. The results reported in **Table 3** are achieved with f_r = 1/600 Hz and $f_c = \frac{f_r}{2} = 1/1200Hz$. The filter cutoff frequency is chosen as large as possible (equal to its upper bound) in order to limit the consequent phase delay and hence to make the controller more reactive.

Sensor	Occupancy band	Aliasing	f_s^{min}	δ_s^{max}
Temperature	$B_{-20dB} = 0.3$ mHz	1%	0.6 mHz	1667 s
Wind speed	$B_{-20dB} = 3.0$ mHz	1%	3.8 mHz	261 s

Sensor	Occupancy band	Aliasing	f_s^{min}	δ_s^{max}
Wind direction	B_{-20dB} = 6.0 mHz	1%	6.8 mHz	146 s
Air speed	B_{-20dB} = 10.0 mHz	6%	10.8 mHz	92 s
CO_2 concentration	B_{-20dB} = 0.7 mHz	1%	1.4 mHz	714 s
PM_{10} concentration	B_{-20dB} = 2.0 mHz	1%	2.8 mHz	353 s

Table 3. Sampling frequencies and sampling intervals for each sensor type.

Based on the spectrum analysis, a sampling interval $\delta_s \doteq 1/f_s = 60s$ is selected as the final value for all the sensors involved in the control. In this way, the sampling interval is large enough to limit the network traffic and the storage requirements, but it is also small enough to avoid significant aliasing in acquired information.

In order to exploit the disturbance rejection capability of the closed loop, the control interval, that is the interval used for updating the control action, is selected as the fastest synchronous data update rate available, that is the re-sampling rate $f_r = 1/600\text{Hz}$ ($\delta_r \doteq \frac{1}{f_r} = 600s$).

Finally, the prediction interval, that is the step used for updating predictions, is selected as the slowest available prediction update rate, which is the weather forecast update rate $\delta_w = 1$ h. This allows prediction horizons of hours to be used without introducing excessive computational burden and with better prediction accuracy (lower propagated uncertainties). Since, as will be shown in following Section 5.3, satisfactory control results and energy savings have been obtained with a prediction horizon of one step $p = 1$, a prediction horizon of 1 h is finally adopted.

From now on, post-processing functions will be intended to be applied to filtered and resampled values.

4.5. Post-processing functions

Post-processing functions were used to convert data processed as described in Section 4.4 into a format that is compliant with the controller unit of the MPC system. In the case of PdG station, the most important indoor environmental parameters, which were sent to the controller in order to estimate the current state of the controlled domain at each iteration of the MPC, were as follows: air change rates; air temperature values; dust (PM_{10}) concentration.

4.5.1. Air change rates

Thanks to the layout of PdG station, that is made up of a series of corridors, if air flow rates through the corridors leading to the PdG's platform are estimated, their balance will give back the total amount of air change rates across the platform, that is of interest because it is the most crowded room in the station and it is polluted by the passage of trains. As a consequence, an accurate evaluation of air speed flowing through corridors is of utmost importance. This measure was collected by means of the "high-speed anemometer" reported in Section 4, whose records are filtered and re-sampled in real-time. However, this is just correlated to the air flow rate, whose value is still unknown and must be estimated, instead. In addition, it must be estimated by means of a straightforward algorithm because it must be implemented in real-time. Among the factors that make this conversion task quite cumbersome, we cite the sensor's sheltering by a pipe and by a net at the pipe's ends, and its location to one of any room's top corners. So, preliminary numerical and experimental surveys were carried out in order to find out an accurate conversion procedure. More specifically, numerical simulations supported by experimental evidence showed that obstacles that may be found in corridors (e.g. people) affect just locally air speed field in any cross section of corridors, and do not change the overall balance estimated in the case of unobstructed corridor's cross section [32]. In other words, any air speed value on the middle cross section of corridors could be correlated with the average air speed across corridors. These values were then multiplied by the cross section's area in order to estimate the overall air flow rates across any corridor. However, the disturbance caused by presence of the sensor's sheltering was corrected by means of a calibration process, that adjusted real-time measurements of high-speed anemometers (Q') through a relation including an y-offset (q) and a scale factor (m):

$$Q = m \cdot Q' + q \tag{4}$$

The two coefficients were estimated from a set of on field measurements performed in PdG station by means of hand-held instruments. The dataset was then split into the first 75%, which was used for estimating the coefficients q and m, and the second 25%, which was used for validation purposes. Technically, the estimation was based on an OLS (ordinary least square) algorithm [33]. Six calibration curves were worked out for as many sensors placed in corridors. Each curve was based on two sets of measurements taken for about 15 min at two different times of the day. The calibrated measurements of air speed were then multiplied by the cross section, so as to work out air flow rates. The validity of this procedure was already demonstrated by the authors in a previous research paper [32].

In **Figures 5** and **6**, an example of the inputs and outcomes from this calibration process is provided. **Figure 5** compares the plot of the data logged by the hand-held instrument (i.e., benchmark) and the data plotted by the installed Seam4us sensor, where the benchmark presents peaks higher than the Seam4us sensor, and its average value is slightly higher than the other series. Those plots are the result of filtering and resampling, as reported in Section 4.4. Then, the y-offset (0.1510 m/s) and scale factor (1.2719) of the calibration curve were estimated by means of OLS analysis, like in Eq. (4). Similarly, the calibration curves for all the other corridors were worked out. In the case of node no. 18, **Figure 6** shows that the calibration brought the two curves to almost superimpose. At this juncture, air flow rates through corridors are known and they are ready to be combined one another in order to estimate outdoor air supplied to the platform (PL3), which is air change per hour from outdoor air (ACO):

http://dx.doi.org/10.5772/62679

$$M = ACO_{PL3} = Q_{as} + Q_{CNl} + \left(Q_{CNe} - Q_{SLb}\right)^{+} \tag{5}$$

where Q_{as} is the air supplied by the mechanical ventilation system; Q_{CNl} is air flow rate entering across the corridor called CNl, and the last two terms computes the difference between air flow rate flowing through corridor CNe and another corridor called SLb. The difference was due to the evidence that only the air flow coming from CNe, but that was not directed toward SLb, entered the platform PL3. The plus apex indicates that this contribution was taken into account just in case the balance is positive.

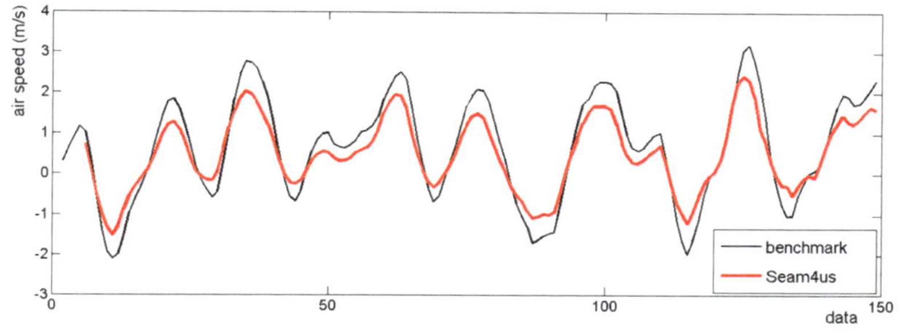

Figure 5. Raw data at node no. 18.

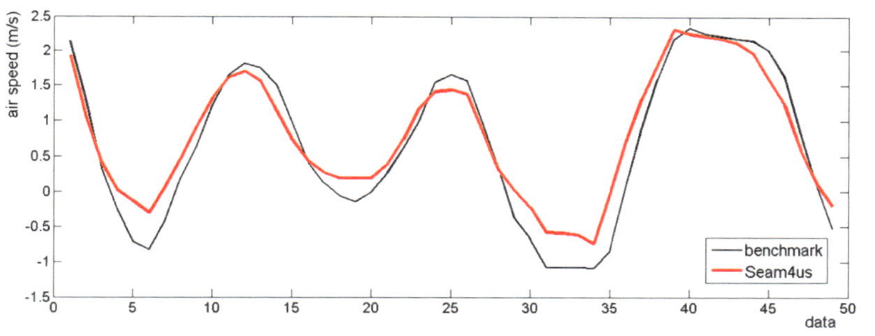

Figure 6. Transformed data compared with the dataset used for verification.

Another finding was that trains in tunnels affect the amount of air flow rates flowing across tunnels. For that reason, air flow rates estimated in tunnels by means of sensors' measurements were reduced by a factor included in post-processing functions, which was computed as a result of an overall air flow balance in the station. Although no contribution to the platform's daily ventilation came from the two Pdg's tunnels, because they always worked in extraction mode, the reduction determined on air flow rates due to the presence of trains was estimated just for the purpose of general knowledge. The overall air flow balance in the station around the platform can be written as:

$$-Q_{as} = Q_{CNl} + Q_{CNq} + 2 \cdot Q_{CNop} + \alpha \cdot Q_{tun} \quad (6)$$

where, Qas is the same as mentioned above, Q_{tun} is the air flow rate of the fans extracting air from tunnels and CNl, CNq, and CNop are corridors. The overall air flow balance brought to determine the coefficient $\alpha = 0.7$, that is the reduction due to the presence of trains in tunnels.

4.5.2. Air temperature

Similarly to what described in Section 4.5.1, air temperature plots provided by the Seam4us' WSN were compared with those ones measured by accurate hand-held instruments. We checked two types of deviation: an y-offset of the respective average values of the two plots; peaks of the Seam4us networks were lower than the peaks of the hand-held instruments. The latter was probably due to the packaging inside which the Seam4us sensors were sheltered. But it was deemed as not relevant, because just average temperatures over time steps of 1 h were needed by the intelligent control module, whereas peaks were due just to trains passing by, whose consequences lasted for a few minutes. The former was corrected by comparing the two average measures from the two plots and applying an y-offset factor to every Seam4us sensor. So, one specific y-offset conversion for each Seam4us temperature sensor was estimated.

4.5.3. Dust concentration

The raw measurements provided by the PM_{10} sensors were relative to the number of particles counted within 0.283 l of air volume (u.o.m. is pcs/0.283 l). The purpose of the post-processing function was twofold: firstly, to extend particles' count over the whole spectrum, due to the fact the sensor was able to sense only particles sized more than 0.5 μm; secondly, PM_{10} concentration should be measured in standard unit of measure, that is, μg/m^3. In order to pursue that, a post-processing function made of six steps was set up. Given that raw data (rawPM) were measured as pcs/0.283 l, the first step turned it into n measures in pcs/m^3, through the factor k = 3534 l/m^3, hence n = k*rawPM. The second step assessed the ratio of particles out of their total number, which was not considered in the raw measures (because limited above 0.5 μm). So an on-site survey through a hand-held instrument (i.e., "Fluke particle counter") was done, and the distribution in **Table 4** was had. As a result, if the sum of particles measured by the WSN between 0.5 and 10 μm is 100%, which number must be increased by 79.3% to include even those particles between 0.3 and 0.5 μm.

Range of diameters [μm]	Central value of diameters d_s^j [μm]	Ratio D^j [%]
0.3–0.5	0.4	79.3
0.5–1.0	0.75	62.2
1.0–2.0	1.5	19.1
2.0–5.0	3.5	17.7

http://dx.doi.org/10.5772/62679

Range of diameters [μm]	Central value of diameters d_s^j [μm]	Ratio D^j [%]
5.0–10.0	7.5	0.88
>10.0	12.5	0.13

Table 4. Distribution of particles found in PdG station.

Given the distribution of particles in **Table 4**, in the third step, the number of particles per size was rewritten in the form: $n_j = n^*D_j$, where n_j is the number of particles whose diameter's central value is equal to d_{sj}, n is the raw measure of particles and D_j is the ratio. Steps 4–6 were determined according to literature and used to convert the number of particles in concentration. In particular, step no. 4 computed the volume occupied by n_j particles [34]:

$$vol^j = \frac{\pi}{6} \cdot \left(d_s^j\right)^3 \cdot n \tag{7}$$

As a fifth step, the concentration m^j [μg/m³] will be computed as [35]:

$$C_{PM10}^{'} PM_{10} = m^j = C_F \cdot \rho_{eff}^j \cdot vol^j \tag{8}$$

where the coefficient $C_F = 1$ in our case and an overall value of ϱ_{eff} was assessed experimentally according to the relationships [36]:

$$\rho_{eff} = \frac{PM_{10}}{\sum_{j=1}^{5} vol^j \cdot F_{PM_{10}}^j} \tag{9}$$

The coefficients F are provided by the literature [36], while PM_{10} was measured in the station, at the same time, when the counting in **Table 1** was done. It came out that $PM_{10} = 320$ μg/m³, all the other values are known, hence $\varrho_{eff} = 3.15 \cdot 10^{12}$ μg/m³. By combining all the steps described

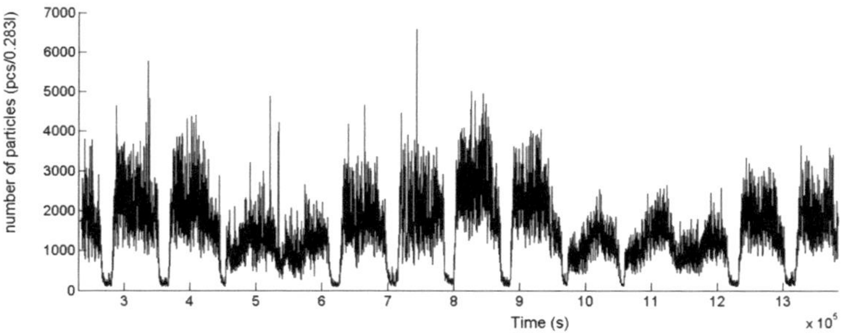

Figure 7. Raw data collected about PM10.

above, the conversion of the kind depicted on **Figures 7** and **8** were performed automatically by the Seam4us system, and in real-time during monitoring.

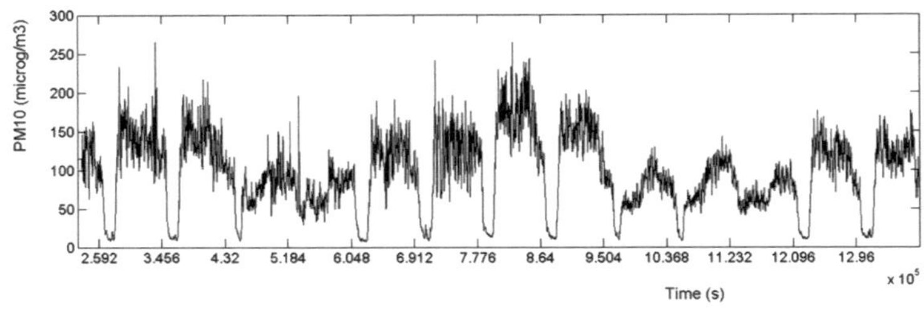

Figure 8. PM10 post-processed and converted into concentration.

5. Implementation of the MPC

5.1. MPC installed in the case study

In the considered station (PdG-Line3), the air exchange and thermal comfort is achieved by two fans located in the station and two fans situated in the middle of the two tunnels. The original control policy, hereafter referred to as baseline (BSL), requires the station fans to inject air into the station in the daytime, and the tunnel fans to extract air from the platform in the daytime (between 07.00 and 22.00) and inject air at night (between 22.00 and 07.00 of the next day), when the station fans are switched off. All the fans are driven by an inverter based on the input frequency on the basis of a day/night schedule and a seasonal schedule set by the station operator as follows (the sign of the frequency input represents the air flow direction: positive when entering platform):

- Winter (January, February, March) and Autumn (November, Decdmber) modes: tunnel fans at −25 Hz in the daytime and +25 Hz at night, station fans at +25 Hz only in the daytime;
- Spring (April, May, June) and Summer (July, August, September, October) modes: tunnel fans at −50 Hz in the daytime and +25 Hz at night, station fans at +50 Hz only in the daytime.

Since the tunnel fans serve different contiguous stations, their control must be implemented at a higher level in order to coordinate multiple stations on the same line. On the contrary, the station fans can be controlled locally (even if they must be driven in parallel in order to avoid falling into stall conditions) and are driven by the MPC agent. Therefore, the ventilation controller has to manage power consumption and indoor comfort by acting on only one actuator that is the driving frequency of the two station fans. MPC control is active only when the fans are active for the baseline; therefore, MPC is ON between 07.00 and 22.00 (daytime).

While the standard approach adopted by the station operator is to drive the devices solely based on time schedules, with MPC the problem is tackled in a dynamic way: the information

http://dx.doi.org/10.5772/62679

coming from the monitoring network and from the models are used to decide on the optimal ventilation control to be applied at any given time.

Weather conditions and forecasts are obtained by means of online web-service wunderground.com©. A software proxy is in charge of querying this service and periodically, thus providing weather conditions and forecasts. The quality of the current weather condition is improved by using a local weather station connected to the wireless sensor network. The CCTV-based crowd density estimator (see [37, 38]) is used here to detect people, since it is the main source of data for modeling passenger behavior, and it is based exclusively on the video streams of the CCTV surveillance system (which usually exists in a station).

Based on what was stated in Section 2.2 and is shown in **Figure 9**, at each re-sampling instant (i.e., every $1/f_r$ seconds), the MPC algorithm collects information about the station by taking re-sampled data from the monitoring, evaluates the best control action by using hourly predictions over a predefined prediction horizon p and applies it to the station. Data acquisition is carried out by waiting a maximum defined time-out interval after each re-sampling instant: when time-out is reached, MPC proceeds to compute the control action corresponding to that interval and applies it via the actuator proxy. The generation of the candidate control policy is strongly related to the adopted searching technique. In the case study, since the controlled actuators have the same input values that are discretized from 0 to 50 Hz with a resolution of 1 Hz {0, 1,…, 49, 50}, and the prediction horizon is set to p = 1, an exhaustive case generation is used as a simple solution for determining the optimal control action to be applied.

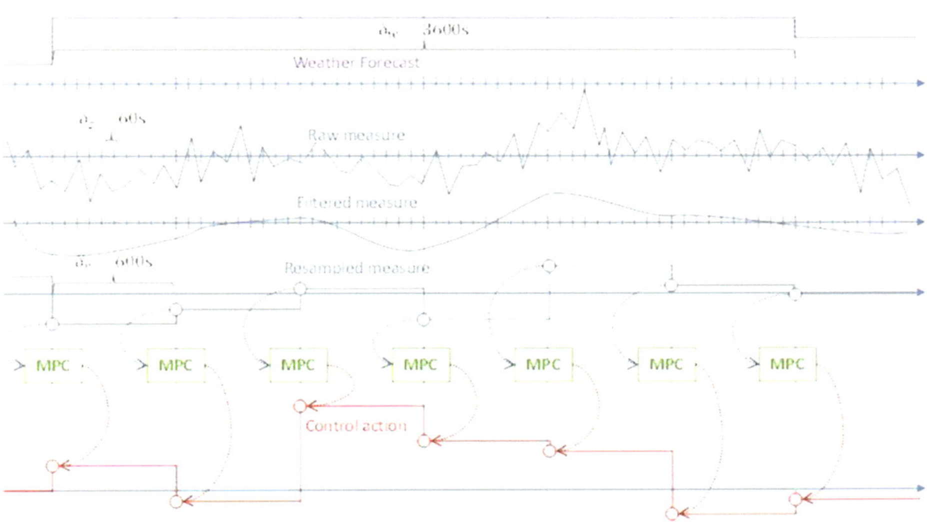

Figure 9. Timing of the control system.

For the sake of generality, parameters and variables are normalized here with respect to the maximum value of the related term in the cost function. Therefore, all the physical variables identified with tilde in their raw version, will be represented in the MPC problem formulation with their normalized versions (without tilde).

The total absorbed electric power has to be minimized while keeping thermal comfort and air quality parameters as close as possible to the desired values (soft constraints). Moreover, the thermal comfort and air-quality parameters must be kept strictly inside the bound constraints:

- Air exchange level on platform greater than a minimum threshold: $M(t) > M^{LO}(t)$
- Difference between inside and outside CO_2 level lower than a maximum level: $C_{CO_2}(t) - C^{O}_{CO_2}(t) < \Delta C^{U}_{CO_2}$
- Particulate level lower than a maximum threshold: $C_{PM_{10}}(t) < C^{U}_{PM_{10}}$
- Temperature lower than a maximum threshold: $T(t) < T^{U}$

The sum of squares of the total absorbed electric power of tunnel fans P_T and station fans P_S have to be minimized. The temperature in platform T should be as close as possible to the outside temperature T^O and to the desired value $\acute{T}$ and it must be lower than the upper bound T^U. The air change rate with outdoor air M should be as big as possible and it must be bigger than the lower bound M^LO, which takes into account for the current occupancy also. Pollutant concentrations in platform C_{CO2} and C_{PM10} should be minimized, moreover C_{CO2} must be lower than the outdoor concentration C^{O}_{CO2} plus an allowed increase ΔC^{U}_{CO2} and C_{PM10} must be lower than the upper bound C^{U}_{PM10}. In order to achieve these multiple conflicting objectives over the fixed prediction horizon p, the single objectives are combined in a global objective by arbitrary weighting factors α_{P_T}, α_{P_S}, $\alpha_{\Delta T}$, α_T, α_M, α_{CO_2}, $\alpha_{PM_{10}}$, $\alpha_{\Delta F}$. Therefore, the following cost function is defined and evaluated:

$$J(t)=\sum_{k=1}^{p}\Big[\alpha_{P_T}P_T(t+k)^2+\alpha_{P_S}P_S(t+k)^2+\alpha_{\Delta T}\left(T^O(t+k)-T(t+k)\right)^2+\alpha_T\left(\acute{T}-T(t+k)\right)^2 \\ +\alpha_M\left(1-M(t+k)\right)^2+\alpha_{CO_2}C_{CO_2}(t+k)^2+\alpha_{PM_{10}}C_{PM_{10}}(t+k)^2+\alpha_{\Delta F}\left(F(t+k-1)-F(t+k-2)\right)^2\Big] \tag{10}$$

The last term in cost function has been added for considering the amplitude of change in frequency F that drives the actuators. It is a stability objective that could be useful to smooth the control movements. Denoting with superscripts $\cdot^{L}$ and $\cdot^{U}$ lower bound and upper bounds, respectively, the previous minimization is subject to the following comfort constraints $\forall\ t \in Z$:

$$M(t) > M^{LO}(t),\ C_{CO_2}(t)-C^{O}_{CO_2}(t) < \Delta C^{U}_{CO_2},\ C_{PM_{10}}(t) < C^{U}_{PM_{10}},\ T(t) < T^{U} \tag{11}$$

and to the following operative constraints $\forall\ t \in Z$ that considers the physical limits of the actuators:

$$F^L < F(t) < F^H \tag{12}$$

Once the bounds are derived from regulations or operative limits and set point $\acute{T}$ is fixed by comfort requirements, the remaining degrees of freedom for tuning the controller are the weights of the different cost terms $\alpha_.$ and the prediction horizon p. At each control step t, the MPC problem consists in finding the optimal control sequence that minimizes the cost function (10), under constraints (11) and (12). The presence of constraints makes the optimization problem not trivial, however, as reported in literature [39–41], barrier functions can be used to transform the constraints into objectives. In constrained optimization, a barrier function is a continuous function whose value increases to infinity when approaching the boundary of the feasible region: it is used as a penalizing term for the violations of constraints.

The logarithmic barrier function is used here to implement a generic upper bound constraint $x \le x^U$, thus transforming the original constrained optimization problem into an unconstrained equivalent one. Then, by exploiting the predictive models, all the possible scenarios are evaluated and the best one is selected for controlling the fan.

Further details about the control approach can be found in [12].

5.2. The predictive models

Two dynamic Bayesian networks (DBN) were embedded in the MPC scheme in order to act as the control models [42]. The main benefits deriving from their use consist in: having established a formalism for dealing with uncertain and incomplete information; their graphical representation explicitly states causal relations between variables; the causal assumptions allowed us to limit the amount of data needed to define joint probability distributions; when additional data are available, the "belief updating" process can be applied, that is, conditional probability tables can be updated and refined when new evidence is available.

All the afore-listed features dramatically match with the needs typically arising in contexts monitored in real-time. For instance, data coming from sensors are always affected by uncertainty; even more important, while monitoring is in progress, new knowledge is available and it should be used to refine the parameters of the nonlinear probability distribution functions embedded in DBN, etc.... So, the choice of DBN fits particularly well in this case, when simpler models (e.g., auto-regressive) cannot work, due to the complexity of the domain. The word "Dynamic" means that these networks are able to make inference about some variables of the state of a system at time "t + 1", once the state of the same system at time "t" is known, thanks to the data provided by the WSN environmental monitoring system.

A detailed description of the two DBNs embedded in the whole control architecture is out of the scope of this contribution, although it was provided by another book chapter [43]. However, it is worth recalling that the two DBNs were relative to:

1. The first DBN estimated indoor air temperature in the station halls and in the platform; the temperature values at selected nodes is estimated based on the temperature values

recorded at various places in the station and outdoors, number of trains passing per hour and occupation density during previous hours;

2. The second DBN estimated air flow rates in the station and the rate of air changes in the platform, starting from the temperature values forecasted by the first DBN, expected mechanical air supply, outdoor forecasts, and the state of some variables of the station in previous hours, namely airflow rates in some corridors and in tunnels, outdoor air supplied by the mechanical air supply system, number of trains per hour.

3. Both networks were trained on a set of data generated by means of a lumped parameter simulation models. But their parameters were being gradually improved by means of datasets made up of measurements by the WSN.

5.3. Performances of MPC

The described MPC strategy was successfully applied to control the forced ventilation of the PdG-Line3 station for 5 months (from August to December 2014). Some relevant measures collected by the monitoring system, representing filtered, re-sampled and post-processed quantities, are depicted in **Figures 10** and **11**.

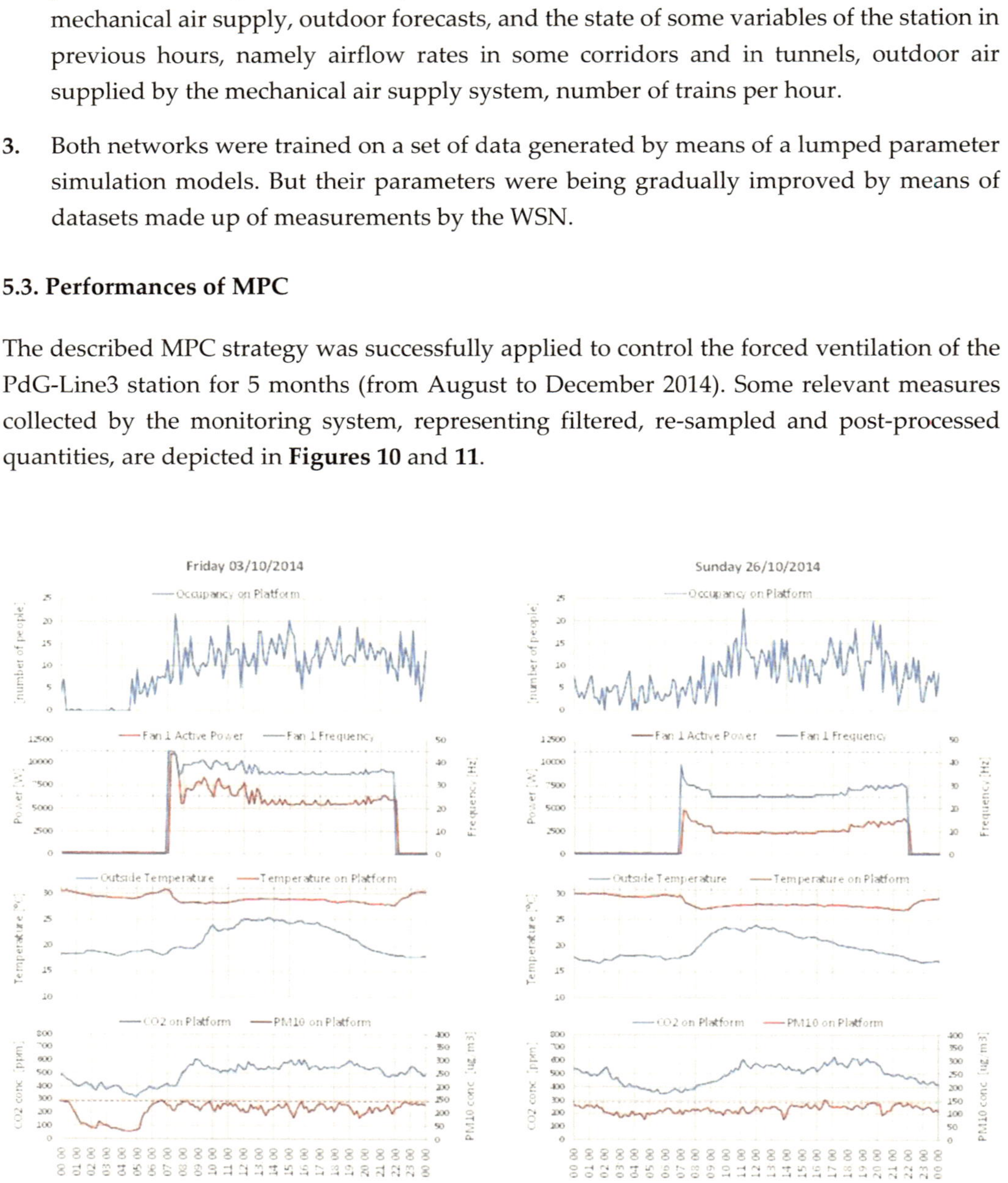

Figure 10. Performances measured during a working day (left) and a weekend (right) in October.

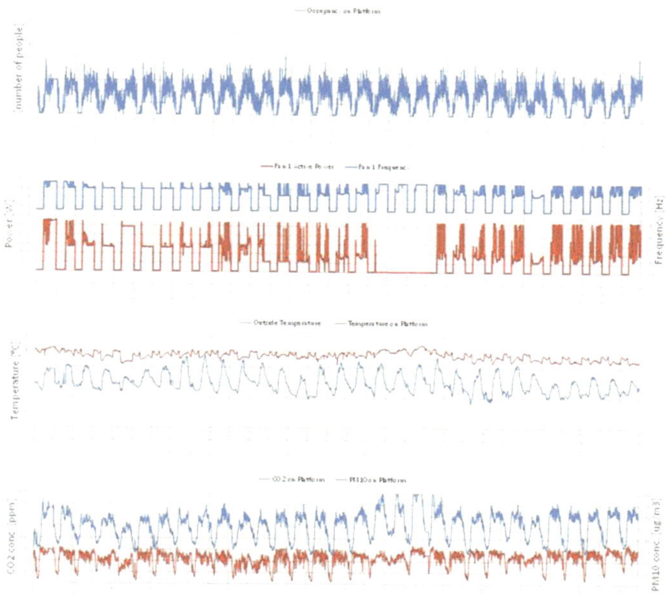

Figure 11. Performances measured during the whole month of October.

Figure 10 refers to the system operating in the summer mode during a working day (when the station opens at 05:00 and closes at 24:00) and during a weekend (when the station remains open all the time). Similarly, **Figure 11** refers to the whole month of October. Note that from October 18th to 21st there is an interruption due to maintenance on the station and the fans were switched manually off. The corresponding comfort levels in the station were significantly worsened in that period, showing the control effectiveness.

Note that, during the working days, irrespective of the summer or winter modes, the higher number of people and trains passing through the station makes the indoor climate less comfortable and the savings margins become smaller, albeit still relevant w.r.t the weekend. The comfort indexes all remain acceptable: temperature is kept stable and at acceptable levels while pollutants comply with constraints.

Permanently installed energy meters where used for monitoring energy consumption before and after the installation of the SEAM4US system. The total energy saving with respect to the baseline $S \doteq E_{MPC} - E_{BSL}$ is defined as the difference between the energy consumption achieved with the MPC strategy E_{MPC} and the energy consumption obtained with the baseline strategy E_{BSL}. The percent energy saving S is the same value S divided by the baseline energy consumption E_{BSL}.

The resulting values for energy saving relative to the direct and continuous measures taken during the 4 months of full operation are reported in **Table 5**. These periods are representative of the different operating conditions occurring in PdG-Line3 station and produce global savings of about 33% without significantly affecting passenger comfort.

Months	S (kWh)	$S_{\%}$
September	2304	30
October	3859	48
November	240	11
December	297	14
Total	6701	33

Table 5. Monthly and total energy saving produced by the MPC.

6. Conclusions and lessons learnt

The experimental results and lessons learnt reported in this chapter, confirm the importance of the pre-evaluation of the environment, and of a careful pre-deployment design for a wireless real-time environmental monitoring system. Several are the technologies and protocols available to build the wireless system, allowing to accomplish many tasks, from the periodical sensing to the recovery from PL at the gateway. However, the selection of those to be used is highly dependent on the scenario and must be a trade-off between requirements and limitations. An essential aspect is accessing the nodes remotely, and to implement the network with the capability of self-configuration and recovery after failure, so as to reduce human intervention. However, we also showed that knowing the complete architecture of the building, and the details of the operational condition, is of utmost importance for identifying the source of unexpected problems or sudden changes of operation (e.g. unusual event, such as city festival). From the data forwarding point of view, our results confirm the challenging signal propagation, especially in tunnel at rush hours, and observe the importance of installing redundant nodes for both sensing and connectivity objective. Ensuring redundant paths from a node to the gateway has shown to be of paramount importance for keeping data loss below a reasonable value.

Once WSNs are in place and real-time monitoring is running, several control applications can be developed on top of them. However, the controller needs filtered, re-sampled, and processed datasets with no missing values, hence post-processing must be implemented to this purpose. In the specific case described in this chapter, real-time monitoring was used in support of MPC and was tested in a subway in Barcelona. Not only did the system show to be able to comply with air quality and comfort requirements set for these places, but it determined energy savings as high as 33%, too. In conclusion, considering the affordability and wide availability of monitoring technologies nowadays, much research should be devoted to the development of intelligent control logics that can determine very high energy savings, even when installed in existing buildings.

Author details

Alessandro Carbonari[1,3*], Massimo Vaccarini[1,3], Mikko Valta[2,3] and Maddalena Nurchis[2,3]

*Address all correspondence to: alessandro.carbonari@staff.univpm.it

1 Department of Civil and Building Engineering and Architecture (DICEA), Polytechnic University of Marche, via Brecce Bianche, Ancona, Italy

2 VTT Technical Research Centre of Finland – Kaitoväylä, 1, Oulu, Finland

3 Department of Information and Communication Technologies (DICT), University of Pompeu Fabra, Barcelona, Spain

References

[1] Mayne D.Q., Rawlings J.B., Rao C.V., Scokaert P.O.M. Constrained model predictive control: Stability and optimality. Automatica. 2000;36(6):789–814.

[2] Mayne D.Q. Model predictive control: Recent developments and future promise. Automatica. 2014;50(12):2967-2986.

[3] Maciejowski J.M. Predictive control with constraints. Prentice Hall, England; 2002.

[4] Borrelli F. Constrained Optimal control of linear and hybrid systems. Springer, Heidelberg; 2003.

[5] Zhang X., Grammatico S., Margellos K., Goulart P.J., Lygeros J. Randomized nonlinear MPC for uncertain control-affine systems with bounded closed-loop constraint violations. Proceedings of: IFAC World Congress, Cape Town, South Africa, 2014, August.

[6] Zhang X., Schildbach G., Sturzenegger D., M.Morari. Scenario-based MPC for energy-efficient building climate control under weather and occupancy uncertainty. Proceedings of: European Control Conference, Zurich, Switzerland, 2013, July: 1029–1034.

[7] Oldewurtel F., Parisio A., Jones C.N., Gyalistras D., Gwerder M., Stauch V., Lehmann B., Morari M. Use of model predictive control and weather forecasts for energy efficient building climate control. Energy Build. 2012;45:15–27.

[8] Mesbah A., Streif S., Findeisen R., Braatz R.D. Stochastic nonlinear model predictive control with probabilistic constraints. American Control Conference (ACC), 2014, IEEE, 2014:2413–2419.

[9] Kwak Y., Huh J.H., Jang C. Development of a model predictive control framework through real-time building energy management system data. Appl. Energy. 2015;155:1–13.

[10] Casals M., Gangolells M., Forcada N., Macarulla M., Giretti A. A breakdown of energy consumption in an underground station. Energy Build. 2014;78:89–97.

[11] Henze G., Kalz D. Experimental analysis of model-based predictive optimal control for active and passive thermal storage inventory. HVAC&R, 2005;11(2):189–213.

[12] Vaccarini, M., Giretti, A., Tolve, L. C., & Casals, M. Model Predictive Energy Control of Ventilation for Underground Stations. Energy and Buildings, Volume 116, 15 March 2016, Pages 326-340

[13] Oldewurtel F., Sturzenegger D., Morari M. Importance of occupancy information for building climate control. Appl. Energy. 2013;101:521–532.

[14] Langendoen K., Baggio A., Visser O. Murphy loves potatoes: Experiences from a pilot sensor network deployment in precision agriculture. Proceedings of: 20th IEEE International Parallel & Distributed Processing Symposium. IEEE, 2006.

[15] Barrenetxea G., et al. Sensorscope: Out-of-the-box environmental monitoring. Proceedings of: Information Processing in Sensor Networks, 2008. IPSN'08. International Conference on., IEEE, 2008.

[16] Hakala, Ismo, et al. Evaluation of Environmental Wireless Sensor Network-Case Foxhouse. International Journal on Advances in Networks and Services. Vol 3, no. 1 & 2, special issue, 2010.

[17] Szewczyk R., et al. An analysis of a large scale habitat monitoring application. Proceedings of: 2nd International Conference on Embedded Networked Sensor Systems. ACM, 2004.

[18] A. Silva, and M. Vuran. Development of a Testbed for Wireless Underground Sensor Networks. EURASIP Journal on Wireless Communications and Networking. Volume 2010, Article ID 620307, 14 pages doi:10.1155/2010/620307.

[19] Cardell-Oliver R., et al. Field testing a wireless sensor network for reactive environmental monitoring [soil moisture measurement]. Intelligent Sensors, Sensor Networks and Information Processing Conference, 2004. Proceedings of the 2004. IEEE, 2004.

[20] Turner J.S.C., et al. The study of human movement effect on Signal Strength for indoor WSN deployment. Wireless Sensor (ICWISE), 2013 IEEE Conference on. IEEE, 2013.

[21] Ceriotti M., et al. Monitoring heritage buildings with wireless sensor networks: The Torre Aquila deployment. Proceedings of: 2009 International Conference on Information Processing in Sensor Networks. IEEE Computer Society, 2009.

[22] Peralta L.M.R., de Brito L.M.P.L. An integrating platform for environmental monitoring in museums based on wireless sensor networks. Int. J. Adv. Netw. Serv. 2010;3(1 & 2).

[23] Li X., et al. A feasibility study of the measuring accuracy and capability of wireless sensor networks in tunnel monitoring. Front. Struct. Civil Eng. 2012;6(2):111–120.

[24] M. Nurchis, M. Valta, M. Vaccarini, and A. Carbonari. A Wireless System for Real-time Environmental and Energy Monitoring of a Metro Station: Lessons Learnt from a Three-year Research Project. Proceedings of the 32nd ISARC Symposium, 15–18 June 2015.

[25] Bennett P.J., et al. Wireless sensor networks for underground railway applications: Case studies in Prague and London. Smart Struct. Syst. 2010;6(5–6):619–639.

[26] G. Martins, S. Oechsner, and B. Bellalta. A Centralized Mechanism to Make Predictions Based on Data from Multiple WSNs. "Multiple Access Communications": Volume 9305 of the series Lecture Notes in Computer Science pp 19–32, 25 August 2015.

[27] Koskela P., Valta M., Frantti T. Energy efficient MAC for wireless sensor networks. Sens. Transducers. 2010;121(10):133.

[28] Dunkels A., The ContikiMAC Radio Duty Cycling Protocol, SICS, Tech. Rep. T2011:13, 2011.

[29] Hiltunen J., Valta M., Ylisaukko-oja A. and Nurchis M. Design, Implementation and Experimental Results of a Wireless Sensor Network for Underground Metro Station. International Journal of Computer Science & Communication Networks. Vol. 4(3), 58–66; 2014.

[30] Žáčeková E., Váňa Z., Cigler J. Towards the real-life implementation of MPC for an office building: Identification issues. Appl. Energy. 2014;135:53–62.

[31] Shannon C.E. A mathematical theory of communication. ACMSIGMOBILE Mobile Comput. Commun. Rev. 2001;5(1):3–55.

[32] Di Perna C., Carbonari A., Ansuini R., Casals M. Empirical approach for real-time estimation of air flow rates in a subway station. Tunn. Undergr. Space Technol. 2014;42:25–39.

[33] Wonnacott T.H., Wonnacott R.J.. Introductory statistics. 5th ed. John Wiley and sons; New York. 1990. 705 p.

[34] Hinds W. C. Aerosol Technology. John Wiley and Sons; New York. 1999.

[35] Kulkarni P., Baron P. A., Willeke K. Aerosol measurements: Principles, Techniques and Applications. John Wiley & Sons; New York, 3rd ed. 2011.

[36] De Carlo P.F., Slowik J.G., Worsnop D.R., Davidovits J.L., Jimenez J.L. Particle morphology and density characterization by combined mobility and aerodynamic diameter measurements. Part 1: Theory. Aerosol Sci. Technol. 2004;38(12):1185–1205.

[37] Rahmalan H., Nixon M.S., Carter J.N. On crowd density estimation for surveillance. 2006

[38] Chow T.W.S., Yam J.Y.F., Cho S.Y. Fast training algorithm for feedforward neural networks: application to crowd estimation at underground stations. Artificial Intelligence in Engineering, Vol. 13, Issue. 3, July 1999, pp. 301–307.

[39] Nash S.G., Polyak N.R., Sofer A. A numerical comparison of barrier and modified barrier methods for large-scale bound-constrained optimization. In: Large scale optimization, Springer; 1994. pp. 319–338.

[40] Hauser J., Saccon A. A barrier function method for the optimization of trajectory functionals with constraints. Proceedings of: 45th IEEE Conference on Decision and Control, 2006. IEEE; 2006. pp. 864–869.

[41] Wright S.J., Nocedal J. Numerical Optimization. Springer-Verlag; New York; 2nd ed. 1999.

[42] Korb K.B., Nicholson A.E. Bayesian artificial intelligence. 2nd ed. Chapman & Hall, London; 2011.

[43] Carbonari A., Vaccarini M., Giretti A. Bayesian networks for supporting model based predictive control of smart buildings. In: Nezhad M.S.F., editor. Dynamic programming and Bayesian inference, concepts and applications. In Tech; 2014. pp. 3–37.